More Windows Vista for SENIORS

Studio Visual Steps

More Windows Vista for SENIORS

Customizing and Managing Your Computer

www.visualsteps.com

This book has been written by Yvette Huijsman, Henk Mol and Alex Wit, using the Visual Steps™ method.
Translated by Yvette Huijsman and Chris Holingsworth
Edited by Jolanda Ligthart, Marleen Vermeij and Ria Beentjes
Copyright 2007 by Visual Steps B.V.
Cover design by Studio Willemien Haagsma bNO

First printing: November 2007
ISBN 978 90 5905 055 6

Would you like more information?
www.visualsteps.com

Do you have questions or suggestions?
E-mail: info@visualsteps.com

Website for this book:
www.visualsteps.com/morewinvista
Here you can register your book.

Register your book
We will keep you aware of any important changes that are necessary to you as a user of the book. You can also take advantage of our periodic newsletter informing you of our product releases, company news, tips & tricks, special offers, etcetera.
www.visualsteps.com/morewinvista

Table of Contents

Foreword

This book is suitable for every computer user with basic computing skills. You can acquire these skills by working through the beginner book *Windows Vista for SENIORS.*

In *More Windows Vista for SENIORS* you will continue expanding your knowledge of your computer and *Windows Vista.* You will learn how to create backups of your personal files and how to write (burn) CDs and DVDs. You will learn more about security issues relating to your computer and how to set up '(grand)*Parental Controls*'. Finally, you will learn more about the many different settings in *Windows* that you can adjust yourself, to make your computer do exactly what you want.

You can work through this book on your own and at your own pace. Use this book right next to your computer and follow the tasks step by step. With the clear instructions and the many screenshots you will know exactly what to do.

We wish you a lot of fun learning more about computers and *Windows Vista*!

The Studio Visual Steps authors

P.S.
Your comments and suggestions are most welcome.
Our e-mail address is: mail@visualsteps.com

Visual Steps Newsletter

All Visual Steps books follow the same methodology: clear and concise step by step instruction with screenshots to demonstrate each task.
A complete list of all of our books can be found on **www.visualsteps.com**
On this website you can also subscribe to the **free Visual Steps Newsletter** that is sent by e-mail.

In this Newsletter you will receive periodic information about:
- the latest titles and previously released books, special offers and free guides.
Our Newsletter subscribers have access to free information booklets, handy tips and guides which are listed on the webpages **www.visualsteps.com/info_downloads** and **www.visualsteps.com/tips**.

Please be assured that we will never use your e-mail address for any purpose other than sending you the information you have requested and we will not share this address with any third-party. Each newsletter contains a one-click link to unsubscribe from our newsletter.

Introduction to Visual Steps™

The Visual Steps manuals and handbooks offer the best instructions available to learn how to work with computers. Nowhere else in the world you will find better support while getting to know the computer, the Internet, *Windows* and other computer programs.

Properties of the Visual Steps books:

- **Comprehensible contents**
  In each book the wishes, knowledge and skills of beginner or intermediate computer users have been taken into account.
- **Clear structure**
  Well written, easy to use, easy to follow instructions. The material is broken down in small enough chunks to be readily absorbed.
- **Screenshots of every step**
  Uses clear, concise text and screenshots. You can be sure you are always in the right place and know what to do next.
- **Format**
  The text is formatted to allow easy readability.

In short, I believe these manuals will be excellent guides for you.

dr. H. van der Meij

Faculty of Applied Education, Department of Instruction Technology, University of Twente, the Netherlands

Register Your Book

You can register your book. We will keep you updated on any important changes that are necessary to you as a user of the book. You can also take advantage of our periodic newsletter informing you of our product releases, company news, tips & tricks, special offers, etcetera.

What You Will Need

In order to work through this book, you will need a number of things on your computer:

The primary requirement for working with this book is having the US version of **Windows Vista** on your computer. You can check this yourself by turning on your computer and looking at the opening screen. *Windows Vista* is available in various editions. This book can be used with the editions:

- *Windows Vista Home Basic**
- *Windows Vista Home Premium*
- *Windows Vista Ultimate*

*Windows Vista Home Basic does not contain *Windows DVD Maker* and *Windows Media Center*.

Windows Vista includes the following programs:

Windows contains the folder *Accessories*. Here you find the word processing program:

- *WordPad*

To work with the Internet you use the following program:

- *Internet Explorer*

A functioning **Internet connection** is needed for working with *Internet Explorer.*
If you do not have an Internet connection yet, contact your Internet Service Provider.
Depending on the type of connection you use, certain settings are made on your computer. Most Internet Service Providers offer a CD-ROM and/or manual with the right data for your type of subscription.
You can also ask your computer supplier to arrange this for you.

Other necessities, for instance blank, writable CDs and DVDs, are mentioned in the applicable chapters.

Prior Computer Experience

In order to work through this book successfully, you need to be able to perform the following tasks on your computer:

***Windows*:**
- Start and stop *Windows*.
- Click, right-click, double-click and drag.
- Open and close programs.
- Use a scroll bar.
- Use tabs.

***WordPad*:**
- Open and close *WordPad*.
- Type text.
- Create a new line and remove it again.
- Move the cursor.
- Save a text and open it again.
- Select words and lines.
- Start a new document.
- Choose a different font and font size.

***Internet Explorer*:**
- Open and close *Internet Explorer*.
- Use a web address.
- Browse websites.
- Use a *Favorite*.

If you do not have these basic skills, you can work through the following book:

Windows Vista for SENIORS

Author: Studio Visual Steps

ISBN 978 90 5905 274 1
400 pages
Paperback

With accompanying support website:
www.visualsteps.com/vista

How to Use This Book

This book has been written using the Visual Steps™ method. The method is simple: have the book near you as you work on your computer, read the relevant section and perform the tasks as described. By using concise instructions with screenshots to visualize each step, you will quickly be able to do what you want with your computer.

In this Visual Steps™ book, you will see various icons. This is what they mean:

Techniques
These icons indicate an action to be carried out:

⌨ The mouse icon means you should do something with the mouse.

▦ The keyboard icon means you should type something on the keyboard.

☞ The hand icon means you should do something else, for example insert a CD-ROM in the computer. It is also used to remind you of something you learned before or when a specific task needs to be performed.

Extra help is given when we want to alert you about a particular topic.

Help
These icons indicate that extra help is available:

⇨ The arrow icon warns you about something.

�֍ The bandage icon will help you if something has gone wrong.

✓ The check mark is used with the exercises. These exercises directly reinforce what you have learned in the chapter you just read.

👣1 Have you forgotten how to do something? The number next to the footsteps tells you where to look it up in **appendix B How Do I Do That Again?**

In separate boxes you find tips or additional, background information.

Extra Information
Information boxes are denoted by these icons:

 The book icon gives you extra background information that you can read at your convenience. This extra information is not necessary for working through the book.

 The light bulb icon indicates an extra tip for using *Windows*.

How This Book Is Organized

The book is set up in such a way that you do not necessarily need to work through the book from beginning to end. You can read the table of contents to see which subjects interest you first. Work through the chapters at your own pace and in the order you want.
It is advisable to work through a complete chapter though, since the content of subsequent paragraphs may pertain to a previous section.

The Screenshots

The screenshots in this book were made on a computer running *Windows Vista Home Premium*. Depending on the *Vista* edition you have on your computer, the screenshots may look a little bit different from what you see on your screen.
This makes no difference however in performing the requested actions.
In the text it will be noted when a difference could occur and in which *Vista* edition a certain feature or specific program may not be available.

For Teachers

This book is designed as a self-study guide. It is also well-suited for use in a group or a classroom setting. A free teacher's manual (PDF file) is available.

The teacher's manual and other additional materials regarding this book can be found on the website: **www.visualsteps.com/morevista**
You can use this free service after registering on this website.

The Website That Accompanies This Book

This book is accompanied by a website with current information. The web address is:
www.visualsteps.com/morevista
Simply click on the buttons on the right side to navigate through the website.

Clicking the button News displays a webpage where you can find the latest news and possible supplements to this book.

In the event of changes to the *Windows Vista* edition described in your book, pertinent information will be found here as well.

Do you see something in your book that does not correspond with what you see on your screen? Then check this webpage to find out if something has changed.

Test Your Knowledge

When you have worked through this book, you can test your knowledge by doing one of the free tests available online on the website **www.ccforseniors.com**

These multiple choice tests will show you how thorough your knowledge of *Windows Vista* is. If you pass the test, you will receive your free computer certificate by e-mail.

There are **no costs** involved for taking part in these tests. The test website is a free service provided by Visual Steps to subscribers of the free Visual Steps Newsletter.

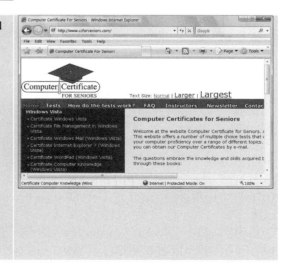

How to Continue After This Book?

When you have worked through **Windows Vista for SENIORS** and **More Windows Vista for SENIORS**, you have gained ample knowledge about the *Windows Vista* operating system and some of the accompanying programs. This gives you a solid base to be able to work with the computer as you see fit and to have fun while your at it!

The computer offers many more possibilities. For instance, you can view and edit your digital photos and videos, or listen to music on your computer. *Windows Vista* has several interesting programs to handle different types of *media*. You can also learn a lot more about surfing the Internet and working with *Windows Mail*.
Would you like to expand and deepen your knowledge of computers? Then you can continue with the other volumes in the *Windows for SENIORS* series. At the end of this book you will find more information.

All Visual Steps books have been written using the same easy, step by step method. If you like this method, there is no need to hesitate to buy another Visual Steps book. More information about other Visual Steps books, including the complete table of contents and chapter excerpts, can be found on the website **www.visualsteps.com.**

Do you have questions regarding a certain subject or book, or would you like more information? Then send an e-mail to **mail@visualsteps.com**

The CD-ROM in This Book

This book comes with a CD-ROM. The CD-ROM contains exercise files, free guides and tips (PDF files) and free programs like *Adobe Reader 8* and the *Visual Steps Alarm Clock* gadget. Complete instructions regarding these files and programs are found in the book.

In **Appendix A Copying the practice files to your computer**, you can read how to copy the practice files to the hard disk of your computer.

Storage advice
The CD-ROM is stored in a sleeve that is bound between the pages of this book. It is advisable to leave the CD-ROM in this sleeve. Do **not** try to rip the sleeve out of the book as you may risk damaging the book or its pages.
When you need the CD-ROM you can carefully open the sleeve and take the disc out.
Put the CD-ROM back into the sleeve in the book right after use. This will help you avoid misplacing the CD. Then you will have it available when you want to use it.

1. Adjusting Your Work Area

You can customize the *Windows Vista* operating system to look and function exactly how you want. In the book **Windows Vista for SENIORS** you learned for example how to change the appearance of the desktop with a new background, how to make text larger or smaller, even how to adjust the speed of your mouse pointer. But there are more possibilities.

Windows Vista contains many useful features that make working with the computer easier and more pleasant. For example, you can place a shortcut to a program that you frequently use on your desktop. To open this program, just double-click the shortcut. You can also place a shortcut in a special section of the taskbar called the *Quick Launch* toolbar. Then it takes just one click to start the program.

You can decide to have the taskbar and the *Windows Sidebar* displayed 'on top' or behind other windows that are opened. If you have a widescreen monitor for instance, you may want to keep *Windows Sidebar* 'on top' because you have more space available on your desktop.

In this chapter you will learn more about adjusting your work area to better suit your needs.

In this chapter, you will learn how to:

- place shortcuts on the desktop;
- arrange, move and delete icons on the desktop;
- add icons to the *Quick Launch* toolbar and remove them again;
- keep the taskbar always on top of other windows;
- adjust the notification area of the taskbar;
- add programs to the *Start menu*;
- keep *Windows Sidebar* in view.

➡ **Please note:**

The windows that appear on your computer may look different than the screenshots in this book. This will depend on the settings of your computer and which edition of *Windows Vista* you are using, but will not interfere with carrying out any instruction or performing any exercise as needed.

1.1 Desktop

The *Windows Vista* desktop is the screen you see after you have started your computer and typed the password (if necessary) for your user account.

☞ **Turn on your computer**

☞ **Turn on the monitor**

☞ **If necessary, enter the password for your user account**

You may see the *Welcome Center* of *Windows Vista*:

When you click to remove the check mark at

☑ Run at startup (Welcome Center can

this window will no longer appear when you start your computer:

☞ **Click** [X]

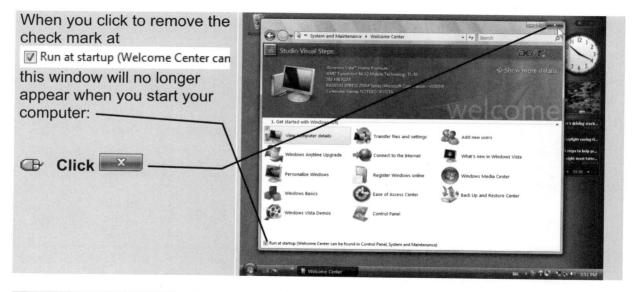

You see the *Windows Vista* desktop containing one or more icons:

On the right side you see *Windows Sidebar* containing several 'gadgets':

The desktop on your computer may look different, depending on your settings.

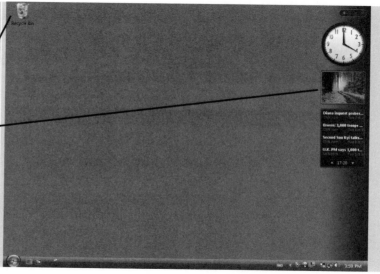

1.2 Creating Shortcuts

It is quite handy to place a shortcut on the desktop to a program you frequently use. This enables you to quickly start the program. Shortcuts in *Windows Vista* look like small images. These images are called *icons*.

To create a shortcut to a program, you start by looking up the program in the *Start menu*. As an example you are going to create a shortcut to the program *WordPad*. You can find *WordPad* in the folder *Accessories*:

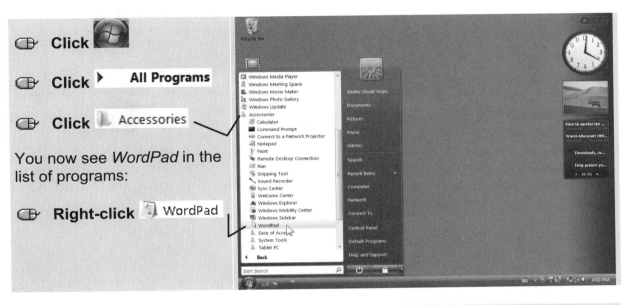

This menu appears:

You can create the shortcut using the option **Send To** :

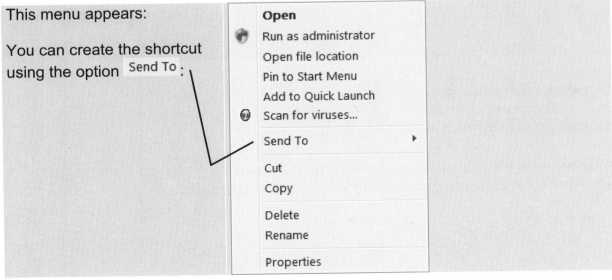

☞ Click Send To

A submenu appears:

☞ Click
▪ Desktop (create shortcut)

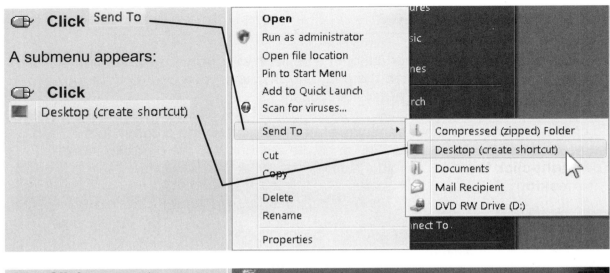

☞ Click an empty area on your desktop

The *Start menu* disappears and the shortcut to *WordPad* is placed somewhere on the desktop:

The shortcut is displayed as

an icon WordPad .

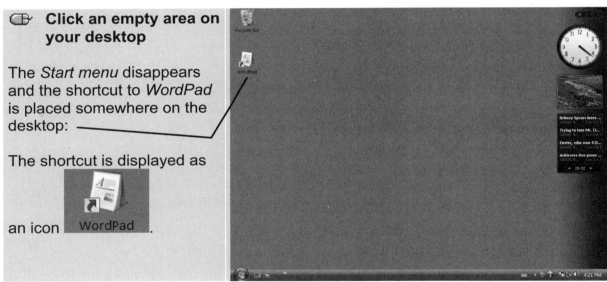

The **small arrow** in the lower left corner of the icon indicates this is a shortcut.

You can also place shortcuts to other frequently used programs on your desktop. Double-clicking the shortcut icon starts the program right away.

1.3 Moving Icons

When there are many shortcuts on your desktop, it will appear cluttered. Perhaps you want to arrange them differently. It is very easy to move your shortcuts to another place on your desktop.
Before you start, you need to make sure the setting *Auto Arrange* is turned off. Otherwise you will not be able to move the icons.

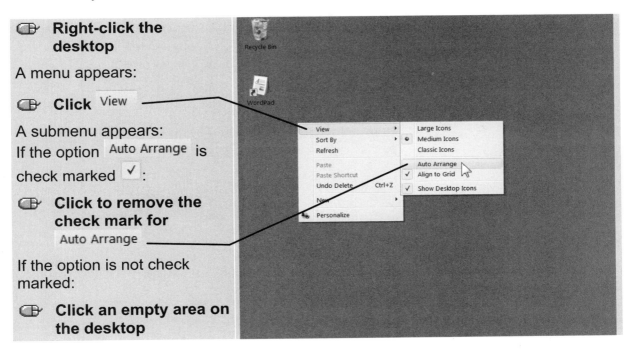

- **Right-click the desktop**

A menu appears:

- **Click** View

A submenu appears:
If the option Auto Arrange is check marked ✓:

- **Click to remove the check mark for** Auto Arrange

If the option is not check marked:

- **Click an empty area on the desktop**

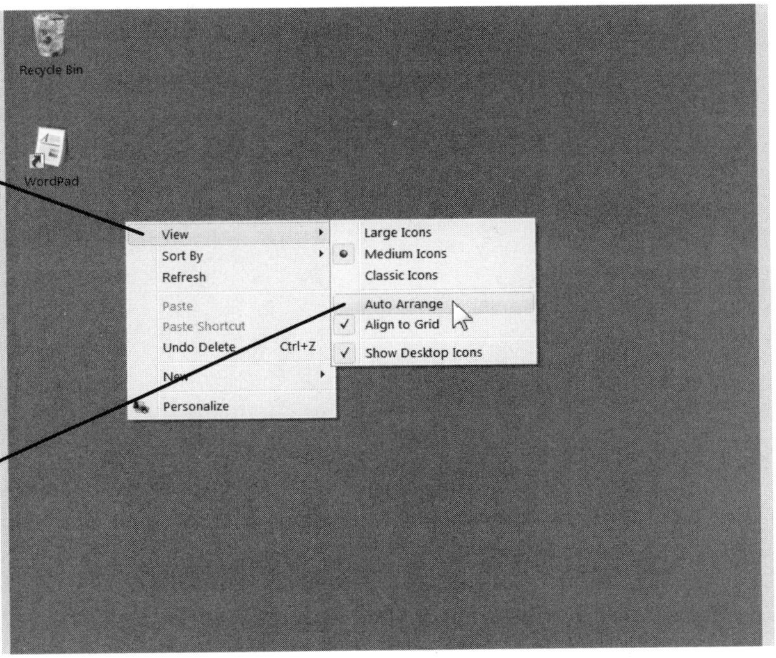

The setting *Auto Arrange* is no longer active. Now you can freely move the icons on the desktop.

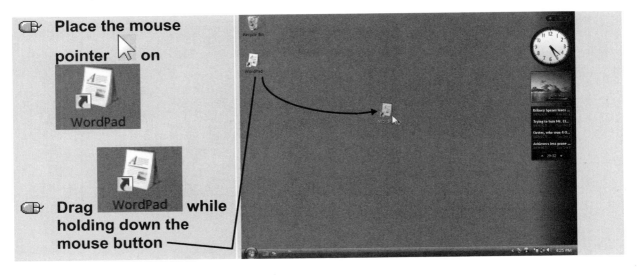

- **Place the mouse pointer** on

- **Drag**

while holding down the mouse button

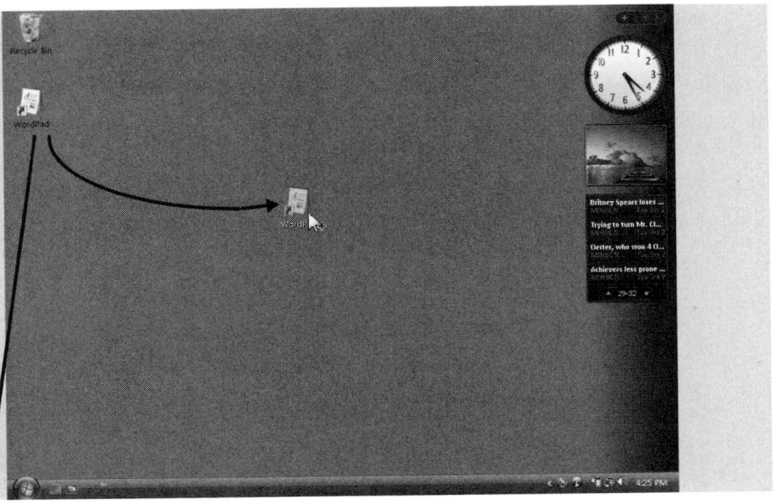

Please note:

When the icon disappears while you are dragging it and you see the 'No entry' sign ⊘, you have dragged it to a location where the icon can not be placed, like inside *Windows Sidebar*.

The *WordPad* icon has been moved:

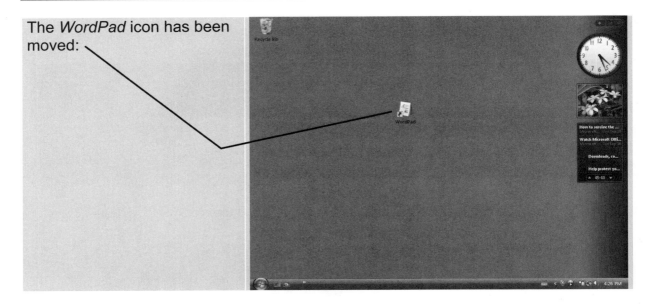

You see how easy it is to arrange the icons on your desktop just the way you want.

1.4 Turning On Auto Arrange

If you would rather have your icons displayed in a straight line, you can have them arranged automatically. This is how you do that:

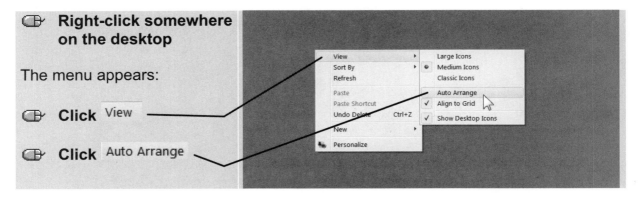

The *WordPad* icon is now neatly aligned with the other icons: ⟍

In this manner you can keep all of your icons neatly aligned with one another. Even if you try to move one to a different place. Try it:

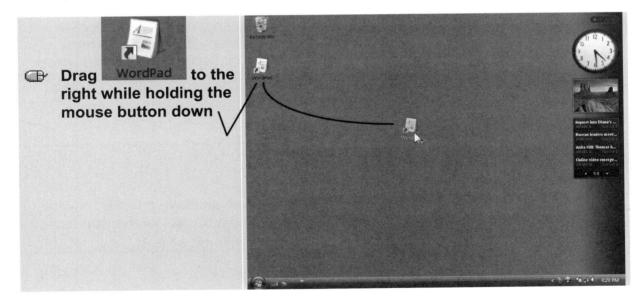

Drag WordPad to the right while holding the mouse button down ⟍

You see the *WordPad* icon
jump right back to its previous
position:

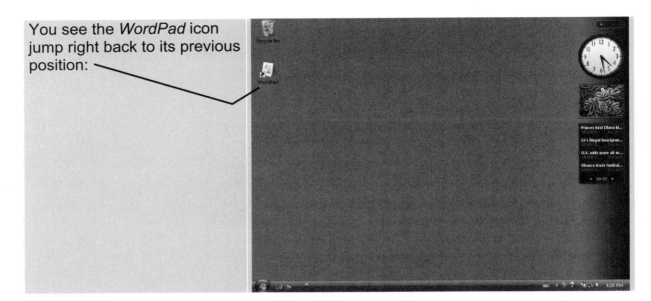

 Tip

Drag in line

Moving an icon when the *Auto Arrange* option is turned on causes all of the other
icons to be moved as well. Icons are not allowed to overlap. Dragging an icon
completely outside the existing pattern moves it to the last spot in the pattern, after
rearranging all other icons accordingly.

 Tip

Drag into a folder

Some users like to keep folders on their desktop. If you have a folder on your
desktop, make sure not to drag an icon into the folder. It will look like the icon has
disappeared, but in fact it has simply been stored in the folder.

1.5 Changing the Shortcut Icon

You can change the icon for your shortcuts. This is very useful when you have similar looking icons.

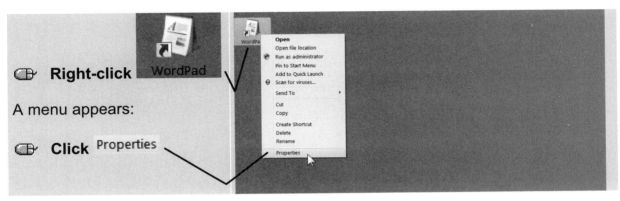

Right-click WordPad

A menu appears:

Click Properties

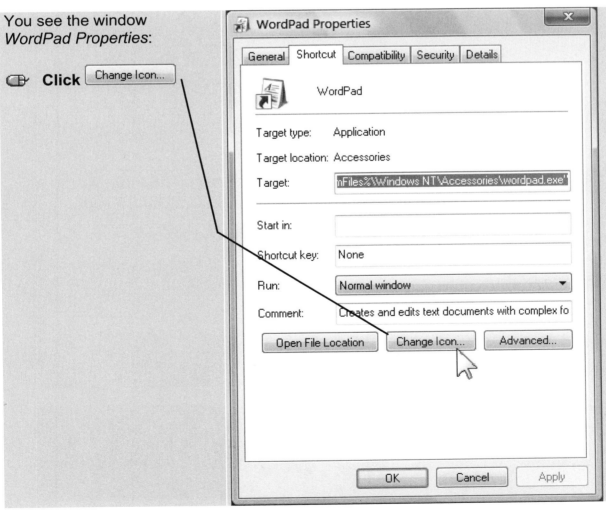

You see the window *WordPad Properties*:

Click Change Icon...

You see a window with different icons:

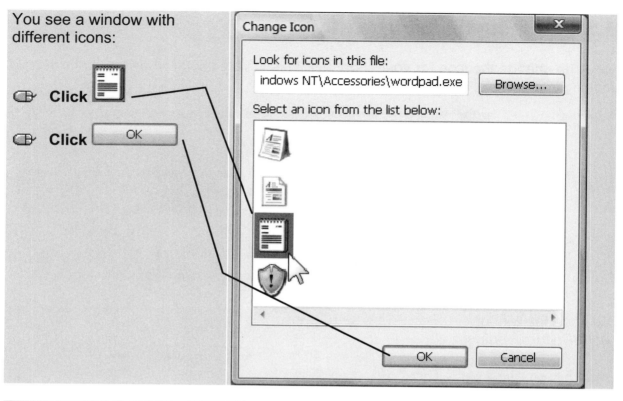

👆 **Click** 📄

👆 **Click** OK

You see the window *WordPad Properties* again:

👆 **Click** OK

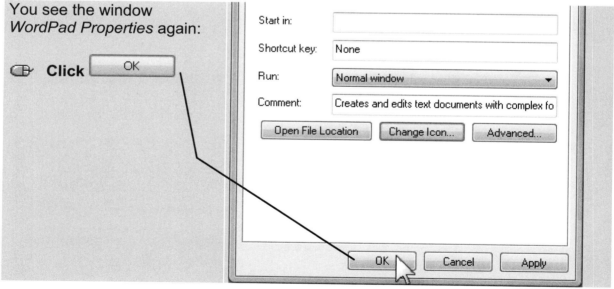

The icon has changed:

1.6 Deleting an Icon

Deleting an icon from your desktop is very easy:

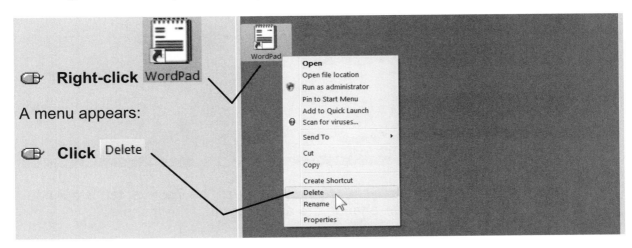

☞ **Right-click** WordPad

A menu appears:

☞ **Click** Delete

Windows asks if you are sure you want to move this file to the *Recycle Bin*:

☞ **Click** Yes

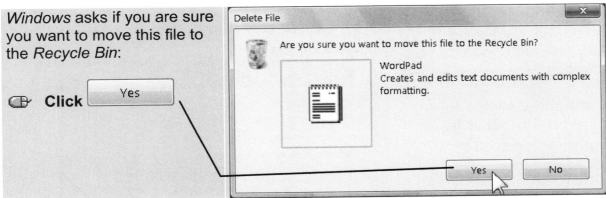

The *WordPad* icon has been moved to the *Recycle Bin*:

If your *Recycle Bin* was empty before, you will now see something in it:

1.7 Adjusting the Taskbar Settings

You can alter the way the taskbar is displayed by adjusting its settings. To see the properties of the taskbar, do the following:

Right-click an empty area on the taskbar

A menu appears:

Click Properties

You see the window *Taskbar and Start Menu Properties*. The *Taskbar* tab is opened. Selecting any of these options will change the appearance of the taskbar:

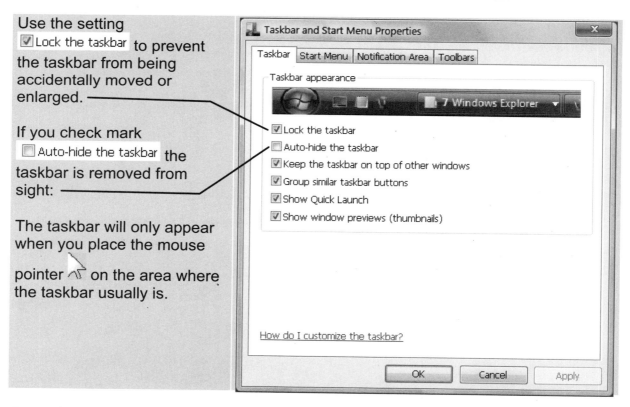

Use the setting ☑ Lock the taskbar to prevent the taskbar from being accidentally moved or enlarged.

If you check mark ☐ Auto-hide the taskbar the taskbar is removed from sight:

The taskbar will only appear when you place the mouse pointer on the area where the taskbar usually is.

There are more settings in this window.
When the option ☑ Keep the taskbar on top of other windows is check marked, the taskbar will always be displayed, even if you maximized a program window. This setting allows you to quickly switch back and forth between program windows using the buttons on the taskbar.

A taskbar button represents a program or file you opened. You always see these buttons displayed on the taskbar.

When the option ☑ Group similar taskbar buttons is check marked, similar taskbar buttons are stacked when the taskbar is full. For example, when you are working on multiple documents in *WordPad* at the same time, the taskbar buttons of these documents

are shown as one button: 📄 3 WordPad ▼ . The arrow and the number indicate that there are more documents open.

If you would rather display similar taskbar buttons separately, make sure to remove the check mark by *Group similar taskbar buttons*.

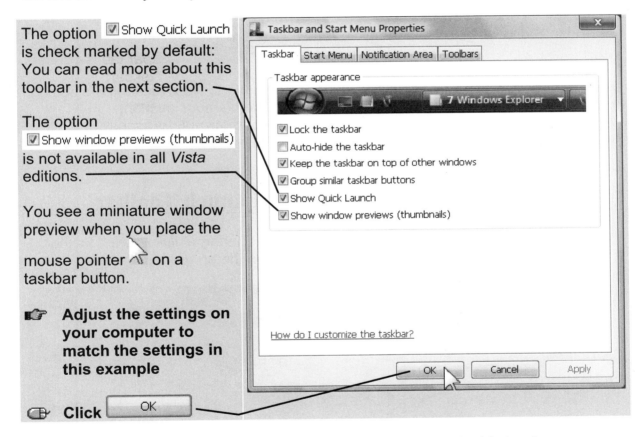

The option ☑ Show Quick Launch is check marked by default: You can read more about this toolbar in the next section. ⟍

The option ☑ Show window previews (thumbnails) is not available in all *Vista* editions. ⟍

You see a miniature window preview when you place the mouse pointer ⭦ on a taskbar button.

☞ **Adjust the settings on your computer to match the settings in this example**

☞ **Click OK**

The taskbar on your computer now has the same settings as in this book.

1.8 The Quick Launch Toolbar

The *Quick Launch* toolbar is the section of the taskbar next to the *Start button* where you can add shortcuts to programs.

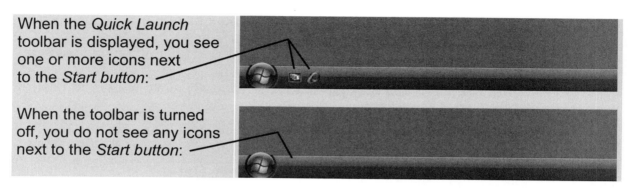

When the *Quick Launch* toolbar is displayed, you see one or more icons next to the *Start button*:

When the toolbar is turned off, you do not see any icons next to the *Start button*:

The *Quick Launch* toolbar is visible on your computer when you matched the settings on your computer to the settings in the example in the previous section.
The *Quick Launch* toolbar will give you access to programs you frequently use.
You can easily add or remove shortcut icons from this toolbar.

1.9 Adding a Shortcut to the Quick Launch Toolbar

If you use *WordPad* often, you can add a shortcut to it in the *Quick Launch* toolbar. Then you need only to click the shortcut once to open the program.

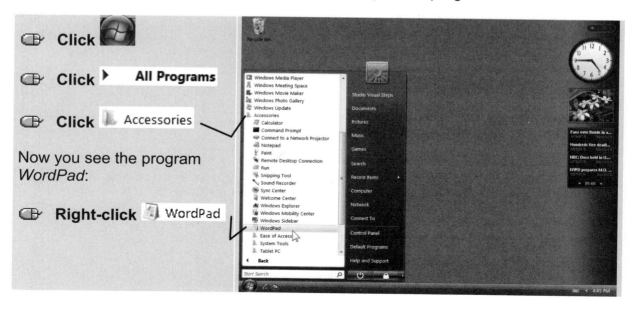

Click

Click ▶ **All Programs**

Click Accessories

Now you see the program *WordPad*:

Right-click WordPad

This menu appears:

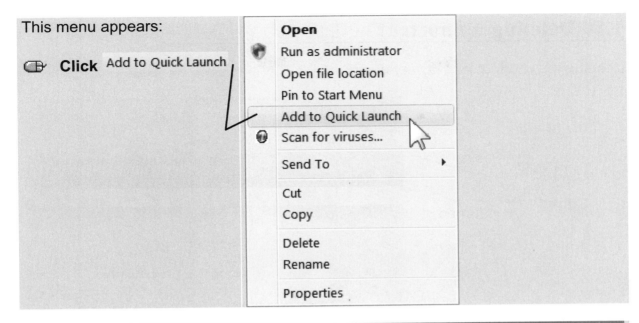

 Click Add to Quick Launch

| Open |
| Run as administrator |
| Open file location |
| Pin to Start Menu |
| Add to Quick Launch |
| Scan for viruses... |
| Send To ▶ |
| Cut |
| Copy |
| Delete |
| Rename |
| Properties |

The *WordPad* icon has been added to the *Quick Launch* toolbar: ———

💡 **Tip**

Copying icons from the desktop to the Quick Launch Toolbar

If you want to add an icon from the desktop to the *Quick Launch* toolbar, you can also drag it there: ———

Release the mouse button when you see the icon appear next to the *Start button*. The shortcut is copied. The icon on the desktop will stay in place.

1.10 Deleting a Shortcut

Deleting the shortcut icon is very easy:

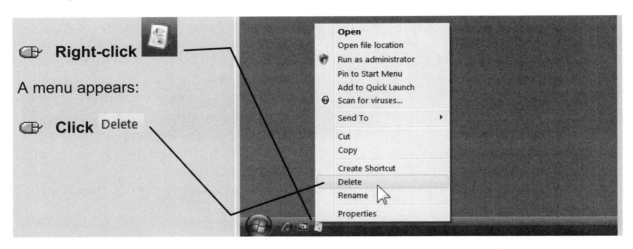

Windows asks for a confirmation:

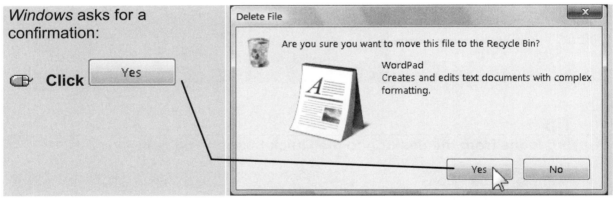

Tip

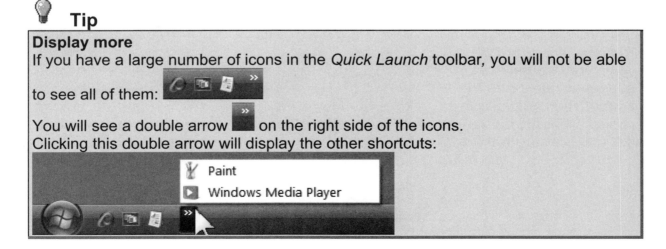

1.11 Adjusting the Notification Area

The *notification area* is the area on the right side of the *Windows* taskbar. The notification area is sometimes called the *system tray*. The notification area contains shortcuts to programs and other information.

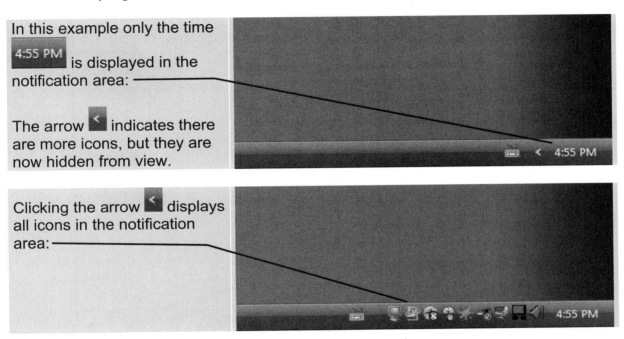

You will of course see other icons on your computer. Which icons you see, depends on the programs you have installed on your computer.

You can choose which icons you want to display in the notification area:

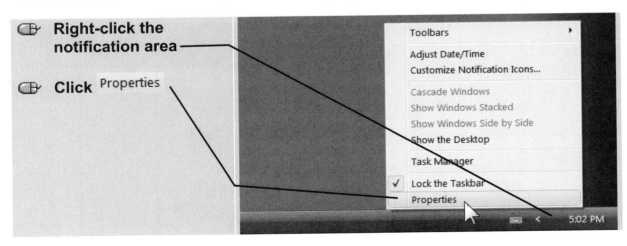

You see the properties of the notification area where you can select which icons to display. For example, you can choose to hide the time in the notification area if you have a clock already running in *Windows Sidebar*.

In this example the item Clock
has a check mark ☑: ⎯

☞ **Click to remove the
check mark for** Clock

☞ **Click** [Apply]

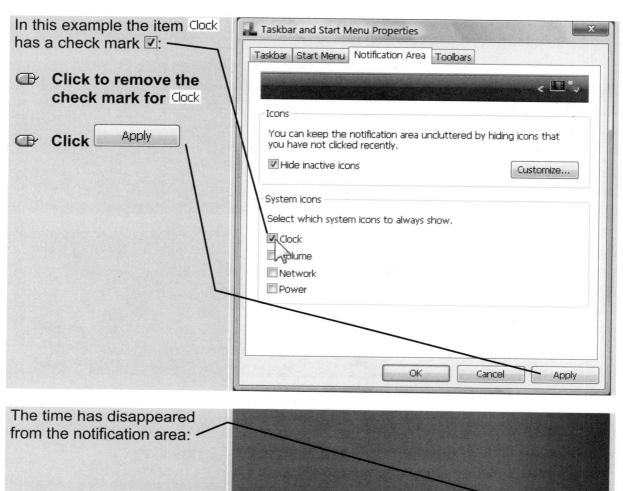

The time has disappeared
from the notification area: ⎯

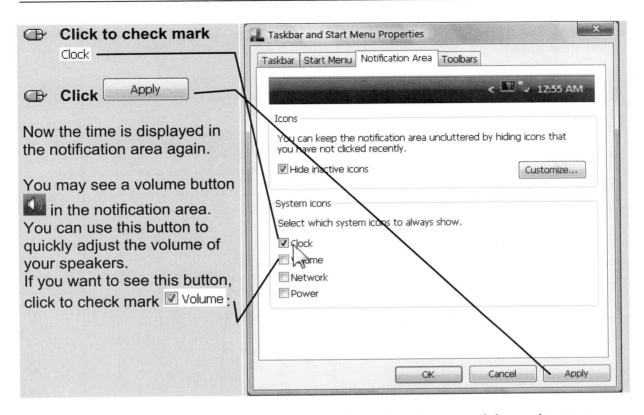

- ☞ **Click to check mark** Clock

- ☞ **Click** Apply

Now the time is displayed in the notification area again.

You may see a volume button in the notification area. You can use this button to quickly adjust the volume of your speakers.
If you want to see this button, click to check mark ☑ Volume:

You can use the other options to show icons for network connectivity and power settings. This last option is only available if you use a laptop.

In addition to these icons for system functions like time, volume, network and power settings, other programs may also show information in the notification area. For example, the status of your antivirus program.

By default, this type of information is hidden, but you can choose to display it in the notification area:

 Click Hide inactive icons

The check mark disappears.

 Click Apply

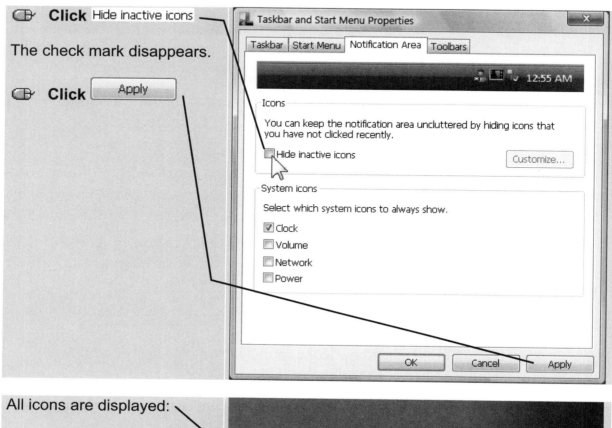

All icons are displayed:

➡️ **Please note:**

Which icons are shown on your screen depends on the programs that are installed on your computer. You will probably see different icons than in the example above.

💡 **Tip**

If you want to take a quick look at the icons in the notification area without displaying them permanently, you can click ◀ on the left side of the notification area. The icons appear and then disappear again after a few seconds.

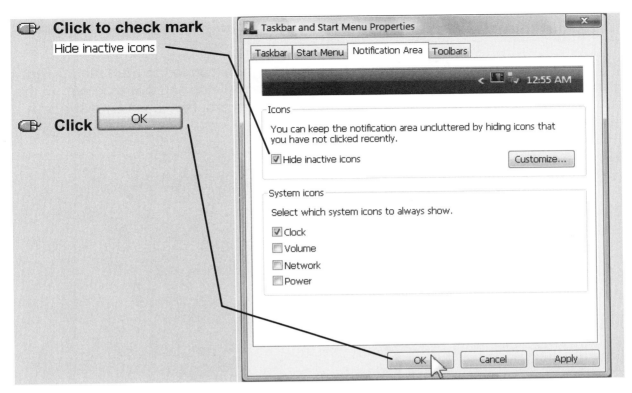

Click to check mark
Hide inactive icons

Click OK

Now you will only see the system icons you check marked earlier in the notification area. These icons give quick access to the corresponding program, for example the date and time settings on your computer:

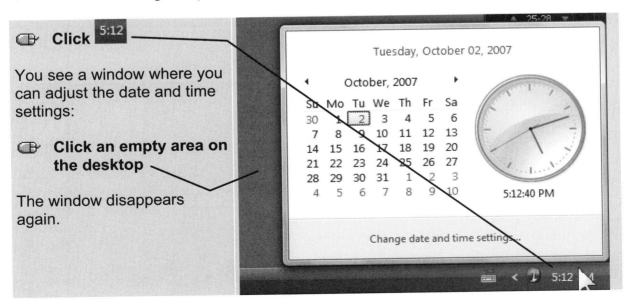

Click 5:12

You see a window where you can adjust the date and time settings:

Click an empty area on the desktop

The window disappears again.

The notification area of the taskbar also displays other information. For example, when you send a file to your printer, a printer icon will appear.

1.12 Customizing the Start Menu

If you use a program regularly, you can pin the program icon to the *Start menu*. Then you no longer need to search through the *All programs* list to find this program. At the top of the *Start menu* you see a horizontal line. Pinned program icons appear above the horizontal line and are always visible.

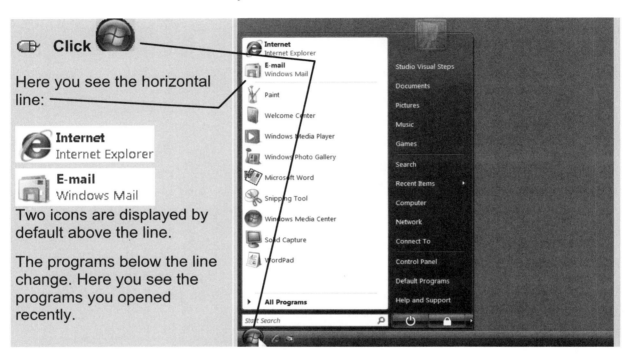

Click 👆

Here you see the horizontal line:

Two icons are displayed by default above the line.

The programs below the line change. Here you see the programs you opened recently.

You are going to pin *WordPad* to the *Start menu*:

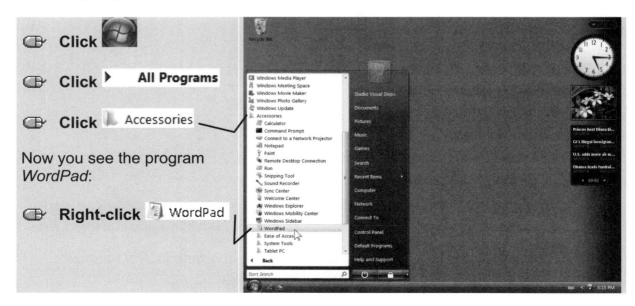

Click 👆

Click 👆 **All Programs**

Click 👆 **Accessories**

Now you see the program *WordPad*:

Right-click 👆 WordPad

You see this menu:

➔ **Click** Pin to Start Menu

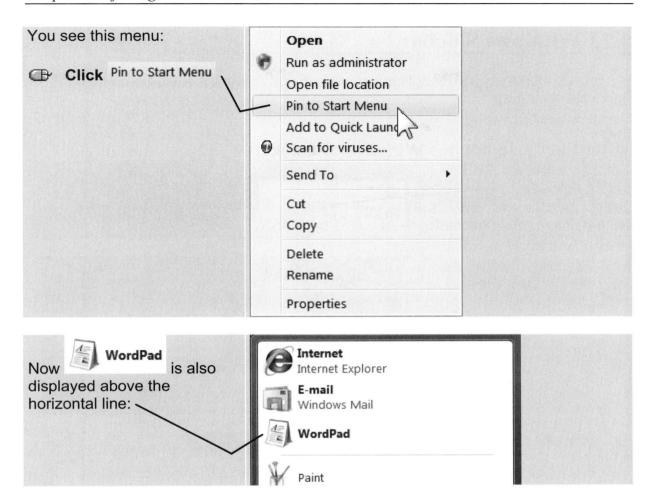

Now [WordPad] is also displayed above the horizontal line:

You can also unpin a program from the *Start menu*:

➔ **Right-click** [WordPad]

➔ **Click** Unpin from Start Menu

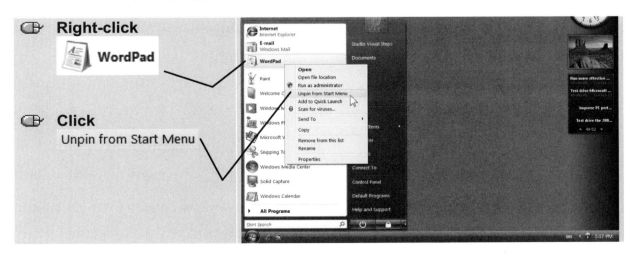

WordPad is no longer displayed above the horizontal line in the *Start menu*. You can use this method to add your favorite programs to the *Start menu*.

1.13 Windows Sidebar

By default, *Windows Sidebar* disappears when you maximize a window. You can change that setting.

 HELP! I do not see Windows Sidebar.

To open *Windows Sidebar*:

☞ **Click successively** 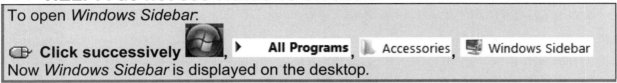 ▶ **All Programs**, ▯ Accessories, ▦ Windows Sidebar

Now *Windows Sidebar* is displayed on the desktop.

☞ **Right-click an empty area on the *Sidebar***

☞ **Click** Properties

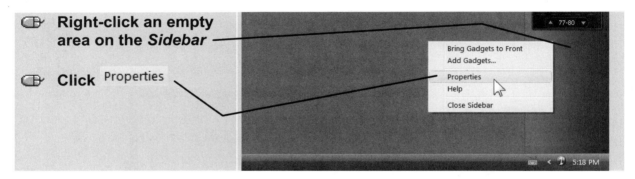

☞ **Click to check mark** Sidebar is always on top of other

☞ **Click** ▭ OK ▭

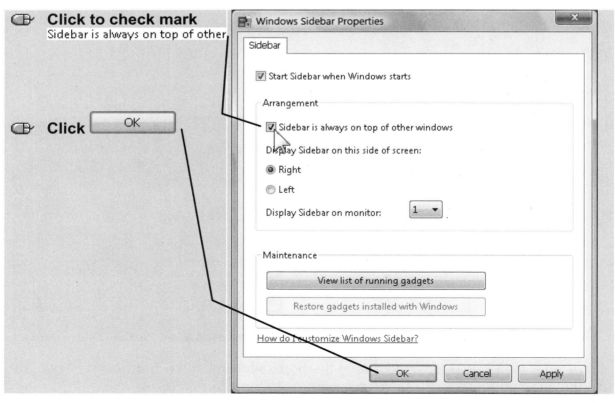

Now *Windows Sidebar* is no longer transparent and always stays visible. You can see that when you open a program and maximize the window:

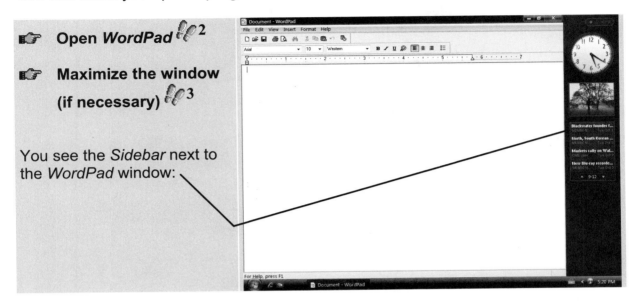

☞ **Open *WordPad*** 🦶²

☞ **Maximize the window (if necessary)** 🦶³

You see the *Sidebar* next to the *WordPad* window:

This way you can keep an eye on important gadgets. To be able to use the full screen for your program, you can turn this setting off like this:

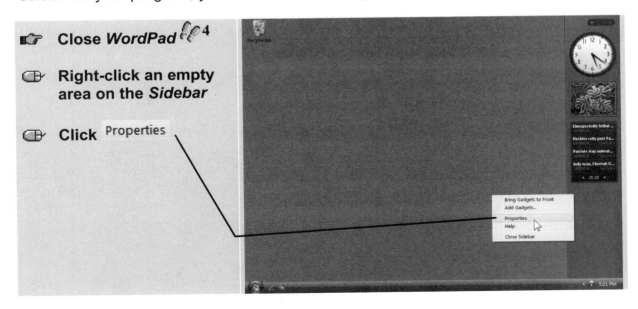

☞ **Close *WordPad*** 🦶⁴

🖱 **Right-click an empty area on the *Sidebar***

🖱 **Click** Properties

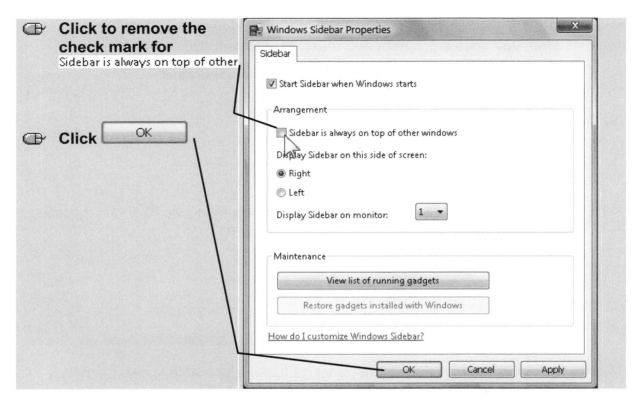

Click to remove the check mark for
Sidebar is always on top of other

Click OK

Windows Sidebar will now disappear behind a maximized window.

💡 **Tip**

Placing gadgets on your desktop

Gadgets do not necessarily need to be in the *Windows Sidebar*. You can also detach them from the *Sidebar* and drag them to another area on the desktop:

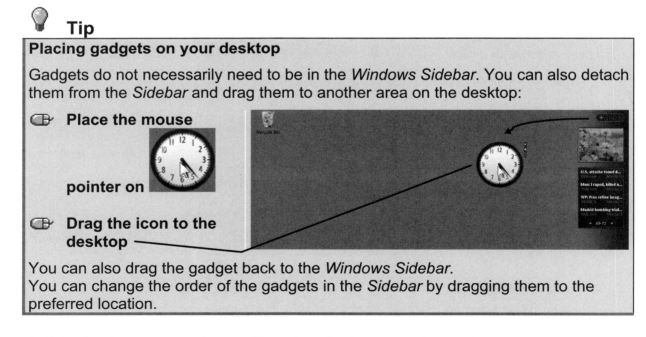

Place the mouse

pointer on

Drag the icon to the desktop

You can also drag the gadget back to the *Windows Sidebar*.
You can change the order of the gadgets in the *Sidebar* by dragging them to the preferred location.

In this chapter you have learned how to adjust your work area to your own preferences. With the following exercises you can practice what you have learned.

1.14 Exercises

Have you forgotten how to do something? Use the number beside the footsteps to look it up in *Appendix B How Do I Do That Again?*

Exercise: Shortcuts

In this exercise, you practice creating shortcuts and arranging icons on the desktop.

✔ Search the program *Windows Photo Gallery* 🖼 Windows Photo Gallery in the list *All programs*.

✔ Create a shortcut on the desktop for the program *Windows Photo Gallery*. 👣⁵

✔ Turn off *Auto Arrange* icons. 👣⁶

✔ Drag the *Windows Photo Gallery* icon to the center of the desktop.

✔ Create a shortcut to *Windows Photo Gallery* in the *Quick Launch* toolbar. 👣⁷

✔ Pin *Windows Photo Gallery* to the *Start menu*. 👣⁸

✔ Delete the *Windows Photo Gallery* icon from the *Quick Launch* toolbar. 👣⁹

✔ Unpin *Windows Photo Gallery* from the *Start menu*. 👣¹⁰

✔ Turn on *Auto Arrange* again. 👣⁶

✔ Delete the *Windows Photo Gallery* icon from the desktop. 👣¹¹

1.15 Background Information

Glossary	
Desktop	The work area on a computer screen that simulates the top of an actual desk. When you open a program, it appears on the desktop.
Gadget	Miniprogram attached to *Windows Sidebar*.
Icon	A small image that represents a shortcut to a file, folder, program, or other object or function.
Notification area	The area on the right side of the *Windows Vista* taskbar that contains shortcuts in the form of icons to programs and important status information. Sometimes also called *System Tray*.
Shortcut	A link in the form of an icon to any item accessible on your computer, such as a program, file, folder, disc drive, printer, or another computer. You can place shortcuts in various areas, such as on the desktop, on the *Start menu*, in the *Quick Launch* toolbar and in the notification area on the taskbar.
System Tray	The area on the right side of the *Windows Vista* taskbar that contains shortcuts in the form of icons to programs and important status information. Better known as notification area.
Taskbar	Horizontal bar at the bottom of the desktop. On the taskbar, taskbar buttons are displayed.
Taskbar button	A button representing an open folder, file or program. These buttons appear on the taskbar. You can click a taskbar button to switch between windows.
Quick Launch toolbar	An area of the taskbar that contains shortcuts in the form of icons to frequently used programs. By default, the *Quick Launch* toolbar is located on the right side of the *Start button*.
Windows Sidebar	Vertical bar displayed on the side of the desktop. This bar contains miniprograms that are called gadgets.

Source: Windows Help and Support

1.16 Tips

 Tip

Icons in the notification area

In this chapter you have learned how to show or hide **all** icons in the notification area. You can also set the display properties for each individual icon separately:

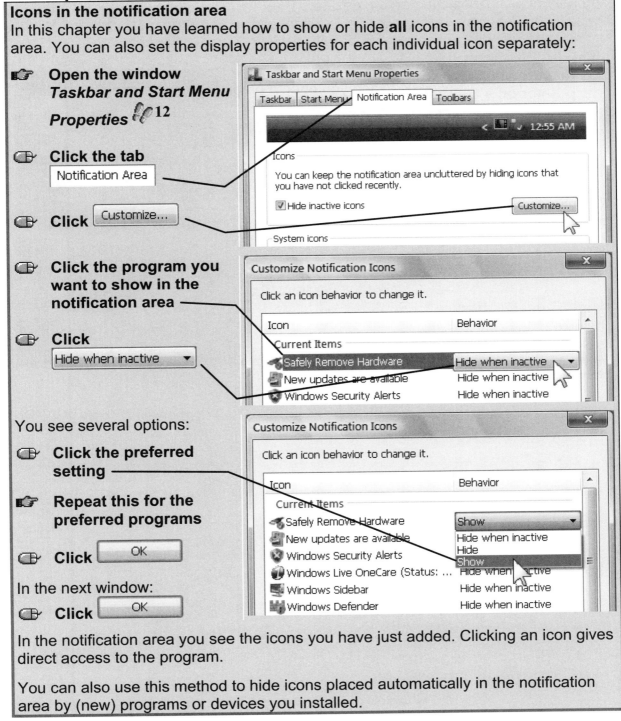

In the notification area you see the icons you have just added. Clicking an icon gives direct access to the program.

You can also use this method to hide icons placed automatically in the notification area by (new) programs or devices you installed.

Tip

Window previews

In general, when you work on multiple programs or documents at the same time, they will not all be displayed on the desktop.

The taskbar displays a taskbar button for every opened program or document. When you place the mouse pointer on this button, a window preview appears:

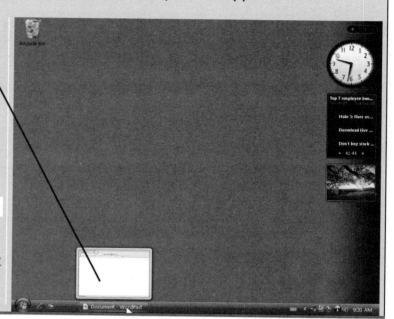

 Place the mouse pointer on a taskbar button ——————

You see the window preview:

If you do not see anything, check the window taskbar and *Start menu properties* to see if the option
☑ Show window previews (thumbnails)
is active.

Please note: this feature is not available in *Windows Vista Home Basic.*

2. Adjusting Windows Settings

You can adjust many of the settings for your programs and devices in *Windows Vista* by going to the *Control Panel*. Here you can adjust settings for your mouse and keyboard, for example, and the date and time on your computer.

You can use the *Ease of Access Center* to make your computer easier to use by changing accessibility options for seeing, hearing and operating the computer.

A useful feature in *Windows Vista* is the ability to manage the settings for programs and file types. The *default* programs are those which are associated with particular kinds of files or groups of files, such as music files or image files. For example, you can associate all your photos and illustrations with *Windows Photo Gallery*.

It is also possible to assign a particular program to a specific file type. For instance, you can specify the text editing program *Word* to be the default program for opening all your *text* documents.

You can also adjust the settings for the different types of media which you use on your computer. For example, the play options for a CD or DVD.

In this chapter you learn how to:

- use the *Control Panel*;
- adjust the date and time;
- use the *Ease of Access Center*;
- set your default programs;
- associate file types with programs;
- set *AutoPlay* options for CDs, DVDs and other media.

2.1 The Control Panel

Many of the settings of your computer can be adjusted in a special window: the *Control Panel.* To open the *Control Panel*:

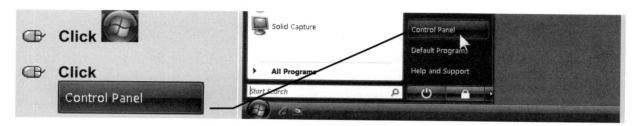

Click [Windows icon]

Click
Control Panel

You see the *Control Panel*:

The items are grouped by subject.

You can change the settings of an item by clicking one of the hyperlinks.

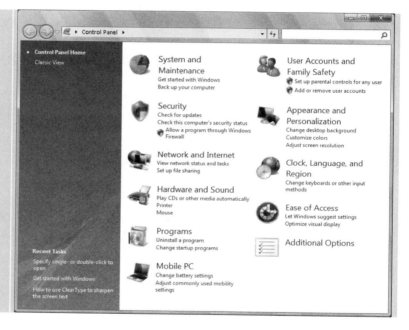

 HELP! My Control Panel looks very different.

If the *Control Panel* on your PC looks like this image, you are using the classic view.

Click Control Panel Home

Now you see the *Control Panel* as it is displayed in this book.

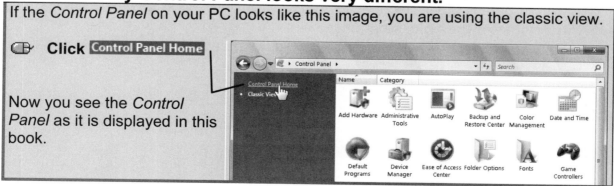

2.2 Adjusting Date and Time

If the clock on your computer no longer displays the current time, you can adjust the time like this:

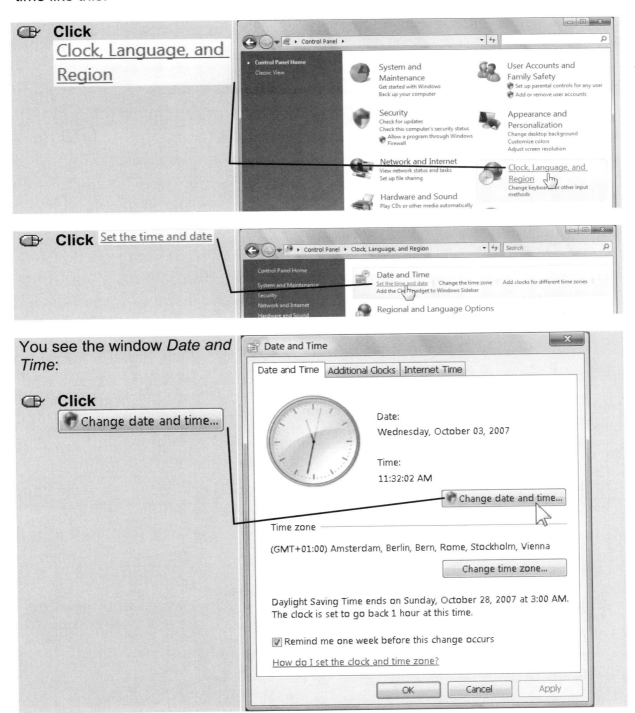

Click
<u>Clock, Language, and Region</u>

Click <u>Set the time and date</u>

You see the window *Date and Time*:

Click
🛡 Change date and time...

Your screen goes dark and the window *User Account Control* appears. Here you have to give your permission to continue:

☞ **Click** [Continue]

Now you see this window:

Here you can click the correct month, year and day:

You can set the time by clicking this box:

When the date and time have been set correctly:

☞ **Click** [OK]

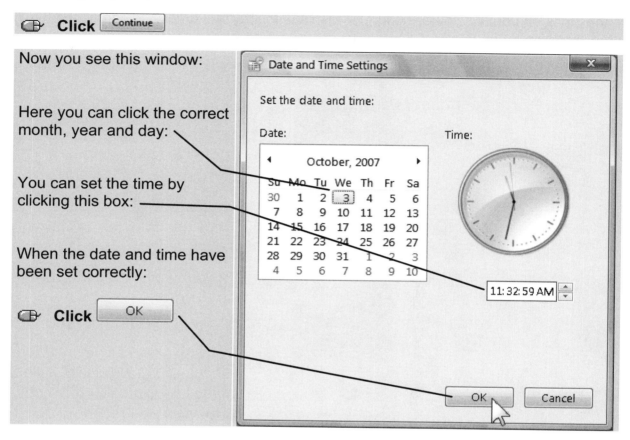

Note that there are different ways to open the same window in *Windows*. In the previous chapter you have learned that you can quickly open this window by clicking the icon [11:35 AM] in the notification area on the taskbar.

☞ **Close the window *Date and Time Settings*** ✍¹

💡 **Tip**

Quickly display the date
Using the notification area you can quickly display the date:

☞ **Place the mouse**

   pointer on [11:35 AM]

After a few seconds the date appears:

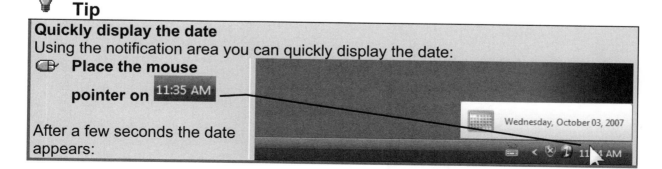

2.3 Ease of Access Center

The *Ease of Access Center* is a centralized location for accessibility settings and programs. Here you can find a questionnaire that you can use to get suggestions for accessibility features that you might find useful. Take a look at it:

Click 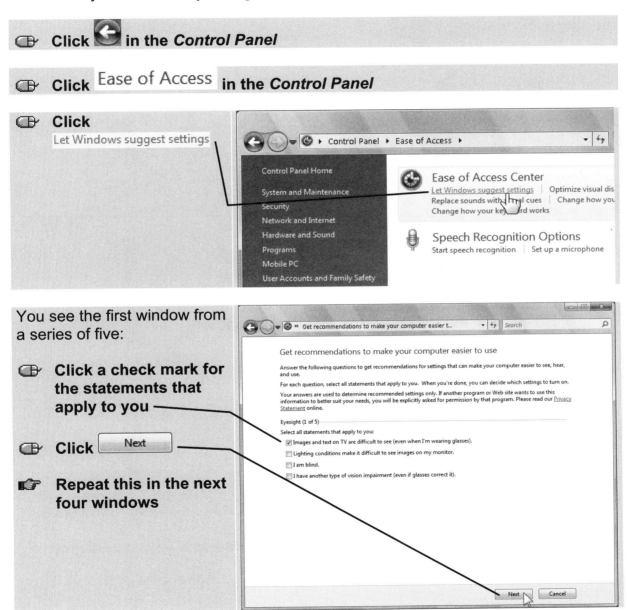 in the *Control Panel*

Click Ease of Access in the *Control Panel*

Click Let Windows suggest settings

You see the first window from a series of five:

Click a check mark for the statements that apply to you

Click Next

Repeat this in the next four windows

After the fifth window, *Windows Vista* will give recommendations for possible solutions and settings that might be applicable in your situation.

☞ **Read the recommendations**

If you want to apply the recommended settings:

☞ **Click** [Apply]

The settings are changed right away. You do not need to open the windows for each setting separately.

If you do not want to change anything, click the button [Cancel].

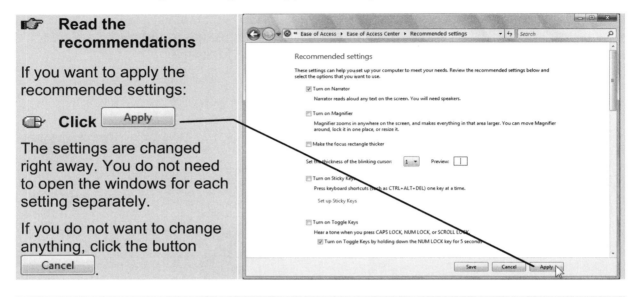

☞ **Close all windows** 🦶¹

If you have specific problems concerning your eyesight or motor skills, it is worth finding out what other possibilities *Windows* offers. You can find more information about these topics in the *Windows Help and Support* section.

☞ **Open *Windows Help and Support*** 🦶¹³

⌨ **Type** Ease of Access Center **in the *Search Box* and click** 🔍

You see a list of all available articles on this subject:

☞ **Read the articles you find interesting**

When you are done:

☞ **Close the window** 🦶¹

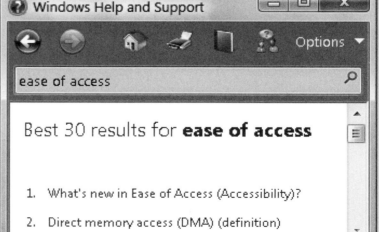

2.4 Setting Default Programs

A default program is the program *Windows* uses to open similar types of files, like images or webpages. For example, if you have more than one e-mail program installed on your computer, you can make one of these programs the default mail program.

You can set a default program like this:

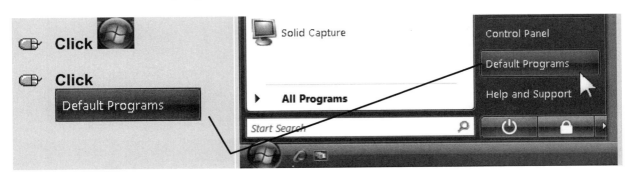

You see the window *Default Programs*:

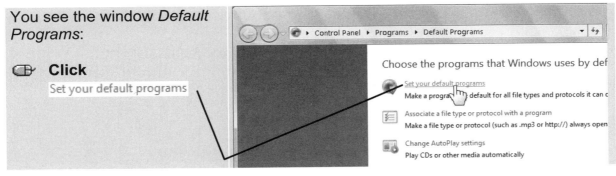

In this window you can set your default programs:

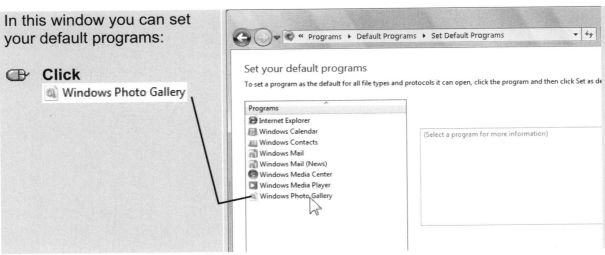

You see a description of the selected program:

Now you can set this program as default program.

☞ **Click**

→ Set this program as de

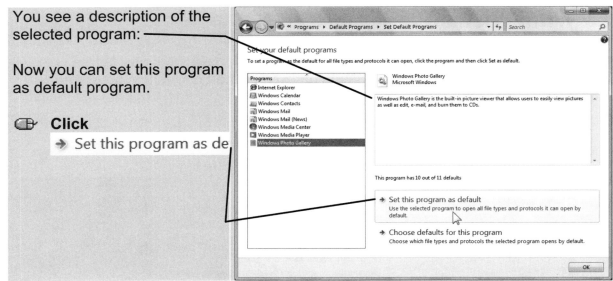

Now *Windows Photo Gallery* has been assigned all default settings:

You can check what these settings are:

☞ **Click**

→ Choose defaults for this pro

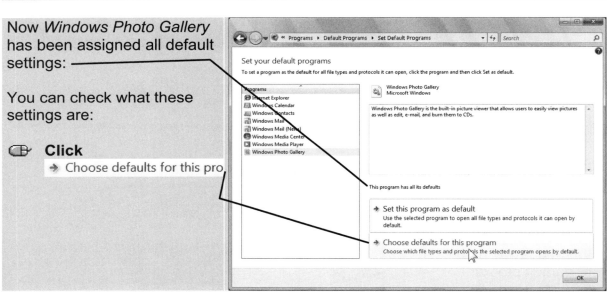

In this window you see the file types that will be opened with *Windows Photo Gallery*:

When you double-click a file with one of these extensions in a folder window, it will be opened in *Windows Photo Gallery*:

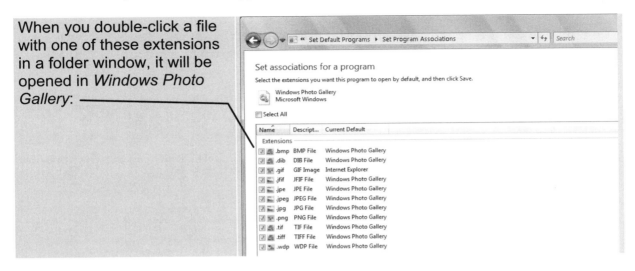

A file extension is the set of characters added to the end of a file name, following the dot. The extension identifies the file type. In the file named *photo.jpg, .jpg* is the extension.

Go back to the previous window:

☞ **Click**

You see the window *Set Default Programs* again:

☞ **Click**

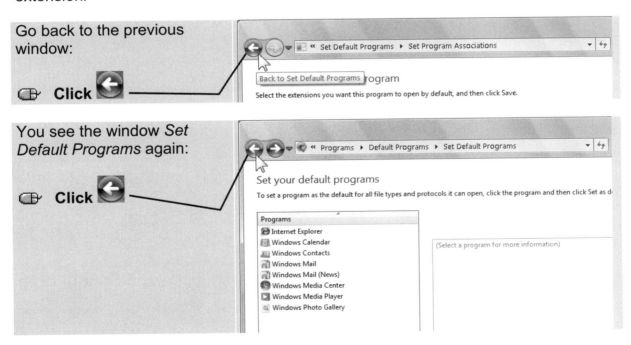

In this section you have learned how to associate a program with certain kinds of files - in this case image files. You can also work the other way round: associate a certain file type with a specific program. You can read how to do that in the next section.

2.5 Associating a File Type with a Program

You can associate a specific file type with one program. That can be useful when you always want to open files of a specific type in your photo editing program. You can adjust this setting in the window *Default Programs*:

You see the window *Default Programs*:

☞ **Click** Associate a file type or protocol with a program

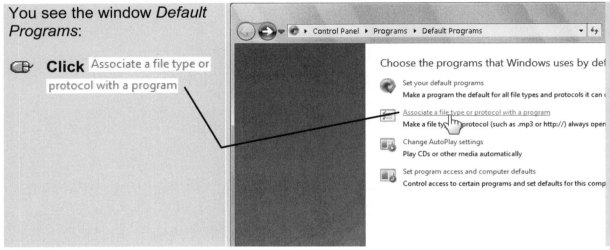

You see the window *Set Associations*:

This long list shows which file types are associated with which programs:

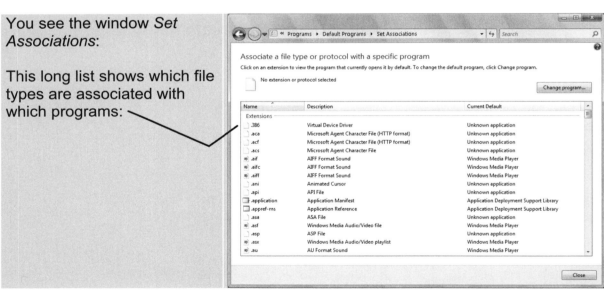

☞ **Drag the scroll bar down until you see the file type** BMP File

☞ **Click** BMP File

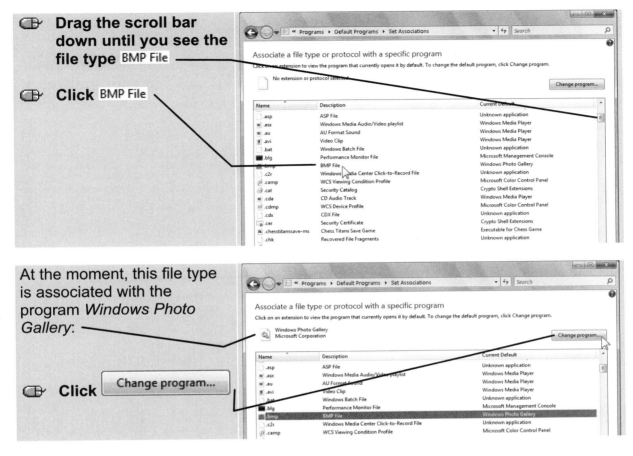

At the moment, this file type is associated with the program *Windows Photo Gallery*:

☞ **Click** Change program...

Now you can specify a different program to be associated with this file type:

Often one or more programs are displayed that you can select right away:

You can also search for a program on your computer yourself:

☞ **Click** Browse...

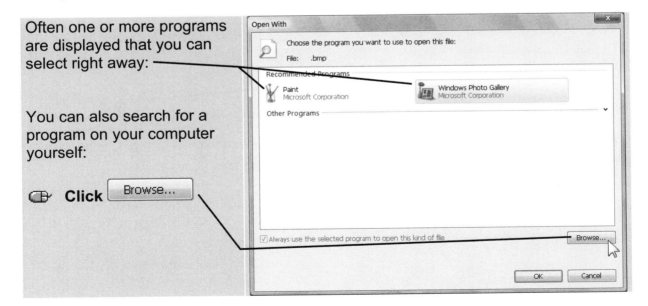

Here you can browse the folders on your hard disk to find the program you want to use, for example your favorite photo editing program.

You do not need to do that in this exercise:

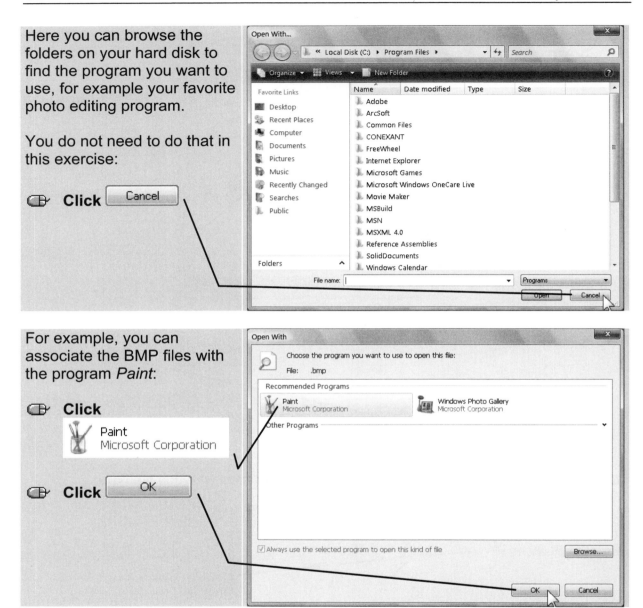

Click | Cancel

For example, you can associate the BMP files with the program *Paint*:

Click

Paint
Microsoft Corporation

Click | OK

Paint is a simple drawing program that can also be used to open images. *Paint* comes packaged with *Windows Vista*.

BMP files are now associated
with the program *Paint*:

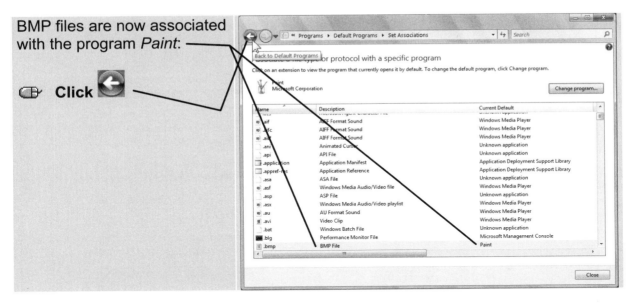

☞ **Click** ⬅

From now on, when you double-click a BMP file (with the extension *.bmp*) in a folder
window, it will be opened in the program *Paint*.

2.6 Changing AutoPlay Settings for CDs and Other Media

When you insert a CD or DVD in the CD/DVD drive of your computer, or insert a USB
stick in one of the USB ports, a window appears where you can choose what you
want to do with the disc/stick and the files on it. You can adjust the *AutoPlay* settings
to choose which program is automatically used for different kinds of digital media,
such as music CDs or DVDs:

You see the window *Default
Programs*:

☞ **Click**
Change AutoPlay settings

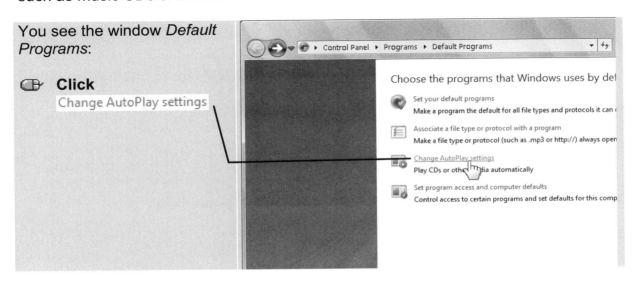

Now you see the window *AutoPlay*:

By default, the option
☑ Use AutoPlay for all media and devices
is active: ―――――――

In this example no other
defaults have been chosen:

This may be different on your
computer.

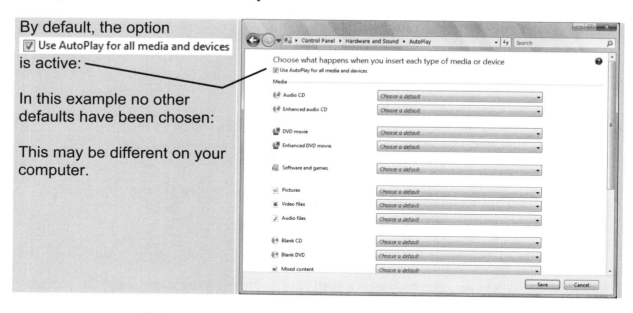

When the option ☑ Use AutoPlay for all media and devices is selected and you insert a CD,
DVD or USB stick, *Windows Vista* will automatically take the selected action. You can
choose a different setting for many kinds of media:

Click ˇ next to
◉ Audio CD ――――――

You see the different actions
for an audio CD:
Which actions are displayed
on your PC, depends on the
programs you have installed
on your computer.

If you like to play music with
Windows Media Player you
choose that option:

Click
▶ Play audio CD using Windows Media Player

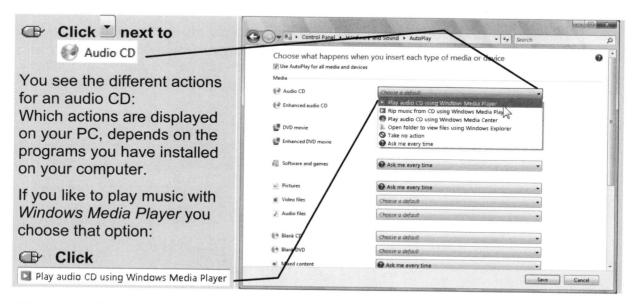

You can select the action to take for the other media the same way:

☞ **Select the action to take for other media**

Using the vertical scroll bar you can also display the media at the bottom of the
window.

Tip

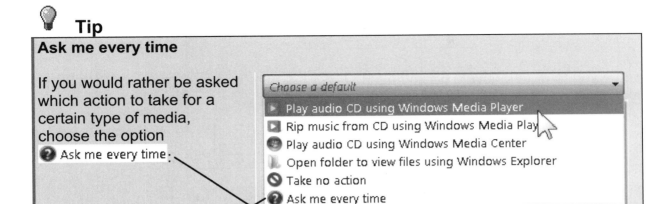

Ask me every time

If you would rather be asked which action to take for a certain type of media, choose the option 🔱 Ask me every time:

When you have finished changing the settings, you can confirm them:

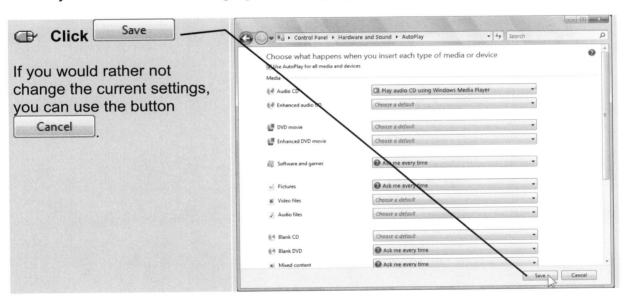

Click [Save]

If you would rather not change the current settings, you can use the button [Cancel].

☞ **Close the *Default Programs* window** 🖱¹

In this chapter you have read how you can associate programs with file types, and the other way round, how you can associate a file type with a program. You have also learned how you can change the *AutoPlay* settings for media like CDs, DVDs and USB sticks. This way you can let *Windows* do exactly what you want.

With the following exercises you can repeat these actions.

2.7 Exercises

Have you forgotten how to do something? Use the number beside the footsteps to look it up in *Appendix B How Do I Do That Again?*

Exercise: Associating a File Type with a Program

In this exercise, you repeat associating a file type with a program.

✔ Open the window *Default Programs.* 14

✔ Open the window *Set Associations.* 15

✔ Associate the file type BMP file with the program *Windows Photo Gallery.* 64

✔ Close the window. 1

Exercise: Setting a Default Program

In this exercise you repeat setting a program as default program.

✔ Open the window *Default Programs.* 14

✔ Set the program *Internet Explorer* as default program. 16

✔ Check which extensions will be opened by *Internet Explorer* by default. 17

✔ Close the window. 1

2.8 Background Information

Glossary	
Built-in clock	The chip (RTC or *Real Time Clock*) in the computer that maintains the date and time using a battery.
Control Panel	Window where you can change the settings for *Windows*, software, hardware and security.
Default program	The standard program associated with files of a certain type. For example, all photo files are opened by *Windows Photo Gallery*.
Ease of Access Center	Centralized location for accessibility settings and programs. You can use it to make your computer easier to use by changing the options for seeing, hearing and operating the computer.
File extension, file name extension	A set of characters added to the end of a file name that identifies the file type. In a file called letter.txt, *txt* is the extension.
File type, file format	The format of a file. The file type indicates which program it was created in and in which program it can be opened.
Protocol	Standard set of formats and procedures allowing computers to exchange information.

Source: Windows Help and Support

The built-in clock
Every computer has a built-in memory chip that maintains the time and date.
This tiny memory is kept running by a battery.
When the time is no longer displayed accurately, you need to have
the battery replaced. Contact your computer supplier to do this.

2.9 Tips

  Tip

Return to the default settings
Sometimes programs set themselves as default programs for certain types of CDs or DVDs when they are installed. This means each disc with files of that specific type will be opened with the newly installed program. This may be undesired especially when you use this program only on occasion and you would rather open your files with a program already familiar to you.

You can go back to the default settings like this:

☞ **Open the *Control Panel***
18

☞ **Click**
Play CDs or other media automatica
below
Hardware and Sound

☞ **Drag the scroll bar down**

☞ **Click** [Reset all defaults]

☞ **Click** [Save]

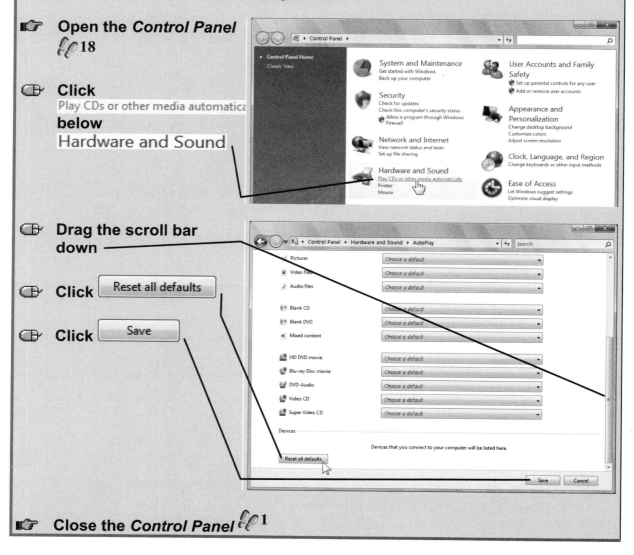

☞ **Close the *Control Panel*** *1*

3. Your Computer

In this chapter you are going to take a look at the different parts of your computer. For example, the hard disk and the devices with removable storage.

You will also learn more about the different types of files on the hard disk. A file can be anything: part of a computer program, or a data file. When you save your own work as a text document or a photo, it is also called a file. There are dozens of file types, each with its own file format. It is helpful to know which file types exist and which programs you can use to open them.

Your computer is constructed in such a way that various kinds of devices (peripheral equipment) can be added to it, for example a printer, scanner, external hard disk, extra memory, etcetera. These devices are called *hardware*.

Windows makes sure this hardware functions correctly. When you start your computer, *Windows* checks if any new items have been added, such as a printer or additional memory. If that is the case *Windows* installs the necessary *drivers* to make these new parts function properly.

In this chapter you will find information about different kinds of devices and the way you can connect them to your computer.

In this chapter you learn how to:

- find out which hard disks are present;
- view the properties of a disk;
- take a look at the DVD drive and removable disc;
- display the parts and performance of your computer;
- display information about your computer;
- look at the contents of a CD;
- see which file types are available;
- view the properties of a file;
- open a file;
- add and remove external hardware.

3.1 What Is Inside Your Computer?

Windows has a special button you can use to open the window that displays the parts of your computer:

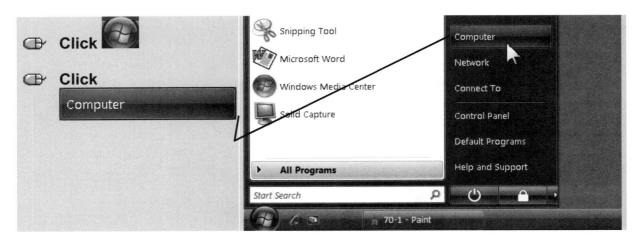

    Click

    Click

    Computer

The window *Computer* is opened. To see the window like it is displayed in this book, do the following:

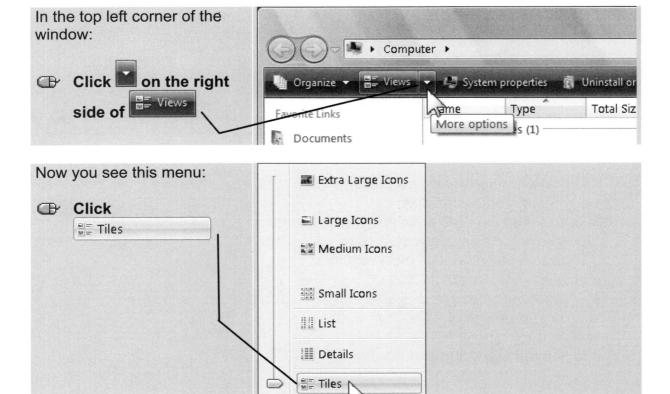

In the top left corner of the window:

    Click ▾ on the right

    side of Views

Now you see this menu:

    Click

    Tiles

You see this window, with the following parts from top to bottom:

The hard disk/disks:

The devices with removable storage: CD/DVD drives and removable disks:

Removable disks are things such as USB sticks or external hard disks.

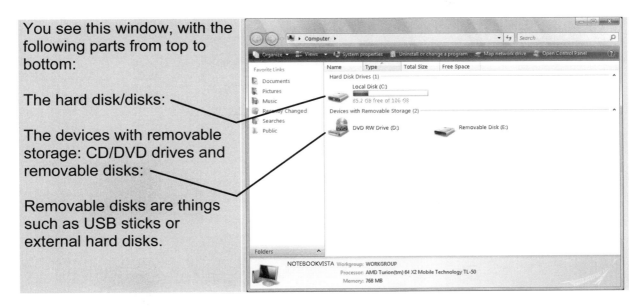

You will see different parts on your computer. Your computer may show more drives and additional devices such as a second CD/DVD drive.

You see that each part is represented by a letter. The hard disk always has the letter C. When there are more hard disks in the computer, the next disk gets the letter D. CD/DVD drives have the letters that follow the hard disk(s) (D in this example) and devices with removable storage the letters that follow that (E in this example). This is different on every computer, depending on the number of drives and devices.

3.2 The Properties of the Hard Disk

In the window *Computer* you can view the properties of each part of the computer like this:

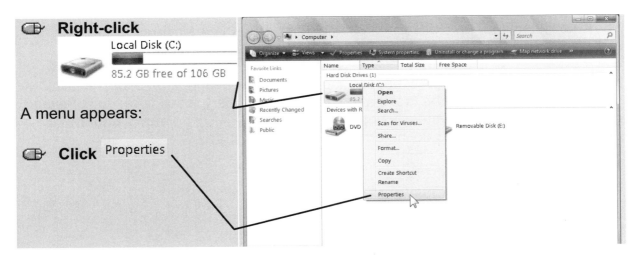

You see this window with the properties of your own hard disk:

The full capacity is expressed in GB:

Below you see a pie chart displaying the division between used and available space:

The capacity and the pie chart will of course look different on your computer than they do in this example.

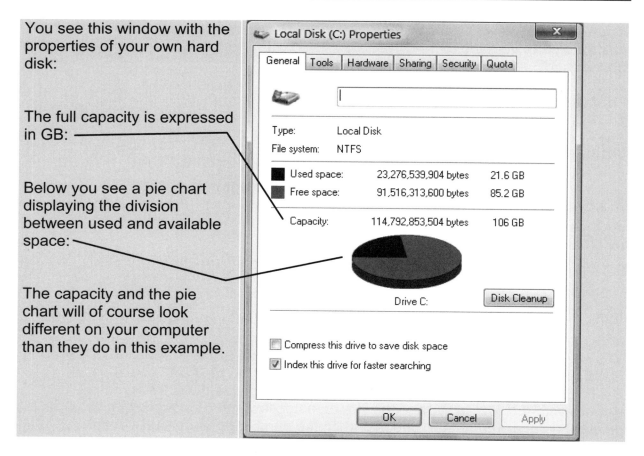

The abbreviation GB stands for Gigabyte, a measure for storage capacity. In the next section you can read more about that.

3.3 Gigabyte, Megabyte, Kilobyte

The smallest unit for data storage on computers is the *bit*. A single *byte* contains eight consecutive bits, and is capable of storing a single ASCII character, like 'h'.

A Kilobyte (KB) is 1,024 bytes, not one thousand bytes as might be expected. This odd number results from the fact that computers use binary (base two) math, instead of a decimal (base ten) system. For simplicity's sake, hard drive manufacturers use a decimal number system to define amounts of storage space:

- 1 Byte is 8 bits
- 1 Kilobyte (KB) is 1000 bytes
- 1 Megabyte (MB) is 1000 Kilobytes
- 1 Gigabyte (GB) is 1000 Megabytes
- 1 Terabyte (TB) is 1000 Gigabyte

There are different kinds of media that can be used to save and store data: USB sticks, memory cards, CDs, DVDs and hard disks. In older computers diskettes may still be used.

The storage capacity of these various types of media is expressed in Megabytes or Gigabytes. For example:

- diskette: 1.4 MB
- CD disc: 650 MB
- DVD disc: 4.7 GB (or double, depending on the type)
- USB stick: 16 MB to 8 GB (or more)
- memory card: 256 MB to 8 GB (or more)
- small hard disk of a computer: 30 to 80 GB
- large hard disk of a computer: 100 to 400 GB (or more)

In the *Properties* window you can see how big the hard disk of your computer is, in other words: what the *storage capacity* is.

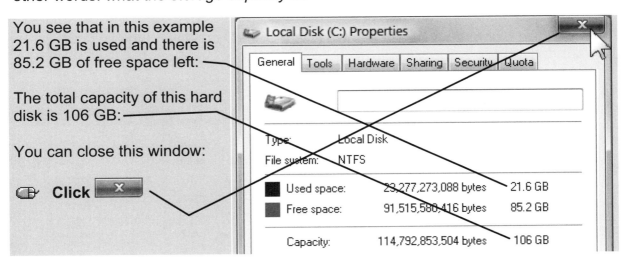

You see that in this example 21.6 GB is used and there is 85.2 GB of free space left:

The total capacity of this hard disk is 106 GB:

You can close this window:

☞ **Click**

3.4 Your DVD Drive

You can also view the properties of your DVD drive. These devices are available in different types:

- DVD player : plays/reads CD-ROMs and DVD-ROMs;
- DVD writer : plays/reads CD-ROMs and DVD-ROMs and writes CD-Recordables (CD-R) and DVD-Recordables (DVD-R);
- DVD rewriter : plays/reads CD-ROMs and DVD-ROMs and writes CD-Recordables (CD-R), DVD-Recordables (DVD-R), CD-Rewritables (CD-RW) and DVD-Rewritables (DVD-RW).

A DVD writer or DVD rewriter is also called a DVD burner.

Types of CD discs

- A CD-ROM disc can only be read/played. A CD is designed to store data in the form of text, graphics, music or even programs. The CD you received with this book is also a CD-ROM. ROM means *Read Only Memory*.
- A CD-Recordable is a CD disc that you can write to only once. These discs are labeled with: CD-R.
- A CD-Rewritable is a CD disc you can write to more than once. These discs are labeled with: CD-RW.

Types of DVD discs

- A DVD-ROM disc can only be read/played.
- A DVD-Recordable is a DVD disc that you can write to only once. These discs are labeled with: DVD-R or DVD+R.
- A DVD-Rewritable is a DVD disc that you can write to more than once. These discs are labeled with: DVD-RW or DVD+RW.

In the window *Computer* you can see what kind of DVD drive you have in your computer:

Right-click a DVD drive

DVD RW Drive (D:)

A menu appears:

Click Properties

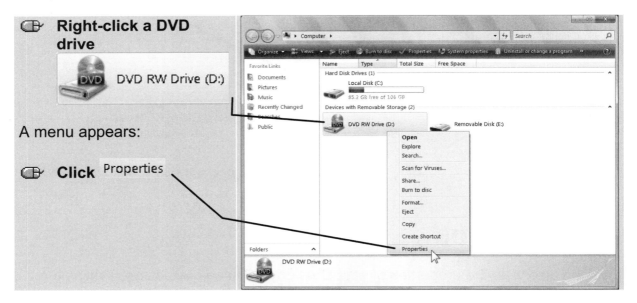

When you have a regular writable DVD station, the window will look like this:

When there is no CD or DVD disc in the player, the capacity is 0 bytes:

 Click OK

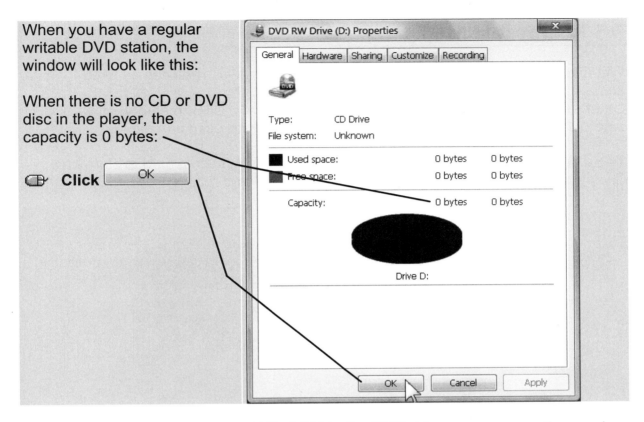

When you insert a CD-ROM or DVD-ROM in the DVD drive, you can see the used capacity of the disc in this window. If you insert a writable CD or DVD in a DVD writer, the storage capacity is displayed.

 Tip

Which DVD drive?
If you are unsure what type of DVD drive you have in your computer, you can go to the window *Computer* to view its label:

 . On the left you see the DVD writer, on the right the DVD player. If you do not see a similar display in your *Computer* window, refer to the documentation you received with your computer. It contains information about the parts of your computer, including the type of DVD drive.

 Tip

Burn CDs or DVDs yourself?
Do you have a DVD writer in your computer? *Windows Vista* allows you to write data to both CD-Recordable or DVD-Recordable discs. This is also called *burning CDs and DVDs.* You can read how to do that in chapter 8.

3.5 Removable Media

Writable CDs and DVDs are also called removable media. They can be used for data storage and are easily connected to the computer.
Other examples of removable media are memory cards, USB (memory) sticks and external hard disks. In older computers diskettes are still used sometimes.

There are different types of memory cards. You can use such a card to store data. They are connected to the computer using a special card reader.

A memory card and a card reader:

You can connect a USB stick to the USB port of a computer. You can read more about using USB sticks in the Visual Steps book **Windows Vista for SENIORS.**

USB sticks can be connected directly to the USB port of a computer:

Memory cards and USB sticks are meant for temporary storage of data and files. When you create a backup of your important files for example, an external hard disk is a more suitable storage device. An external hard disk can be connected by a cable to the USB port of your computer.

You connect an external hard disk to the USB port of the computer:

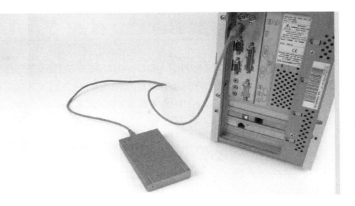

In the window *Computer* you see the different removable media that are connected to your computer:

CD and DVD drives:

Card readers, USB sticks and external hard disks:

When you connect a memory card, USB stick or external hard disk to your computer, you can double-click the device in the window *Computer* to display its contents.
In the folder window you see the files that are stored on the device.

For example, these are the contents of a USB stick:

In the address bar you can see which removable disc is opened. In this example it is
Removable Disk (E:) :

In the *File list* you see the available folders and/or files:

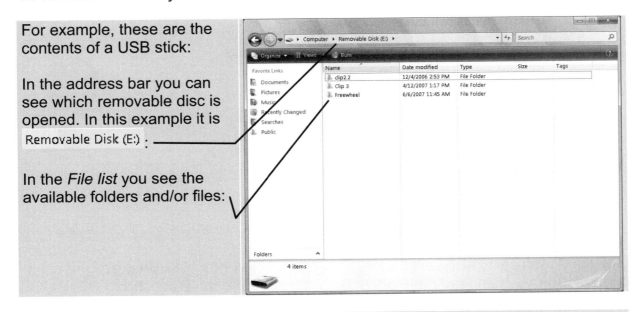

☞ **Close the window** ᶜℓ¹

3.6 Looking at the Parts of Your Computer

Using the *Control Panel* you can see what type of computer you have and what kind of technical components are in use. That includes parts inside the computer case as well as hardware connected to your computer. Take a look:

☞ **Open the *Control Panel* window** ⁄⁄ **18**

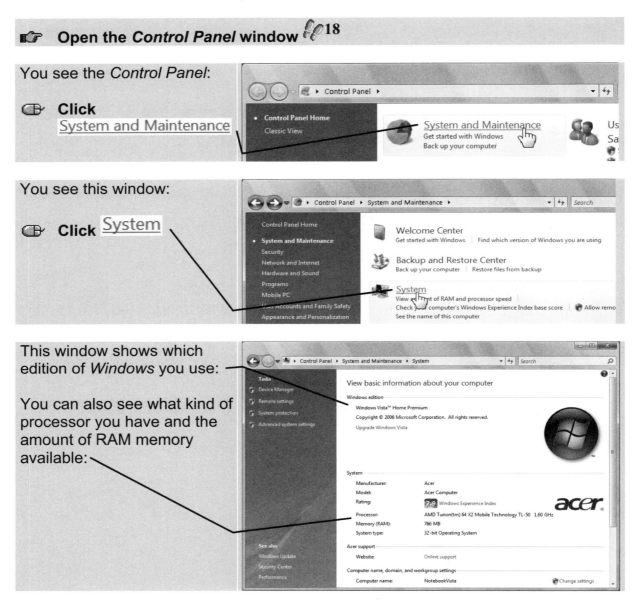

You see the *Control Panel*:

⬉ **Click**
   System and Maintenance

You see this window:

⬉ **Click** System

This window shows which edition of *Windows* you use:

You can also see what kind of processor you have and the amount of RAM memory available:

The RAM memory is also called system memory. In **section 3.12 Background Information** you can read more about RAM memory and the processor.

3.7 Displaying the Performance of Your Computer

Windows Vista can also tell you something about the performance of your computer. This mostly has to do with the speed of the different parts of your computer. If your computer is performing well, your programs should run smoothly and efficiently.

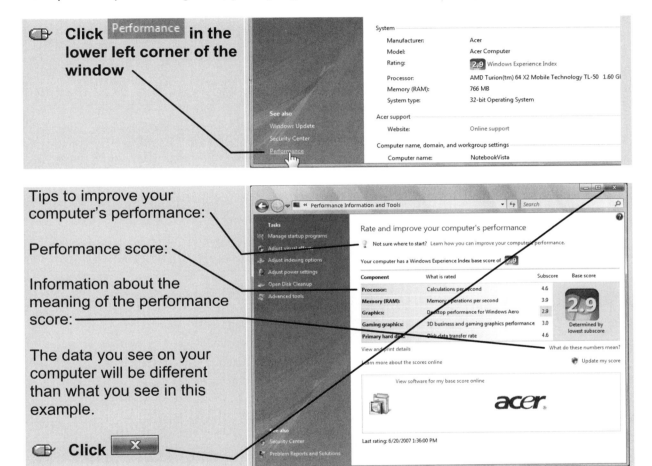

You can improve the performance of your computer by *upgrading* the hardware. For example, you might want to add more memory or install a new graphics card. You can read more about this subject in **section 3.13 New Hardware**.

3.8 Viewing the Contents of the CD-ROM

You can also use the window *Computer* to display the contents of a disc. For example, the contents of the CD-ROM you received with this book.

☞ **Open the *Computer* window** ℓℓ¹⁹

☞ **Insert the CD-ROM you received with this book in your computer**

☞ **Close the window *AutoPlay* (if necessary)** ℓℓ¹

In the window you see the name of the CD-ROM
VISTA_2 :

⊕ **Double-click the DVD drive containing the CD-ROM** ──

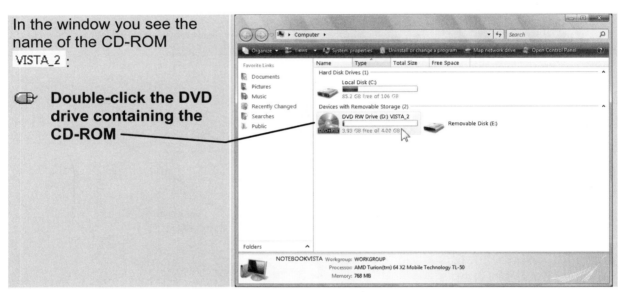

You see this window with files and folders:

⊕ **Double-click**
Examples
File Folder

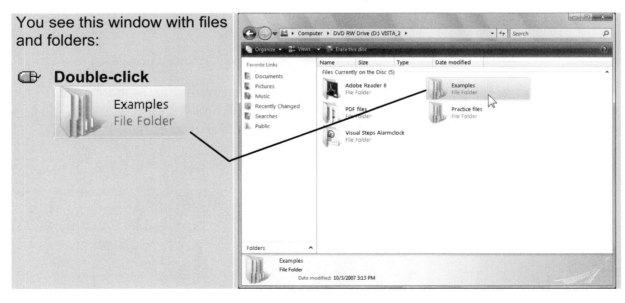

Now you see this window with these folders:

These folders contain examples of different file types. You can open one of the folders:

☞ **Double-click**

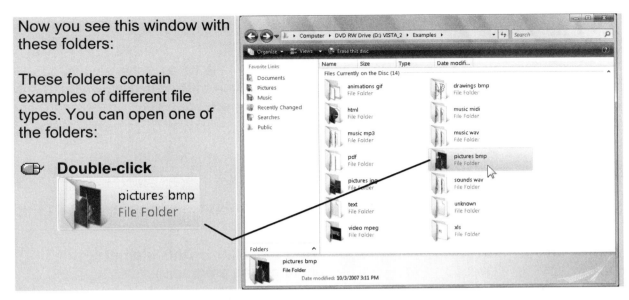

Now you see this window with a list of photo files.
The photos are displayed in miniature form (thumbnails):

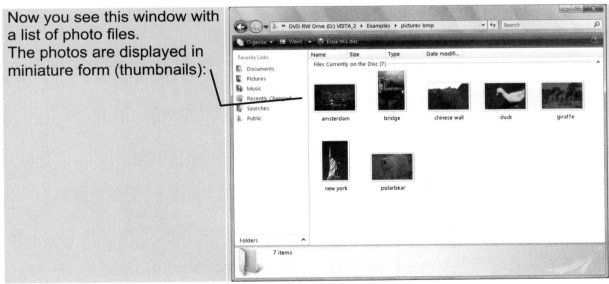

💡 **Tip**

Does the window *Computer* look different on your computer?

☞ **Click** on the right side of Views

☞ **Click** Large Icons

3.9 File Types

The folder *Examples* on the CD-ROM contains different file types. A file always has an extension behind the file name that tells you what type of file it is. Below you see a list of the most commonly used file types, followed (in parenthesis) by one or more programs that can be used to open the file:

BMP   Graphics file for drawings and images. Abbreviation of the word *bitmap* (*Paint, Windows Photo Gallery*, photo editing programs).

GIF   Graphics file for drawings (*Paint, Windows Photo Gallery*, photo editing programs).

JPG of JPEG   Graphics file for images, used very often on the Internet (*Paint, Windows Photo Gallery*, photo editing programs).

TIF, TIFF   Graphics file for images (*Paint,* photo editing programs).

DOC   Text file (*WordPad, Microsoft Word*).

DOCX   Text file - special file format (*Microsoft Word 2007* - other *Word*-versions will need a special 'viewer').

TXT   Text file without text formatting (*Notepad, WordPad, Microsoft Word*).

HTM or HTML   Webpage (*Internet Explorer*).

PDF   Text file, possibly with images, converted to a special format (*Adobe Reader, Acrobat Reader*).

XLS   Spreadsheet (*Microsoft Excel*).

PPS, PPT   Slide show (*PowerPoint* or *PowerPoint Viewer*).

WAV   Audio file (*Windows Media Player*).

MID or MIDI   Audio file (*Windows Media Player*).

MP3   Audio file (*Windows Media Player*).

WMA   Audio file (*Windows Media Player*).

AVI   Video file (*Windows Media Player*).

WMV   Video file (*Windows Media Player*).

MPG or MPEG   Video file (*Windows Media Player*).

Some files are widely used by many types of drawing or photo editing programs, like BMP and JPG files. Other files are associated with a specific program, like *Microsoft PowerPoint* and *Microsoft Excel.* Both programs have their own file types.

The programs mentioned in the list are not the only ones you can use. For example, there are many programs available to play music files (audio files).

3.10 File Properties

Each file has technical properties or *attributes*. For example, a file can have the attribute *hidden* or the attribute *read-only*.
The *read-only* attribute is an important attribute of files stored on a CD-ROM or DVD-ROM. You can read the file, but you can not save it to the same CD-ROM or DVD-ROM. You can not write to a disc with the extension ROM. That is why each file on a CD or DVD-ROM has the attribute *read-only*.

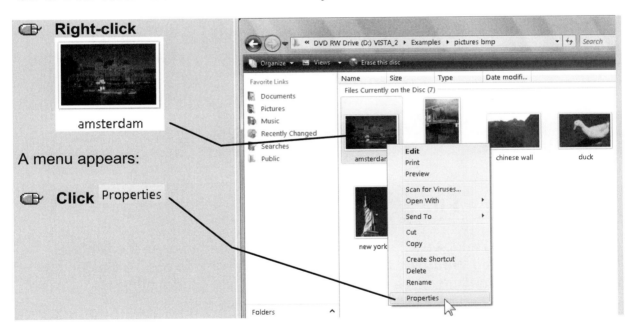

Now you see this window:

At the bottom you see that the attribute Read-only is check marked: ——————

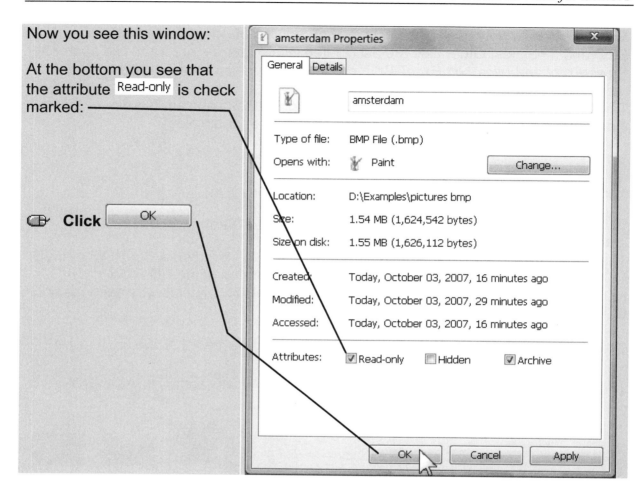

☞ **Click** OK

3.11 Opening a File

For each file type, *Windows* selects the program to be used to open the file (see **chapter 2 Adjusting Windows Settings**). This enables you to open a file directly from the window *Computer*. You can see right away which program this file type is associated with.

☞ **Right-click**

☞ **Click** Open With

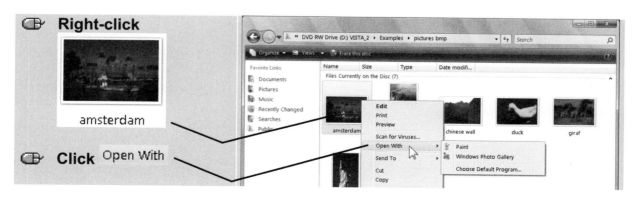

In the menu, you see three programs on the computer that are capable of opening photo files. You can choose which program you want to use. You may see different programs on your computer, for example a photo editing program, if that was installed on your computer.

To make the menu disappear:

Click an empty area in the window

You can use the exercises at the end of this chapter to discover which programs open the other file types in the folders on the CD-ROM. You will notice right away if your computer does not (yet) know the file type. Try that with this file:

First you open

Examples
File Folder

again like
this:

Click

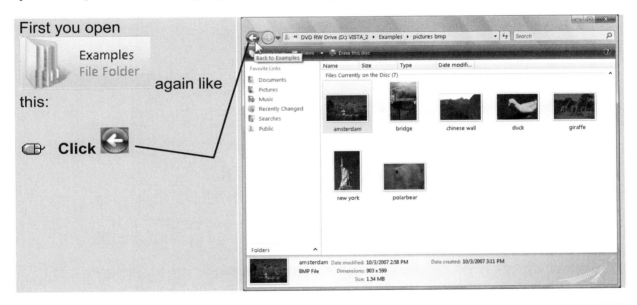

Double-click the folder

unknown
File Folder

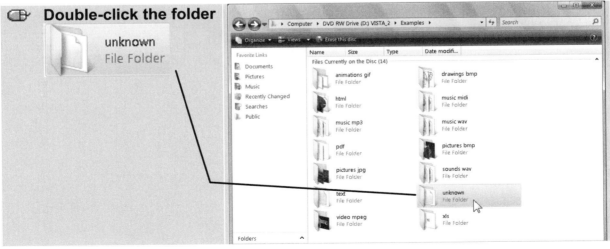

You can try to open this file:

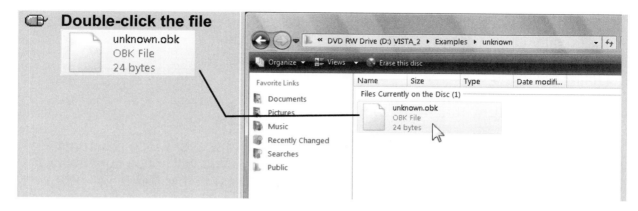

Double-click the file

unknown.obk
OBK File
24 bytes

This file type is not associated with any program:

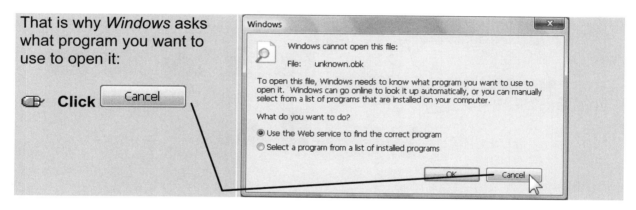

That is why *Windows* asks what program you want to use to open it:

Click Cancel

The extension *obk* does not exist. This file was only made as an example for this book, to show what happens when *Windows* does not recognize a file.

☞ **Close the window *Computer* ᐠᐟ¹**

☞ **Remove the CD-ROM from the CD or DVD drive**

3.12 Background Information

To be able to understand how new devices are installed, it is good to know which components are inside your computer, what kind of devices are available and how everything can be built in or connected.
You can read more about this on the following pages. Take your time to read through the information. Consider it as a reference guide. It may come in handy when you find yourself in a situation needing extra information about your computer.

What is inside your computer?
When you open the system case of your computer, your first impression will be of a chaotic tangle of little boxes, circuit boards and cables.
Many people wonder how such a mess can actually work.

Motherboard
The motherboard is a large circuit board to which all the important parts of the computer are connected.

The most important parts are the *processor*, the *BIOS*, the *RAM memory* and the *expansion slots*.

The processor
The processor is the heart of the computer. Every action you take on the computer, is routed through the processor. In fact, they would not even be possible without the processor. When you type some text in a word processing program, the processor is busy computing. That is what a processor does: computing, even when you are working with text.

- Continue reading on the next page -

Modern processors compute incredibly fast: millions of additions and subtractions per second. The processor also has an excellent sense of rhythm. Everything it does follows a certain beat. This beat is measured in *Megahertz* or *Gigahertz*. This is why the speed of the processor is shown as 800 MHz or 1.8 GHz, for example. The higher the number, the faster the processor can compute and the faster your computer is.

BIOS

The abbreviation *BIOS* means *Basic Input Output System*. It is a small piece of memory that contains important commands necessary to start up the PC. These are commands for the keyboard, the monitor, the hard disk and the DVD drive. Without the BIOS, your computer can not start.

The RAM

The system memory consists of *RAM* memory. RAM stands for *Random Access Memory*. This refers to memory that is accessible at any location at any time.

The computer can save data to the RAM and then read it again. The contents of this memory are stored as long as the computer is on. When you switch the PC off, it all disappears.

The RAM can be extended. You can buy cards of 512 MB or 1 GB for example. They can easily be installed in special memory slots.
Today's computers have a memory of at least 512 MB. You can extend the memory up to 2046 MB. In the (near) future even 4096 (4 GB) or greater will be possible.

Expansion boards

Each motherboard has room for expansion, a series of *slots*.

- Continue reading on the next page

The desired expansion card can generally be inserted in a slot without further technical action.
Types of expansions that are added this way include an internal modem, a network card, a video adapter or a sound card.

Cooling
When you start your PC you should hear a soft hum. This is caused by a small fan that provides the cooling for the system.
A small grill at the back of the system case allows air to be drawn in. If you do not hear anything at all, it is a good idea to check whether the fan is working. Your computer should not overheat.
In addition to the system cooling, another little fan is attached to the processor.
The processor chip produces a lot of heat, which can not be taken away completely by the system cooler. That is why the processor needs its own fan.

Plug and Play
Every time you start a *Windows Vista* computer, the whole system is checked for newly installed components. If you have just connected a scanner for example, *Windows Vista* will notice this. *Windows Vista* will find the accompanying software and you can start using the device right away.

Windows Vista includes a lot of *drivers* for all familiar brands of scanners, printers, keyboards etcetera. A driver is software that enables hardware or devices to function properly with your computer.

It may happen that the software for your device is not included in *Vista*. That is why it is always a good idea to have the device's installation software close by, in case *Windows* asks for it.

Always read the device manual first. Sometimes you have to install the accompanying software yourself rather than letting *Windows Vista* do so automatically.

Your computer's ports

Located on the back, front or side of your computer are several outlets.
Most computers have three different kinds of outlets: a *parallel port*, a *serial port* and
a *USB port*.

Parallel port

A parallel port is a wide outlet at the back
of the system case. It is a 'female' port,
with 25 pins.

This port is also called the printer port or
LPT1 (Line Printer 1) because in the past
most printers were connected to the
parallel port.

The parallel port

The parallel port can also be used to send data from one computer to another, for
example from a desktop to a laptop.
Parallel means data is simultaneously processed over eight lines. That is why a
parallel port is much faster than a serial port.

Serial port

A serial port can be used to connect devices
such as a modem, a mouse, or a scanner.

The serial port is also called the *COM* port
or the *RS-232* port. Computers usually have
two serial ports.

The serial port

Sometimes a device has to be installed manually using the installation software to
guarantee it will work properly. Other devices, like a mouse, have software that
takes care of everything itself. A serial port sends data over a single one-way wire.
A serial port is much slower than a parallel port. These days many devices are
connected using the USB port.

- Continue reading on the next page -

The USB port

Computers have evolved over many years. This has led to some confusion when it comes to ports. There are parallel and serial ports, different ports for all kinds of devices, all built and made to operate according to their own standards. To end this undesirable situation, a new connection standard has been developed. Not to add yet another alternative, but to introduce a new type of universal port that will probably make all others obsolete. This port is called *USB* (Universal Serial Bus).

All kinds of devices can be connected to a USB port. For example a printer or a mouse, but also a digital photo camera.

Most modern computers have at least four or more USB ports.

USB ports   *USB plug*

The USB port is faster than the standard serial port. After the introduction of the first USB ports an even faster version was developed, called USB2.

To connect a device to a USB port, you need a cable.

A USB cable has a flat plug on one end and a square plug at the other end.

Flat USB plug   *Square USB plug*

The other ports

There may be several other ports on your computer.
In this picture, you see two small, round outlets for the keyboard and the mouse.

The port for the mouse is also called a *PS/2* port.

There are also keyboards and mice that connect to a USB port.

The monitor connects to a somewhat wider port.

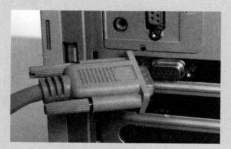

There are usually three round outlets for speakers, microphone in, and line in:

Beside them is a larger port for connecting a joystick:

To connect a digital video camera you need a firewire port:

You can use this very fast port to quickly transfer large video files to the computer's hard disk.

Which device on which port?

You can see the most common devices and the ports they use below. To be able to connect a device to the mentioned port, the device has to be compatible and the right cable must be available. Refer to the device manual for more information about the connection options.

Printer

Parallel port
USB port

Keyboard

Keyboard port
USB port

Digital camera

USB port
(or the computer's built-in card reader)

Scanner

Parallel port
USB port

Monitor

VGA port

Webcam

USB port

Modem (extern)

USB port

Speakers

Speaker port
USB port

Another computer

Network card
USB port

Mouse

Serial port
USB port

Microphone

Microphone port

Digital video camera

Firewire port

3.13 New Hardware

Computers age quickly and newer and faster devices are constantly entering the market. Fortunately, you can easily add or upgrade internal components in a standard computer. Here are several well-known examples:

- adding RAM memory;
- exchanging the hard disk for one with more storage capacity: for example from 100 GB to 200 GB or more, or adding a second hard disk;
- adding a DVD writer or DVD rewriter; perhaps next to the regular DVD player;
- exchanging the internal modem for an ADSL or cable modem;
- installing a faster graphics card with more graphics memory;
- installing a network card: for example to create a home or office network among several computers.

These kinds of improvements are best left to your computer supplier. Many people install expansion cards like a network card or a graphics card themselves. Many of these cards are *Plug and Play*, which makes installation easy.

The *Control Panel* has a special hyperlink

Hardware and Sound .

You can use this to install or remove hardware such as a printer, scanner, or camera.

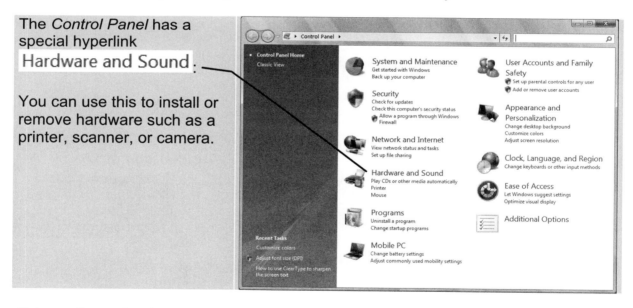

Extra software is often necessary for a component or device to function properly. This software is called a *driver*. This driver is usually stored on the CD-ROM or DVD-ROM that comes with the device.

Many drivers for frequently sold devices come packaged with *Windows Vista* and have already been installed on the hard disk of your computer. Otherwise, *Windows* can usually automatically download the driver from the Internet.

Tip

ReadyBoost
Upgrading the RAM memory can easily be done using the feature *ReadyBoost* and a reasonably fast USB stick.

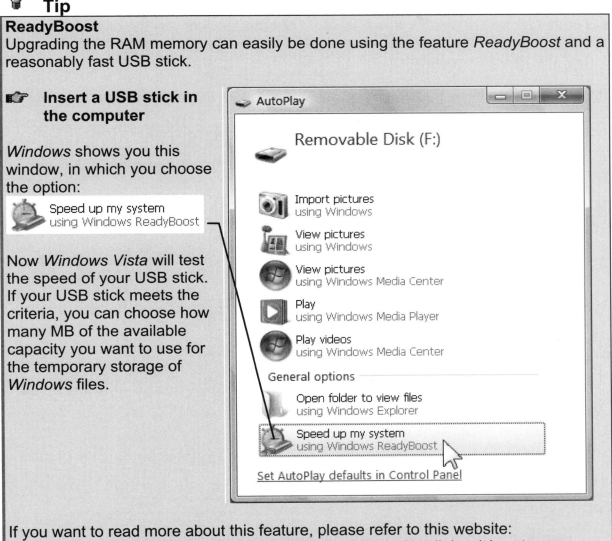

☞ **Insert a USB stick in the computer**

Windows shows you this window, in which you choose the option:

Now *Windows Vista* will test the speed of your USB stick. If your USB stick meets the criteria, you can choose how many MB of the available capacity you want to use for the temporary storage of *Windows* files.

If you want to read more about this feature, please refer to this website:
www.microsoft.com/windows/products/windowsvista/features/details/readyboost.mspx

3.14 Adding External Devices

You can usually connect external devices yourself, especially if they are *Plug and Play* or if they use the USB port. Frequently sold devices include:

- a mouse, such as a new cordless version;
- a larger monitor, such as a 19 inch monitor instead of a 15 inch monitor;
- a printer or a scanner;
- a digital photo camera.

Read the device manual before you connect a device. The manual will tell you in which order the installation should take place. Some devices have to be connected to the computer before the driver is installed. For other devices it is the other way around. There are also devices that have to be connected first and then need to be turned on during the installation.

It is important to follow the right order, otherwise the device may not work properly.

For example, a printer without a USB connection can be installed like this:

☞ Open the *Control Panel* ₰₰18

☞ Click Hardware and Sound

☞ Click Add a printer

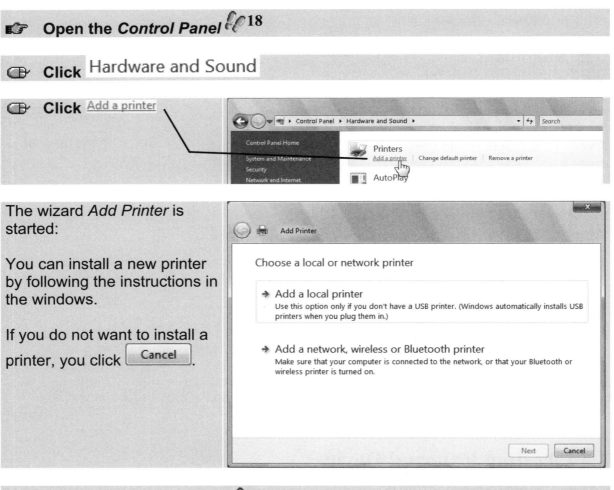

The wizard *Add Printer* is started:

You can install a new printer by following the instructions in the windows.

If you do not want to install a printer, you click Cancel.

☞ Close the *Control Panel* ₰₰1

You can find more information about installing devices in *Windows Help and Support*:

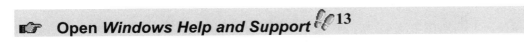 **Open *Windows Help and Support*** $\mathcal{U}$ **13**

⌨ **Type** install hardware **in the *Search Box* and click**

Click the article Installing new hardware: recommended links

You see an overview of the links that are available about this subject:

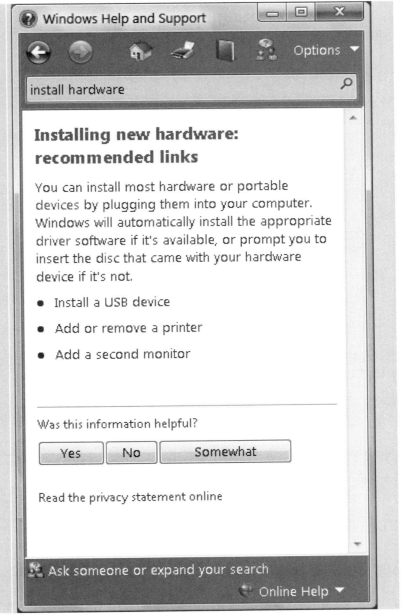

Choose the article you find interesting

When you have finished reading:

Close the window $\mathcal{U}$**1**

3.15 Removing External Devices

Sometimes you want to remove an external device. Disconnecting the cable is enough to physically disconnect the device. You can also remove the device drivers, so the device will no longer be visible in different windows. Usually this is the case with a printer. To remove it:

☞ **Open the *Control Panel*** ¹⁸

👆 **Click** Hardware and Sound

👆 **Click** Remove a printer

You see a window with the printers on your computer:

👆 **Right-click the printer you want to remove**

👆 **Click** Delete

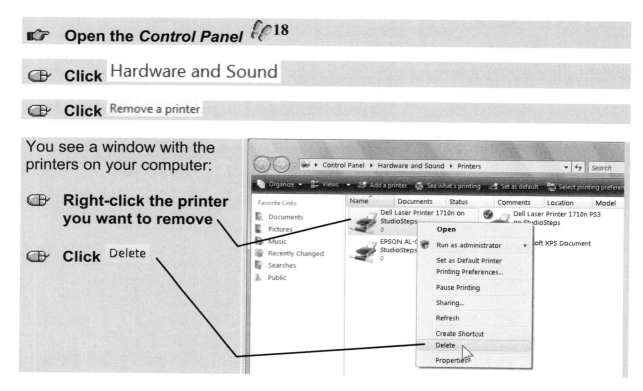

Your screen goes dark and you see the window *User Account Control*, where you need to give your permission to continue:

👆 **Click** Continue

Now you see a window where you are asked if you really want to remove this printer:

👆 **Click** Yes

The printer driver has now been removed.

☞ **Close all open windows** ¹

In this chapter you have learned how to view the different components of your computer. In the following exercises you can repeat what you have learned.

3.16 Exercises

Have you forgotten how to do something? Use the number beside the footsteps to look it up in *Appendix B How Do I Do That Again?*

Exercise: Opening Files

You can use this exercise to find out which program on your computer will be opened when you select a specific file type.

⇨ **Please note:**

Some files may be opened by a different program on your computer than is described here. This depends on the software that is installed on your computer.

✔ Open the window *Computer*. 𝒻𝒻 **19**

✔ Open the CD-ROM you received with this book.

✔ Open the folder *Examples*. 𝒻𝒻 **20**

✔ Open the folder *pictures.jpg*. 𝒻𝒻 **20**

✔ Open the JPG file named *duck*. 𝒻𝒻 **20**

✔ Check which program opens this photo, for example *Windows Photo Gallery*.

✔ Close this program window. 𝒻𝒻 **1**

✔ Go back to the folder *Examples*.

The next file type is an audio file.

✔ Open the folder *music wav*. 𝒻𝒻 **20**

✔ Open the audio file named *FANF01*. 𝒻𝒻 **20**

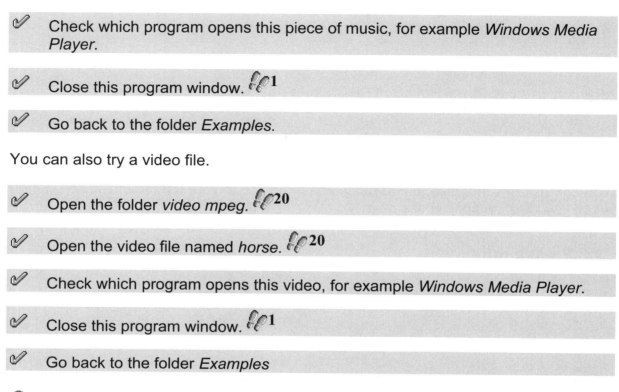

✓ Check which program opens this piece of music, for example *Windows Media Player*.

✓ Close this program window. ℓℓ1

✓ Go back to the folder *Examples*.

You can also try a video file.

✓ Open the folder *video mpeg*. ℓℓ20

✓ Open the video file named *horse*. ℓℓ20

✓ Check which program opens this video, for example *Windows Media Player*.

✓ Close this program window. ℓℓ1

✓ Go back to the folder *Examples*

Tip

Try for yourself
The folder *Examples* on the CD-ROM contains a number of other file types. Find out what happens when you try to open these files.

3.17 Background Information

Glossary	
Computer	Part of *Windows* where you can view the contents of disks and drives.
Driver	Software that enables hardware or devices to work with the computer.
Extension	A set of characters added to the end of a file name that identifies the file type or format.
External hard disk	Portable hard disk that can easily be connected and disconnected.
Gigabyte, Megabyte, Kilobyte	Units for data storage.
Plug and Play	Type of device for which *Windows* will automatically find the accompanying software and correct settings after connecting it.
Read-only	File attribute that indicates a file can only be read.
Removable media	Anything used for information storage that is designed to be easily inserted into and removed from a computer or portable device. Common removable media include CD and DVD discs, as well as removable memory cards.
Upgrade	Improving the computer by adding more or better hardware.
USB stick, USB memory stick	A small device used to store information. USB flash drives plug into computer USB ports so you can copy information to or from them, making it easy to share and transport information. Also called *memory stick*.

Source: Windows Help and Support

3.18 Tips

  Tip

Simpler appearance: faster computer
The default format of *Windows Vista* for windows, menus and other components requires an extra effort from your computer. When your computer performs tasks very slowly, you may want to consider switching to a simpler color scheme:

☞ **Right-click the desktop**

You see a menu:

☞ **Click** Personalize

You see this window:

☞ **Click**
    Window Color and Appearance

Click to remove the check
mark for ☐ Enable transparency :
This feature uses a lot of
computing power.

☞ **Click**
    Open classic appearance properti

☞ **Click another color
    scheme**

☞ **Click** ⬜ OK ⬜

Please note: if you choose a
different scheme, the
windows on your computer
will look different than the
specific examples and
screenshots used in this
book.

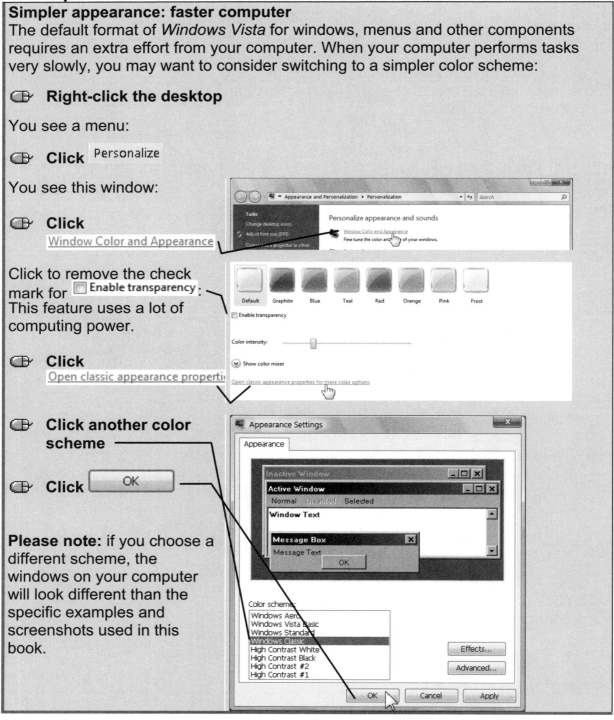

4. Compressing Files

Some files take up a lot of space on your hard disk. For example, certain types of image files, like BMP. Audio files with file type WAV and large illustrated documents also take up a lot of space.

In this chapter you will learn how to compress files in *Windows Vista* using the option *Compressed folder*. Compressing is also called 'zipping'. That name comes from the .ZIP extension that is applied to this file format.

When you use a *Compressed folder*, a folder is created in which you can place files. Each file is packed in the folder and the file size is reduced. A large file will be significantly reduced in size after compression. You can save a lot of space this way, especially with illustrated documents and audio files. If you want to send a file by e-mail using a dial-up connection, it will take much less time to send the compressed version.

A compressed folder must always be extracted, or 'unzipped' before you can open, read or run any file it contains.

In this chapter you will learn how to:

- create a compressed folder;
- add a file by dragging it;
- remove a file from the compressed folder;
- extract a compressed folder using the *Wizard Extract Compressed Folders*;
- extract more quickly by dragging.

⇨ Please note:

To be able to work with this chapter, the folder Practice files should be copied to the folder *Documents* in your *Personal Folder*. See **Appendix A Copying Practice Files to Your Computer** at the end of this book.

4.1 Creating a Compressed Folder

You can find the practice files to use with this chapter in the folder *Documents*.

 Click , Documents

You see the contents of your folder *Documents*. You can open the folder containing the practice files like this:

Double-click Practice files File Folder

HELP! The window looks different.

The folders may be displayed differently in the *Folder window* on your computer. You can change the way they are displayed:

Click ▼ **on the right side of** Views

Click Tiles

Is the *Details Pane* displayed at the bottom of the *Folder window*?

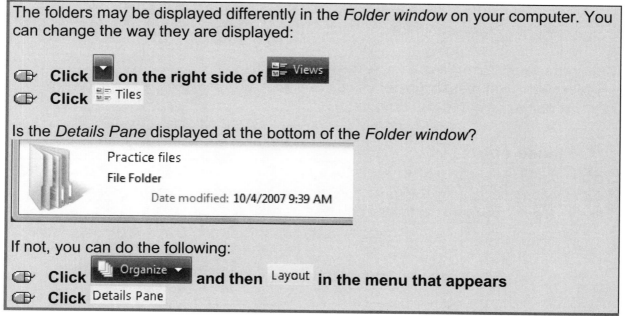

Practice files
File Folder
Date modified: 10/4/2007 9:39 AM

If not, you can do the following:

Click Organize ▼ **and then** Layout **in the menu that appears**

Click Details Pane

The practice files are stored in separate folders for each chapter. Open the folder for this chapter.

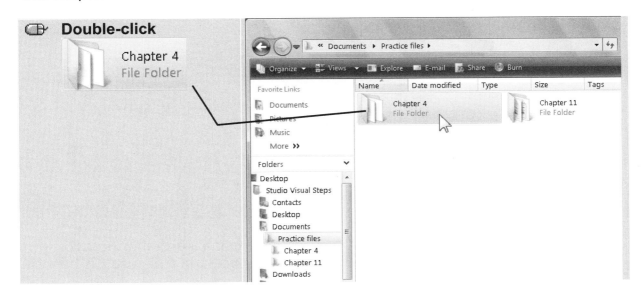

In this folder you see that the file ![Practice File Anne Frank, Rich Text Document, 957 KB] is 957 KB in size. When you open the file, you can see why it is so big:

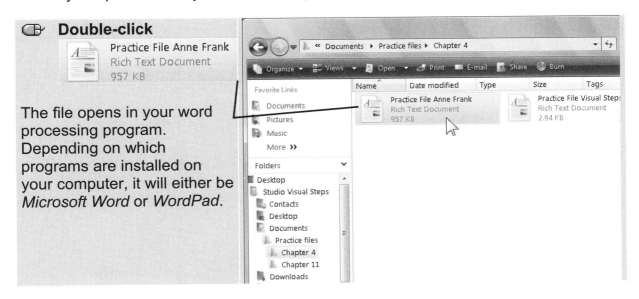

The document contains a small amount of text and two images. These images have increased the size of the document.

You can close the document again:

👉 **Click** [X]

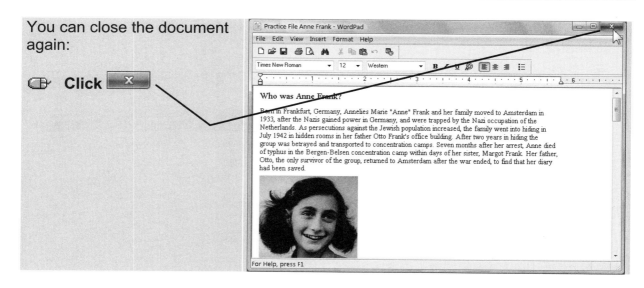

If you were to send this file in an e-mail, and you were using a dial-up connection, it would take some time before it is actually sent (or received!). In that case it is better to compress the file. Like this:

👉 **Right-click**

In the menu that appears, you can choose the option [Compressed (zipped) Folder] to copy the file to a compressed folder:

👉 **Click** Send To

👉 **Click**
[Compressed (zipped) Fol]

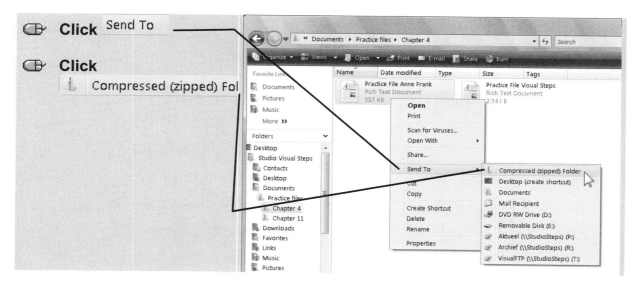

The compressed folder is created and placed in your practice folder.

You recognize a compressed folder by the zipper on the folder icon :

Here you see the compressed folder:

By default, the folder is named after the document. You do not need to change that now.

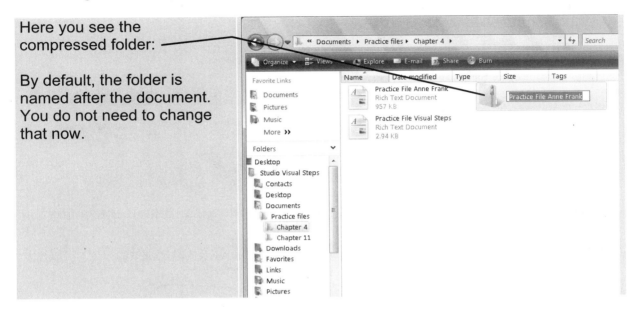

In the *Details Pane* you see the properties of the compressed file:

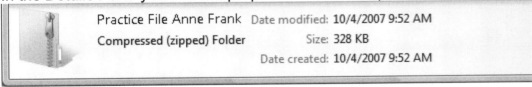

The compressed file has a size of 328 KB. Compressing the text file has shrunk the file from 957 KB to 328 KB.

 Tip

Compressing compressed files?
Some file types, like JPEG images and MP3 audio files, are already heavily compressed. Consequently, compressing several JPEG files in a folder will result in a compressed folder that is approximately the same size as the original image collection.

4.2 Adding Files by Dragging

If you want to add additional files to an existing compressed folder, you can easily do so by dragging a file or folder to the compressed folder. You can add the other text file to the compressed folder like this:

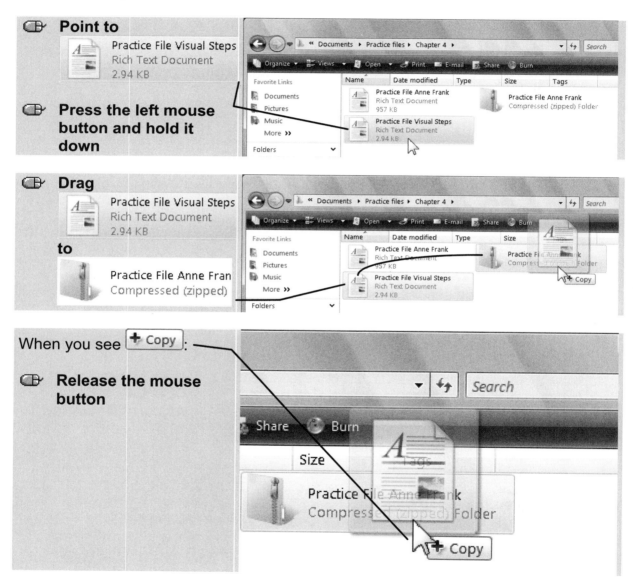

The file has been copied and added to the compressed folder. You see that the original file is still in the *Folder window*.

4.3 Removing Files from a Compressed Folder

If you decide later that you do not need particular a file in the compressed folder, you can remove it. You have to open the compressed folder first:

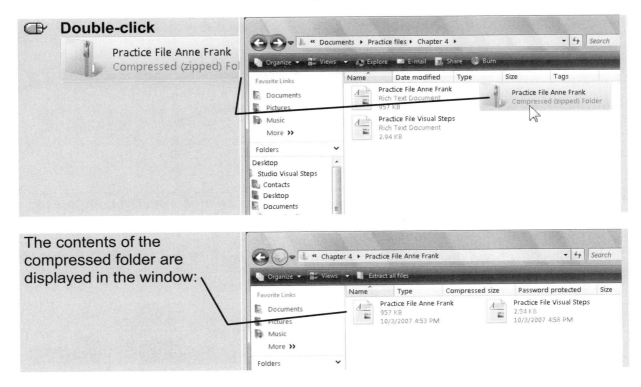

Double-click

    Practice File Anne Frank
    Compressed (zipped) Fol

The contents of the compressed folder are displayed in the window:

Now you are going to remove the second file from the compressed folder:

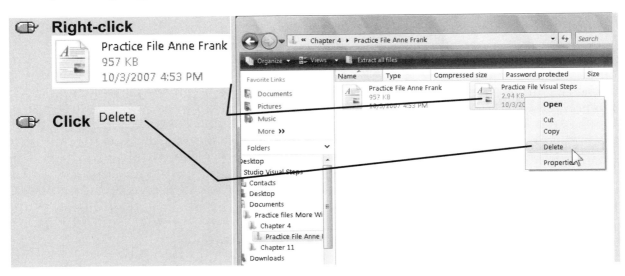

Right-click

    Practice File Anne Frank
    957 KB
    10/3/2007 4:53 PM

Click Delete

Windows Vista asks if you really want to delete the file:

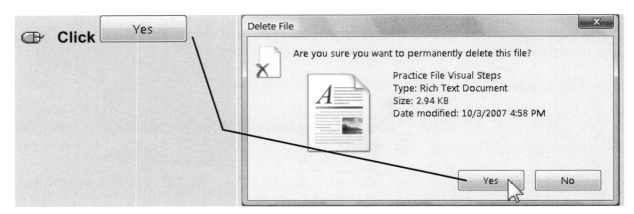

➡️ **Please note:**

When you remove a file from a compressed folder, it is deleted from the compressed folder but not from its original source. The file still remains in the folder *Chapter 4*.

The file has now been deleted from the compressed folder. Now you can return to the practice folder:

4.4 Extracting a Compressed File

To be able to use a compressed file, you first need to extract it. You start by opening the compressed folder:

Then you can give the command to extract the file:

The wizard *Extract Compressed (Zipped) Folders* opens. You can use this wizard to copy the files from a compressed folder.

The wizard *Extract Compressed (Zipped) Folders* asks you where you want to put the extracted file. If you do not specify a location yourself, the wizard creates a new folder in the folder *Chapter 4,* with the same name as the compressed folder.

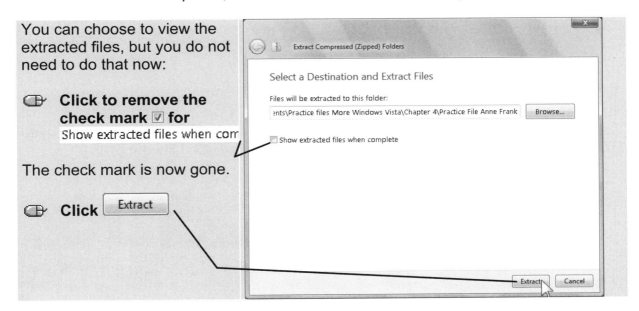

The file is extracted. You can go back to the folder *Chapter 4* to see the result:

In the practice folder you see the new folder

 Please note:

A compressed folder is not deleted when the files are extracted. That means you now have both the compressed folder and the extracted folder in your practice folder.

4.5 Extracting Quicker by Dragging

You can also unpack a compressed file without using the wizard *Extract Compressed (Zipped) Folders*. You do that by just dragging the compressed file out of its compressed folder.

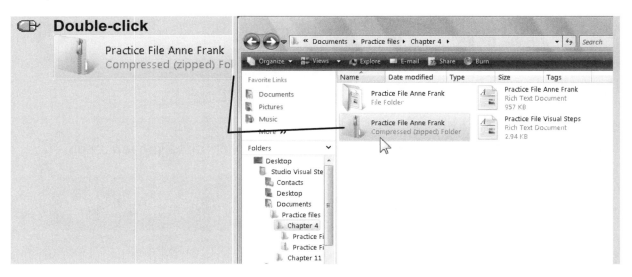

You can place the extracted file on your desktop for example. First, you display the desktop in the *Folders list*:

Drag the vertical scroll bar up (if necessary)

You see ▨ Desktop at the top of the *Folders list*:

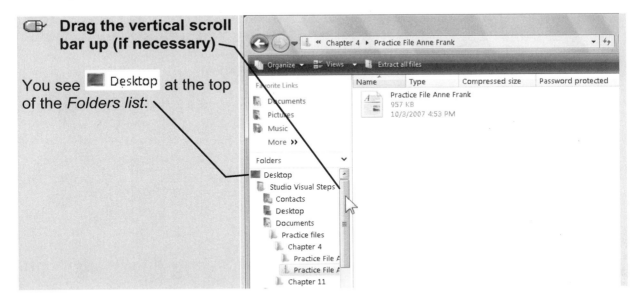

A compressed folder behaves almost the same as a 'normal' folder. Just as with a normal folder, you can drag a file from a compressed folder to another location. A file from a compressed folder is then simultaneously copied and extracted. A file in a normal folder would be moved instead of copied.

Point to

Press the left mouse button and hold it down

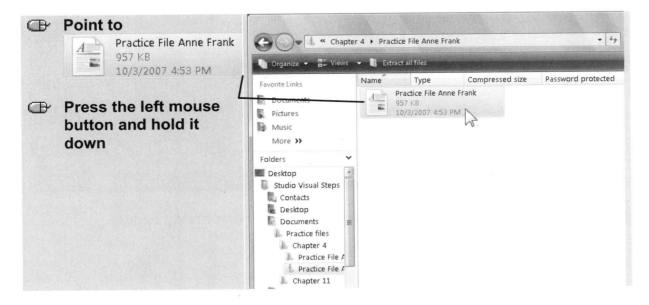

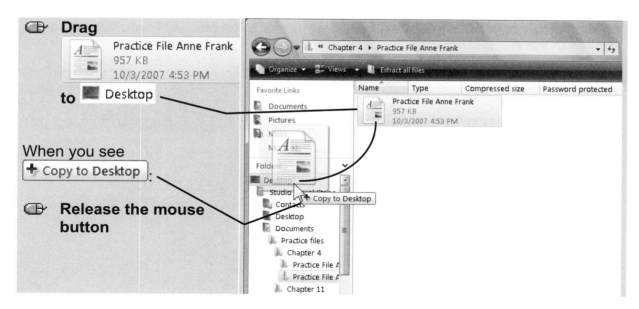

Close the *Folder window* 🐾1

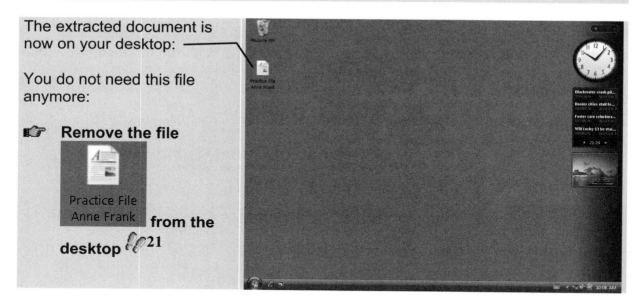

In this chapter you have seen how you can work with compressed folders.

4.6 Exercises

Have you forgotten how to do something? Use the number beside the footsteps to look it up in *Appendix B How Do I Do That Again?*

Exercise: The Compressed Folder

In this exercise you practice creating compressed folders.

✔ Open the practice folder *Chapter 4*. ₡22

✔ Copy the file *Practice File Anne Frank* to a new compressed folder. ₡23

✔ Take a look at the file size of the compressed folder in the *Details Pane*.

Exercise: Adding and Removing a File

In this exercise you add a file to the compressed folder by dragging it, then you remove the file again.

✔ Drag *Practice File Visual Steps* to the compressed folder *Practice File Anne Frank*. ₡24

✔ Open the compressed folder *Practice File Anne Frank*. ₡25

✔ Remove the file *Practice File Visual Steps* from the compressed folder. ₡26

Exercise: Extracting a Compressed Folder

In this exercise you are going to extract the file from the compressed folder.

✔ Use the button on the toolbar to extract the compressed folder *Practice File Anne Frank*. ₡27

✔ Go back to the folder *Chapter 4*. ₡28

✔ Check if a new folder *Practice File Anne Frank* has been created in this folder.

4.7 Background Information

Glossary	
Compressed folder	In *Windows Vista* you can compress files by copying them to a compressed folder. You recognize a compressed folder by the zipper on the folder icon.
Compressing	Reducing the size of a file so it takes up less storage space and is easier to send by e-mail. Compressed files usually have the extension .ZIP.
Details Pane	Part of the *Folder window* that displays more information about the selected file.
Extension	Files have an extension of three characters that identifies the file type or format. For example, photo files are often saved in the JPEG format and get the extension .JPG.
Extracting	Decompressing files that have been saved in a compressed form. When you extract a file, an uncompressed copy of the file is placed in the folder you specify. The original file remains in the compressed folder.
File	The generic name for everything saved on the computer. A file can be a program, a data file with names, but also text you have written or a photo.
Folder window	When you open a folder using the *Start menu*, a *Folder window* appears in which the contents of the folder are displayed. A *Folder window* has specific areas that are designed to help you navigate around the folders on the hard disk of your computer more easily. In this window you can also remove, copy and move files and folders.
Zipping	Another word for compressing, coming from the .ZIP extension compressed files usually have.

Source: Windows Help and Support

4.8 Tips

 Tip

WinZip
The most popular program for zipping files is without a doubt the program *WinZip*:

Folders compressed in *Windows Vista* can be extracted by *WinZip*. Vice versa, *Windows Vista* can extract folders compressed in *WinZip*. That means you do not really need a separate program like *WinZip*.
WinZip does offer more features for working with compressed files than *Windows* does. You can find more information about *WinZip* on **www.winzip.com**.

 Tip

Fast e-mail
In *Windows Vista*, you can quickly send a compressed file by e-mail:

☞ **Right-click the compressed folder**

☞ **Click**
Send To

☞ **Click** Mail Recipient

Now your e-mail program opens automatically.
You see the file as an attachment to a *New message*.

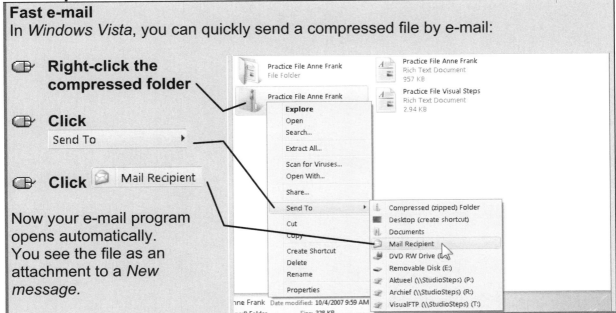

Notes

Write your notes down here.

5. Computer Security

Computer security is very important in *Windows Vista*. You probably already noticed that. You frequently see your screen go dark and you need to give your permission before you can continue. This is controlled by *User Account Control*. This feature will prevent changes being made to your computer by users who do not have permission to do so. You can read more about this in **Chapter 6 User Accounts**.

Windows Vista has more security options, for example to protect your computer from the dangers of the Internet. By default, *Windows Firewall* is used to manage the incoming and outgoing data traffic between your computer and the Internet and/or other networks. Depending on your settings, data traffic is allowed or blocked.

The program *Windows Defender* actively protects your computer against the unwanted installation of spyware or other unwanted software. You can monitor the status of these two programs in the *Security Center*. Here you also find the item *Automatic updating*. This feature continuously checks for available *Windows Vista* updates. Installing these software updates keeps your operating system up to date.

Windows Vista does not include an antivirus program. This means you have to purchase and install an antivirus program yourself. The presence and the status of your antivirus program will be monitored by the *Security Center*.

In this chapter you will learn about:

- protecting your computer;
- *Windows Security Center;*
- *Windows Firewall;*
- *Windows Update;*
- protection against unwanted software;
- *Windows Defender;*
- protection against viruses using an antivirus program.

5.1 Protecting Your Computer

It is very important to effectively protect your computer. Especially when you regularly use the Internet. A good security system reduces the risk of viruses and other malicious software entering your computer.

A computer that is infected with a virus is very annoying: not only for you, but also for other people. When your computer is infected with malicious software, other computers can also become infected. That can happen when you send an e-mail or chat message, or when you exchange files using a CD, DVD or USB stick.

➪ **Please note:**

As a computer user you are responsible for protecting your own computer. Your computer should be protected by a firewall and should also regularly be scanned for the presence of viruses and other malicious software. **Windows Vista does not include a virus scanner!** This means you have to purchase and install an antivirus program yourself.

In the next section you are introduced to the *Security Center* of *Windows Vista*. The *Security Center* is your central location for computer security. The *Security Center* displays the current security status, and you are advised which actions you can take to protect your computer even better.

5.2 Windows Security Center

The *Security Center* checks the security settings of your computer and keeps track of updates to *Vista*. You can open the *Security Center* like this:

☞ **Open the *Control Panel*** ¹⁸

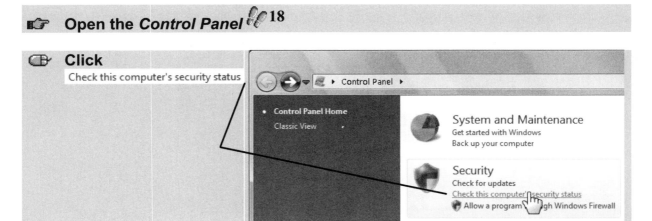

In this window you see the status of the four most important components of your computer's security:

- *Firewall*
- *Automatic updating*
- *Malware protection*
- *Other security settings*

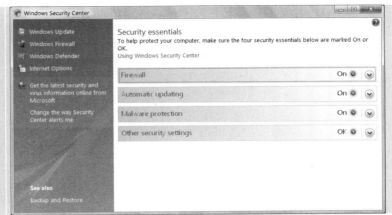

In this example all four items have the status On or OK. These items do not need your attention. The settings of your computer may be different than what you see in this example.

For example, when the malware protection component shows Check settings, it is possible that an antivirus program has not been installed. You see the same message when an already installed program is not recognized by *Vista*.

If you switched off an item manually you see the status Off.

5.3 Windows Firewall

A firewall is software or hardware that manages the incoming and outgoing data traffic between your computer and the Internet and/or other networks. Depending on your firewall settings, data traffic is either blocked or allowed to pass through to your computer.

 Please note:

The word firewall sounds safer than it actually is: a firewall **does not** protect your computer against viruses. If your e-mail program is allowed access to the Internet through your firewall, you can still receive an e-mail with an attachment that contains a virus. The firewall does not check the content of the data traffic.

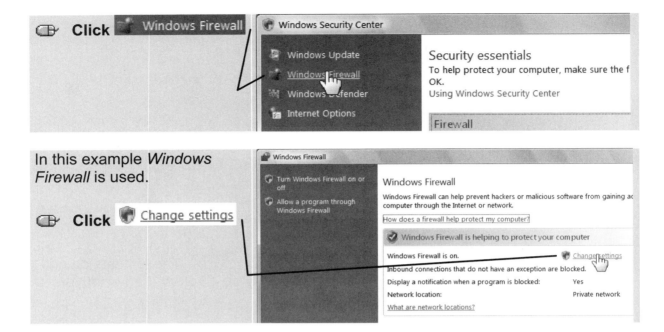

Click ✋ Windows Firewall

In this example *Windows Firewall* is used.

Click 🛡 Change settings

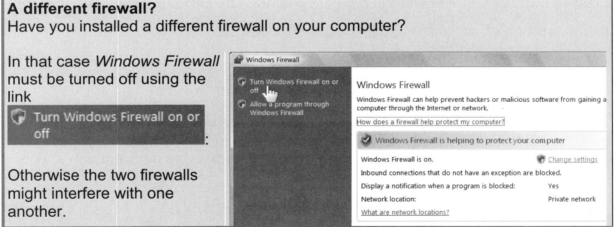

💡 **Tip**

A different firewall?
Have you installed a different firewall on your computer?

In that case *Windows Firewall* must be turned off using the link
🛡 Turn Windows Firewall on or off :

Otherwise the two firewalls might interfere with one another.

Your screen goes dark and you see the window *User Account Control* where you need to give your permission to continue.

Click Continue

Now you see the window *Windows Firewall Settings*:

You see that *Windows Firewall* is on: ─────

You can check the option
☐ **Block all incoming connections**
when you connect to a less secure network such as a public network at an airport:

When this option is not checked, programs on the Exceptions tab are allowed access to your computer.

☞ **Click the tab** Exceptions

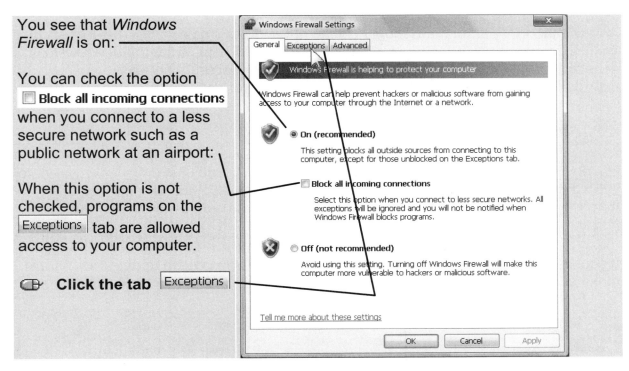

If you are using a program that has to receive data from the Internet or a network, the firewall will ask if you want to allow the connection. For each allowed connection, an exception is added to this list:

You can use the button
Add program... to add exceptions directly: ─────

You do not have to change these settings now:

☞ **Click** Cancel

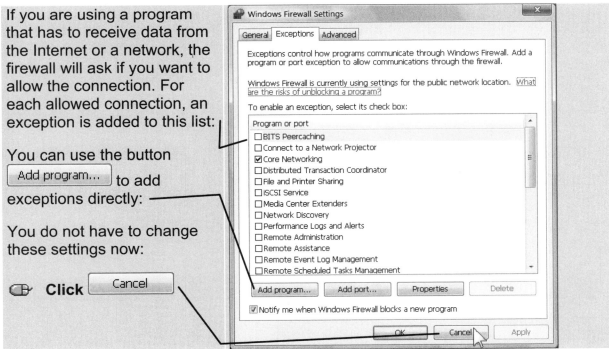

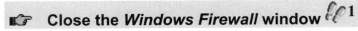

☞ **Close the *Windows Firewall* window** 🦶 1

5.4 Windows Update

A very important part of the *Security Center* is *Windows Update*. This is a system that checks if you are using the most recent version of *Windows Vista*. *Windows Vista* is constantly being modified, expanded and made more secure. The additions and improvements are dispersed by *Microsoft* in the form of *software updates*.

 Please note:

Microsoft **never** sends software updates by e-mail. Anyone who receives an e-mail claiming to contain *Microsoft* software or a *Windows* update is strongly advised not to open the attachment and immediately delete the e-mail. Do not forget to delete it from the folder *Deleted items* as well. Mails like that are sent by criminals who try to install malicious software on your computer.

If you want to make sure your version of *Windows Vista* stays up to date, you should make sure *Windows Update* is turned on. You can turn this option on like this:

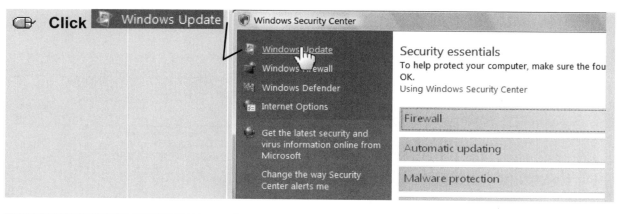

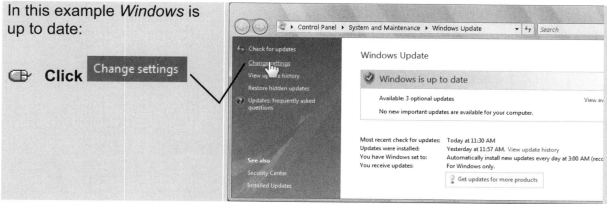

You see the current settings on your computer:

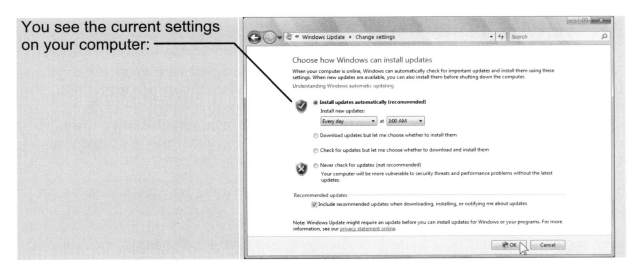

In this example, *Windows Update* is set to check for new updates and install these daily at 3:00 AM. If the computer was turned off at that time, the check will take place the next time the computer is turned on. The updates are then automatically downloaded and installed. *Windows* places a notification about this at the bottom of the screen, but in most cases you can just keep on working. For critical updates it may be necessary to restart your computer.

It is a good idea to select the ⦿ **Install updates automatically (recommended)** setting. You can change the time to a moment that is most convenient for you.

Did you change a setting?

☞ **Click** ⦿ OK

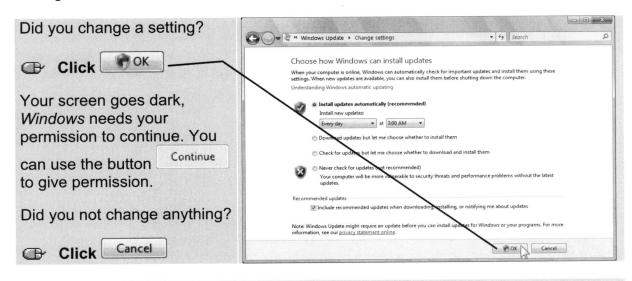

Your screen goes dark, *Windows* needs your permission to continue. You can use the button Continue to give permission.

Did you not change anything?

☞ **Click** Cancel

☞ **Close the *Windows Update* window** 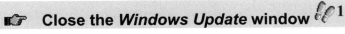1

5.5 Malware Protection

Malware is short for 'malicious software', software that is designed to deliberately harm your computer. Viruses, worms, spyware and Trojan horses are forms of malware. These types of software are an increasing threat to every computer connected to the Internet. The source of infection may be an attachment to an e-mail message or a file downloaded from the Internet. Your computer can also become infected by exchanging USB sticks, CDs or other storage media.

The *Malware protection* component of *Windows Security Center* indicates whether or not an up to date antivirus program is installed on your computer.

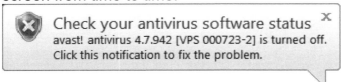

Click

    Malware protection

In this example the antivirus program avast! antivirus is used:

The antispyware program Windows Defender has been installed with *Windows Vista*:

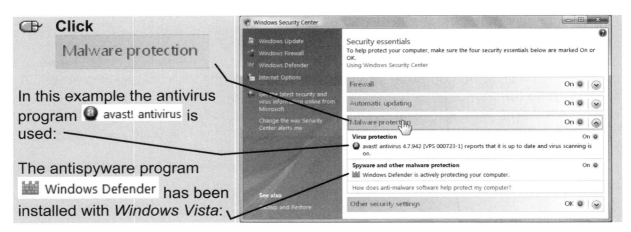

If you did not install an antivirus program, or there is a problem with the program you installed, you will be notified. A message like this will appear at the bottom of your screen from time to time:

> **Check your antivirus software status** X
> avast! antivirus 4.7.942 [VPS 000723-2] is turned off.
> Click this notification to fix the problem.

You will also see Check settings ● if you have installed an antivirus program that is not (yet) recognized by *Windows Vista*. There are excellent programs on the market where this is possible. In that case you can monitor your antivirus program yourself:

Click

Show me my available options.

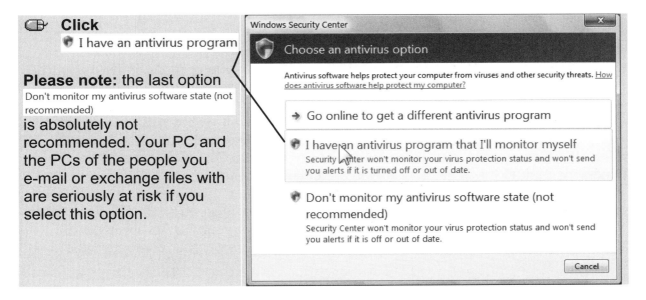

Click 🖰 I have an antivirus program

Please note: the last option
Don't monitor my antivirus software state (not recommended)
is absolutely not recommended. Your PC and the PCs of the people you e-mail or exchange files with are seriously at risk if you select this option.

Your screen goes dark and *Windows* asks for your permission to continue:

Click Continue

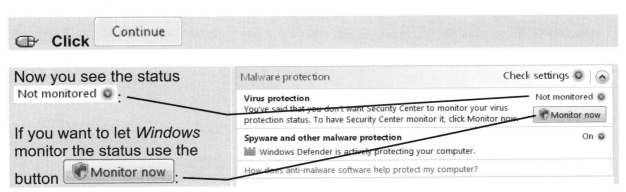

Now you see the status
Not monitored ⊙:

If you want to let *Windows* monitor the status use the button Monitor now:

In the next section, you can read about the antispyware program *Windows Defender*. In the sections after that you can read about the possibilities to protect your computer against viruses and other malware.

👉 **Close all windows** 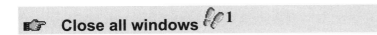¹

5.6 Windows Defender

Most Internet users will occasionally take advantage of one or more of the many free programs available. However, many people do not realize that some of these applications can contain components that gather information about users and send the information to the software's creators, for example about the websites you visit. It is even more annoying when settings on your computer are changed, like a different home page in your Internet browser or the insertion of an extra toolbar. Programs that do these kinds of things are called *spyware*.

Windows Defender is a program from *Microsoft* that is packaged with *Windows Vista*. You can use it to find and remove known spyware from your PC. Its continuous protection prevents the unnoticed installation of spyware on your computer while you surf the Internet.

⇨ **Please note:**

🔲 Windows Defender does **not** protect your computer against viruses! There is no antivirus program packaged with *Windows Vista*. This means you have to purchase and install one yourself. In sections **5.7 Virus Protection** and **5.8 Using an Antivirus Program** you can read more about protecting your computer against viruses.

You can open *Windows Defender* from the *Security Center*.

☞ **Open *Windows Security Center*** 🦶 **29**

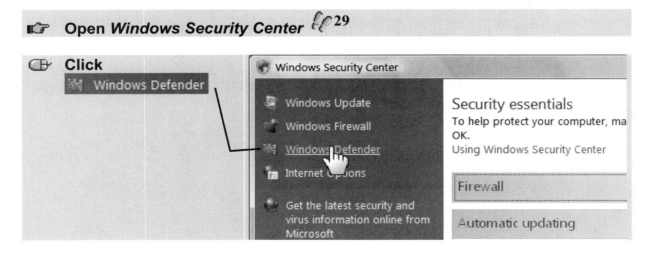

The *Windows Defender* opening screen appears.

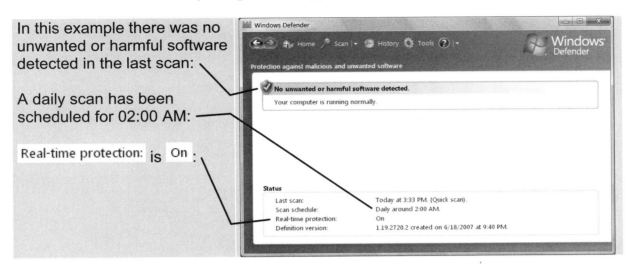

In this example there was no unwanted or harmful software detected in the last scan:

A daily scan has been scheduled for 02:00 AM:

Real-time protection: is On :

The real-time protection will alert you as soon as spyware attempts to install itself on your computer. *Windows Defender* works closely together with *Windows Update*: as soon as there are new spyware definitions available they are downloaded and installed. This way the program always uses the latest information. By default an extra check is made before a scan (automatic or manual) is performed.

You can take a look at the *Windows Defender* settings to verify this:

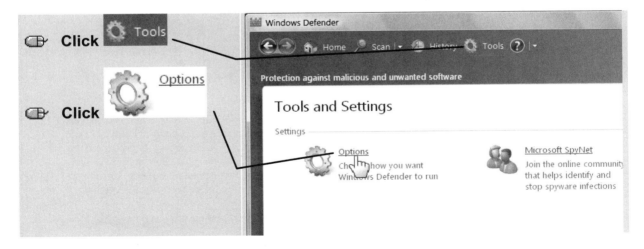

You see a large number of settings for *Windows Defender*. Take your time to read through these settings.

It is recommended to use the default settings.

When you have finished reading:

 Click Cancel

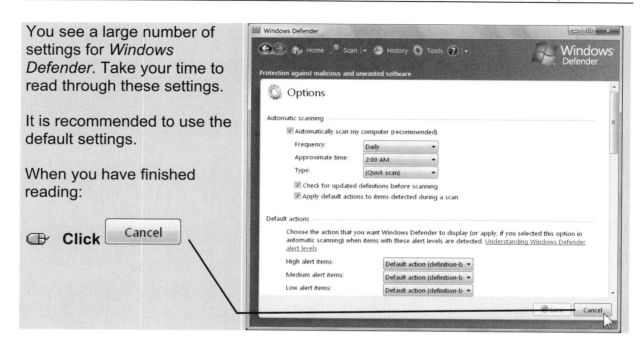

Tip

Help and Support
In *Windows Help and Support* you will find more information about spyware and using *Windows Defender*.

If you use the button 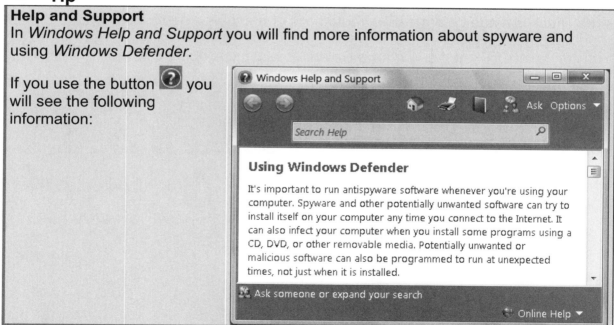 you will see the following information:

In *Windows Defender* you can choose between three scan types:

Quick Scan : only scans locations where spyware is often found.
Full Scan : scans all files and folders on your computer.
Custom Scan... : only scans the folders you specify.

You can start a quick scan like this:

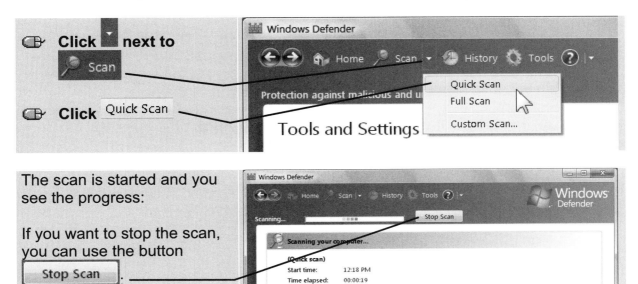

The scan is started and you see the progress:

If you want to stop the scan, you can use the button

A full scan can take fifteen to thirty minutes, depending on the speed of your computer and the number of files. The quick scan takes a lot less time.
If nothing is found, you see this message:

A full scan can take fifteen to thirty minutes, depending on the speed of your computer and the number of files. The quick scan takes a lot less time.
If nothing is found, you see this message:

If something is found, you will see a message like the one in this example:

An item was found with alert level Severe :

Windows Defender advises to remove the item:

In this part of the window you can read detailed information about the item that was found:

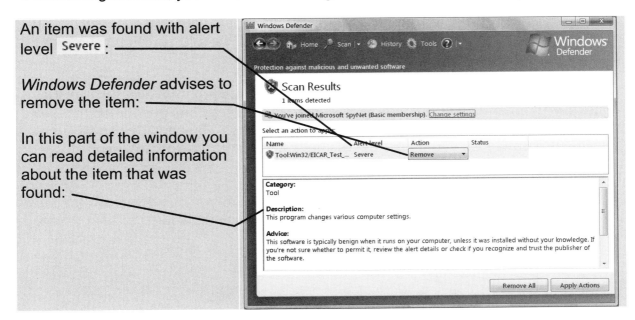

In addition to Remove you have three other options:

Ignore : select this option if you are certain you want to keep the item.

Quarantine : select this option if you are not sure about an item. The item will be placed in a folder where it can do no harm. If it turns out to be something you need, you can put it back where it belongs.

Always allow : select this option if you are familiar with the item and you are sure you want to keep it. The item will no longer be shown in future scans.

If more than one item was found on your computer, you can select a different action for each separate item. With the button Apply Actions you can carry out the selected actions at once. If you would rather just remove all items in one go, you can use the button Remove All .

When you have removed the item for example, you see this:

Name	Alert level	Action	Status
Tool:Win32/EICAR_Test_...	Severe	Remove	Succeeded

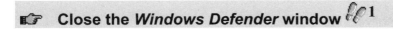 **Close the *Windows Defender* window** $\ell\ell$ 1

5.7 Virus Protection

Windows Vista does not include an antivirus program. It is your own responsibility to purchase and install an antivirus program. If you do not have an antivirus program, you can buy antivirus software from your computer supplier.

You can also download a free trial version of an antivirus program directly from the website of the manufacturer. Many manufacturers offer free trial periods of thirty, sixty or even ninety days. That way you can try before you buy and decide which antivirus program suits you best. Always check if the program you are going to download is compatible with *Windows Vista*.

In this example, you will take a look at the website where you can download the free trial version of *Windows Live OneCare*. This is the complete security solution created by *Microsoft*.

Open *Internet Explorer* $\ell\ell$ 103

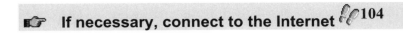

☞ **If necessary, connect to the Internet** 𝓁𝓁**104**

☞ **Go to the website** onecare.live.com 𝓁𝓁**105**

⇨ **Please note:**

You do not have to download and use *Windows Live OneCare*. You can also buy an antivirus program in a computer store. There are more antivirus programs on the market that are also compatible with *Windows Vista.* Other manufacturers will also offer a free trial period.

You see the home page of *Windows Live OneCare.* Due to frequent updates, this website may look different than it does here in this example.

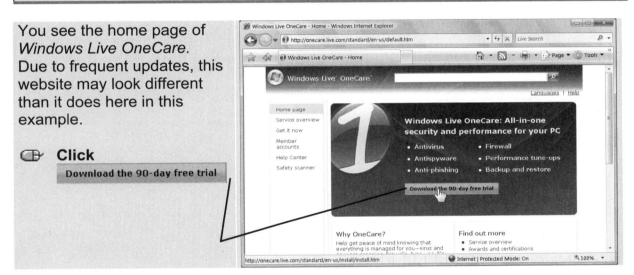

☞ **Click**

Download the 90-day free trial

If you want to install the program *Windows Live OneCare* now, simply follow the instructions that appear on your screen. When the installation of the antivirus program is completed, you must restart your computer.

 Tip

Antivirus software
Well-known manufacturers of antivirus software are:
- McAfee: us.mcafee.com
- Norton: shop.symantecstore.com
- Norman: www.norman.com
- Panda: www.pandasoftware.com
- Kaspersky: www.kaspersky.com

⇨ **Please note:**

Many antivirus programs have their own built-in firewall. This firewall gets priority, and *Windows Firewall* is turned off. When this happens, the *Security Center* will display a warning.

It is possible that the antivirus program you have chosen will have its own *Security Center* and antispyware program. *Windows Vista Security Center* and *Windows Defender* may be turned off. For example, *Windows Live OneCare* uses the *Windows Vista Security Center*. But *Windows Firewall* and *Windows Defender* are replaced by *Windows Live OneCare*'s own programs.

When you open the *Security Center*, you can check the current security status:

☞ **Open *Windows Security Center*** 𝒍𝒍 **29**

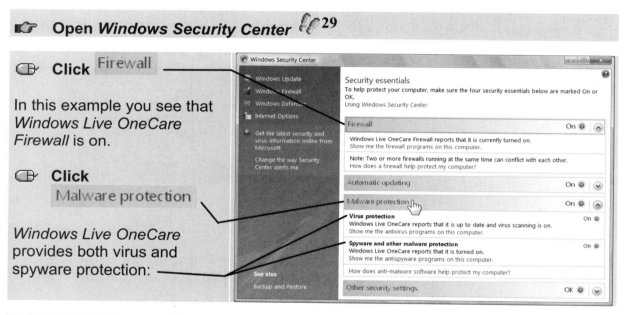

👆 **Click** Firewall

In this example you see that *Windows Live OneCare Firewall* is on.

👆 **Click**
       Malware protection

Windows Live OneCare provides both virus and spyware protection:

☞ **Close the *Windows Security Center* window** 𝒍𝒍 **1**

In the next section you can read more about using an antivirus program. As an example, the program *Windows Live OneCare* is used.

5.8 Using an Antivirus Program

Every antivirus program has a main window where you can view the program settings and make adjustments if necessary. Use the *Start menu*, to open your antivirus program. This is the first window you will see.

In this example you see the main window of *Windows Live OneCare*:

In the top part of the window you see the current status:

Here you see the three components of the program:

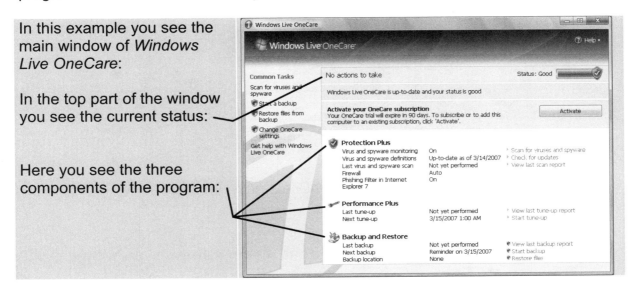

These are the three components of *Windows Live OneCare*:

Protection Plus : this component provides virus, spyware and phishing protection and manages a two-way firewall.

Performance Plus : you can use this tool to perform maintenance tasks to keep your computer running smoothly.

Backup and Restore : this component helps protect your files in case of accidental deletion or hardware failure.

Please note:

Your antivirus program may have other features. Refer to the documentation or the Help section of your antivirus program for more information.

In *Windows Live OneCare* you can let *Protection Plus* scan your computer for viruses and other malware:

Click
▸ Scan for viruses and spyware

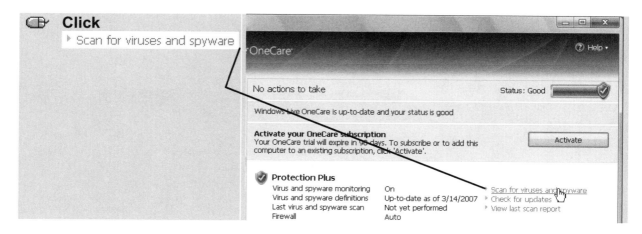

You will find a similar feature in your own antivirus program. Most antivirus programs offer a choice between three types of scans:

⇨ **Quick Scan** : only scans the locations where malware is often found.

⇨ **Complete Scan** : scans all files and folders on your computer.

⇨ **Custom Scan** : only scans the folders you specify.

Choose a scan or click Cancel **if you do not want to scan your computer now**

During the scan you see a window that shows the progress of the scan:

OneCare takes automatic action against potential harmful software rated high or severe. You will be notified about this in the scan report that is displayed when the scan is completed.

For low risk items you can choose between repairing the file, placing the file in quarantine or removing the file. It is possible that your antivirus program asks you what you want to do with each separate harmful file that is found.

Every antivirus program offers the possibility to have the scan performed automatically. To find this option you need to open the program settings. In *Windows Live OneCare* the window *Windows Live OneCare Settings* looks like this:

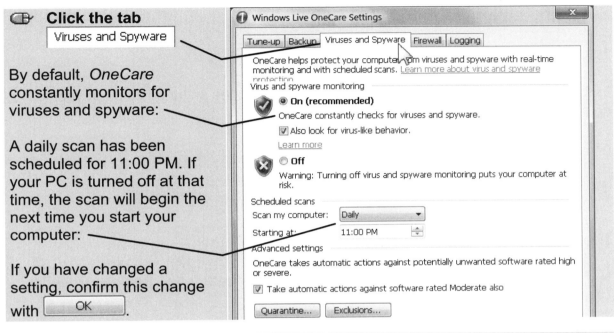

 Click the tab
Viruses and Spyware

By default, *OneCare* constantly monitors for viruses and spyware:

A daily scan has been scheduled for 11:00 PM. If your PC is turned off at that time, the scan will begin the next time you start your computer:

If you have changed a setting, confirm this change with OK.

 **Close the *Windows Live OneCare* window** ᡇᡇ1

♀ **Tip**

Read more?
Would you like to read more about computer security? Then this Visual Steps book is a good choice for you:
Internet and E-mail for SENIORS with Windows Vista
(ISBN 978 90 5905 284 0)

In this book you can read how to e-mail and surf the Internet safely, and how to prevent and fight viruses. The book also describes how to download, install and use the program *Windows Live OneCare*.

In this chapter you have learned how the different program components of *Windows Vista* protect your computer. You also know now that you have to purchase and install an antivirus program yourself.

Make sure you keep your antivirus program updated and buy or renew your license on time. You will be automatically reminded to do so when the license is about to expire. Most antivirus programs require the license to be renewed every year.

5.9 Exercises

Have you forgotten how to do something? Use the number beside the footsteps to look it up in *Appendix B How Do I Do That Again?*

Exercise: The Security Center

In this exercise you use the *Security Center* to check the security status of your computer.

✓ Open the *Security Center.* 🦶[29]

✓ Take a look at the detailed status of *Windows Firewall.* 🦶[30]

Exercise: Automatic Updates

In this exercise you will find out when the automatic check for available updates for *Windows Vista* is performed.

✓ Open the *Windows Update* window. 🦶[31]

✓ Open the *Windows Update* settings. 🦶[32]

✓ Read when the check for available updates is performed.

✓ Close the *Windows Update* window. 🦶[1]

Exercise: Quick Scan for Spyware

In this exercise you perform a quick scan using *Windows Defender*.

✓ Open the *Windows Defender* window. 🦶[33]

✓ Perform a quick scan. 🦶[34]

✓ Stop the scan. 🦶[35]

✓ Close all windows. 🦶[1]

5.10 Background Information

Glossary

Antivirus program	Program you can use to scan your computer for viruses. Found viruses are removed if possible.
Complete Scan	Option in antivirus or antispyware program to scan all files and folders on your computer.
Custom scan	Option in antivirus or antispyware program to scan only the folders you specify yourself.
Firewall	Software or hardware that checks data traffic coming from the Internet or a network to your computer and vice versa, and then either blocks or allows it, depending on your firewall settings.
Malware	Computer program designed to deliberately harm your computer. Viruses, worms and Trojan horses are examples of these harmful programs.
Quick Scan	Option in antivirus of antispyware program to only scan those locations where malware is most likely to be found.
Security Center	Here the current security status of your computer is displayed, and you are advised what actions you can take to protect your computer even better.
Spyware	Computer program that can display advertisements (such as pop-up ads), collect information about your surfing behavior and send the information to the software's creator.
Trojan horse	Unwanted software that comes with an innocent program installed by the user. The program itself appears to be harmless, but is actually harmful when executed.

- Continue reading on the next page -

User Account Control	Feature in *Windows* that can help prevent unauthorized changes to your computer. Before performing actions that could potentially affect your computer's operation or change settings that affect other users, you are asked for your permission or a password. The screen goes dark when that happens.
Virus	A program that attempts to spread from computer to computer and either causes damage (by erasing or corrupting data) or annoys users (by displaying messages or changing the information displayed on the screen).
Windows Defender	Antispyware program that is packaged with *Windows Vista*.
Windows Live OneCare	*Microsoft* program you can use for the complete protection of your computer. The program not only protects your computer against viruses, but also contains a firewall and spyware protection.
Windows Update	System that checks if you are using the most recent version of *Windows Vista*. Available updates can be downloaded and installed automatically.
Worm	Malware in the form of a self-replication program. A typical worm sends out copies of itself to everyone in your *Contacts* folder, then does the same thing on the recipients' computers. This creates a domino effect that could cause your computer or a web or network server to stop responding.

Source: Windows Help and Support

5.11 Tips

Tip

Windows Vista demos
Windows Help and Support contains a narrated video demonstration about the subjects of this chapter: Demo: Security basics

☞ **Open *Windows Help and Support*** [13]

In the *Search Box*:

⌨ **Type:** demo

👆 **Click** 🔍

You see a list of demos.

👆 **For example, click** Demo: Security basics

In the next window:

👆 **Click** ⊙ Watch the demo

The program *Windows Media Player* opens and the demo starts playing automatically:

☞ **Watch the demo**

When the demo is finished, you can close *Windows Media Player.*

👆 **Click** ❌

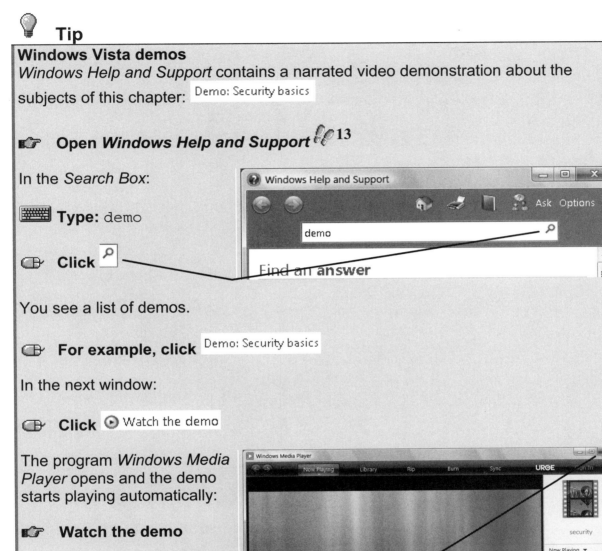

Notes

Write down your notes here.

6. User Accounts

If you share a computer with other people, it is a good idea to create a user account for each user. A user account contains the personal settings and preferences of a user. These settings include the appearance of the desktop, the screen saver, and the way folders are displayed. In addition, each user has their own list of *Favorites* and recently visited websites in *Internet Explorer*. Settings for the e-mail program *Windows Mail* can be specified for each user independently. Users also have their own *Personal Folder*.

It is very easy to work with user accounts. A user clicks his or her own user name in the *Windows Vista Welcome Screen*. Then the user's personal settings are read and applied. Changes to those settings have no effect on other users' settings. In *Windows Vista* you can also quickly switch to another user's account. You do not have to close all your programs and you can just as easily return to your own account.

To prevent others from making changes to your settings, you can protect your account with a password. With *User Account Control* you can protect your computer even further. This feature helps prevent other users from making unauthorized changes to your computer.

Another useful feature in *Windows Vista* is *Parental Controls*. You can use this to control how and when your (grand)children are allowed to use the computer.

In this chapter you will learn how to:

- change the name and picture for a user account;
- create and delete a new user account;
- protect a user account with a password;
- change and remove a password;
- create and use a password reset disk;
- use the *Guest* account;
- quickly switch between users;
- use the features *User Account Control* and *Parental Controls*.

 Please note:

To be able to do the exercises in this chapter you will need a USB stick.

6.1 Types of User Accounts

User accounts make it possible to share a computer with several people, but still have your own files and settings. Each person accesses their user account with a user name and possibly a password.

A user account is a collection of information that tells *Windows Vista* what files and folders you are allowed to access, what changes you can make to the computer, and your personal preferences, such as your desktop background or color theme.

There are three different types of user accounts:

  Standard user account: allows you to use most of the capabilities of the computer, but permission from an administrator is required if you want to make changes that affect other users or the security of the computer. For example, you can not install software and hardware or delete files that are required for the computer to work.

  Administrator account: allows you to make changes that will affect other users. Administrators can change security settings, install software and hardware, and access all files on the computer. Administrators can also make changes to the other user accounts.

  Guest account: an account for users who do not have a permanent account on your computer. It allows people to use your computer without having access to your personal files. People using the guest account can not install software or hardware, change settings, or create a password.

6.2 Changing a User Name

When you start *Windows Vista* for the very first time, for example on a new computer, you enter the information for your user account in a wizard.

A user account shows the name you entered for the user. This name can easily be changed in the window *Manage Accounts.* You reach this window through the *Control Panel*:

☞ **Open the *Control Panel*** 𝒸𝓁 [18]

Click

  Add or remove user accounts

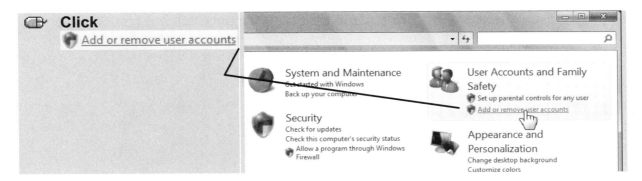

Your screen goes dark and you see the window *User Account Control* where you need to give your permission to continue.

 Click | Continue |

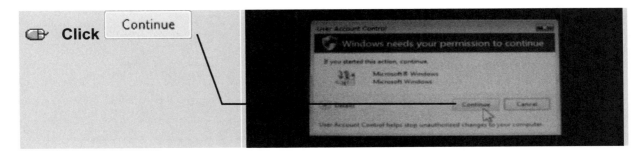

✖ HELP! Do you see this window?

When you see this window, you have a standard user account. With a standard user account you can not access the window *Manage Accounts*.
Users with a standard account need to enter the password that is set for an administrator account to be able to continue this task:

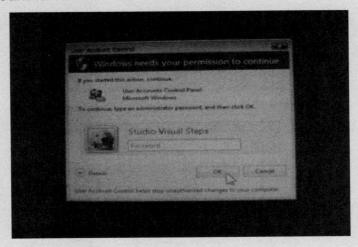

☞ **Ask the user with the administrator account to change your account and help you with the other tasks in this chapter.**

In the window *Manage Accounts* you see the user accounts that are used on this computer. If you did not add any extra user accounts, only your account or the account named *User* is active. The account *User* was created when *Windows Vista* was installed.

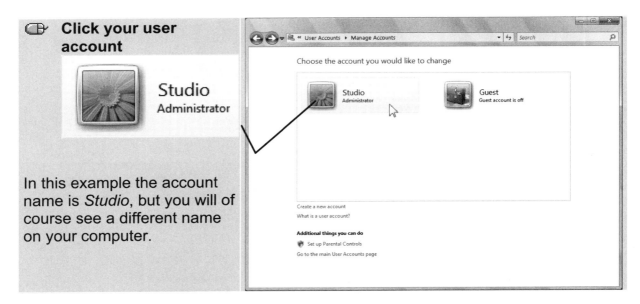

☞ **Click your user account**

In this example the account name is *Studio*, but you will of course see a different name on your computer.

You can change the name of your user account like this:

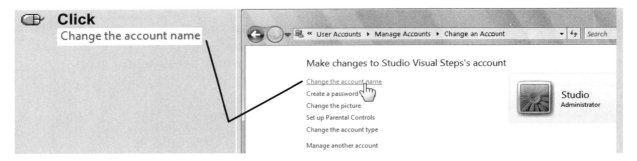

☞ **Click**
Change the account name

Now you can enter a new name for your account:

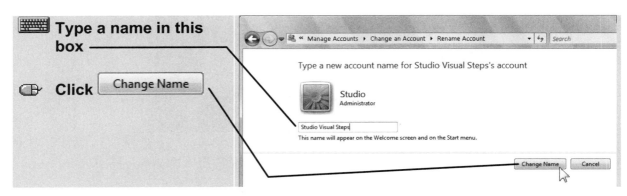

⌨ **Type a name in this box**

☞ **Click** Change Name

The name of your user account has now been changed:

6.3 Choosing Another Picture

Windows Vista displays a small image for every user account. You can change this image like this:

Click Change the picture

In this window you see the images available for user accounts in *Windows Vista*. You are going to change your current picture to the picture of the dog:

Click

Click Change Picture

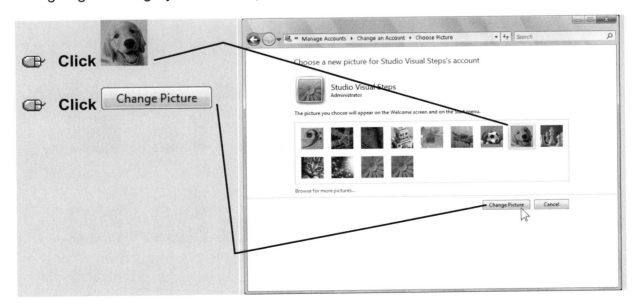

The picture for your user account has been changed to the dog:

☞ **Close the window**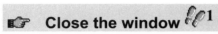

💡 **Tip**

Use your own image
Instead of using the standard images provided by *Windows Vista*, you can also set your own photo or image as the picture for your user account. Like this:

👆 **Click**
Browse for more pictures...

The folder *Pictures* will be opened. You can also choose a different folder like *Sample Pictures*:

👆 **Click** Sample Pictures

👆 **Click a photo**

👆 **Click** Open

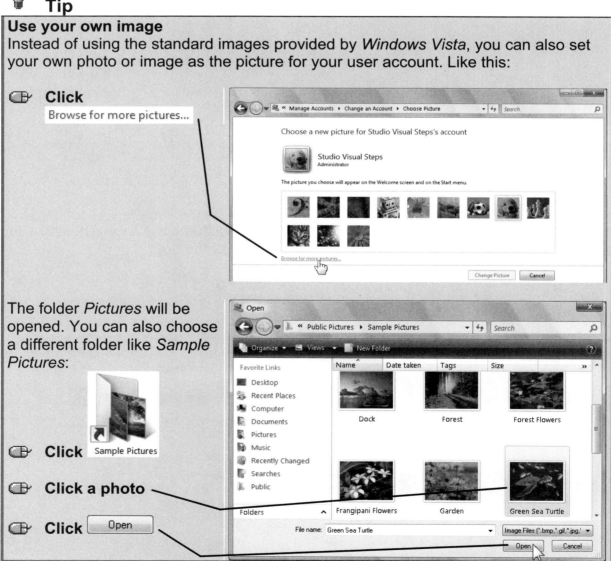

6.4 Creating a New User Account

In just a few steps, you can create a new user account in the window *Manage Accounts*.

☞ **Open the window *Manage Accounts*** 𝓵𝓵**36**

Click Create a new account

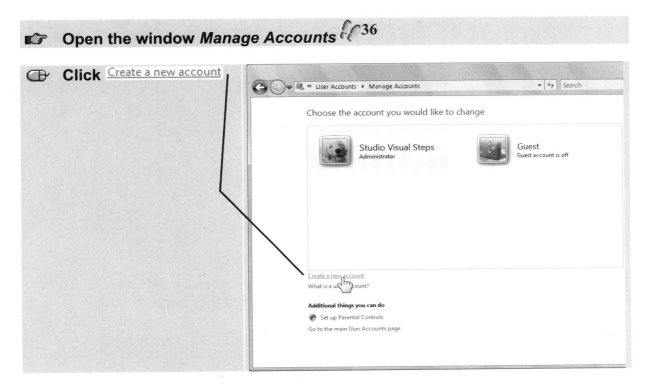

In the next window you can enter the user name and account type for the new user account. For this exercise, choose the standard user account:

⌨ **Type a name in this box, for example:**
Mary

☞ **Click the option**
◉ Standard user

☞ **Click** Create Account

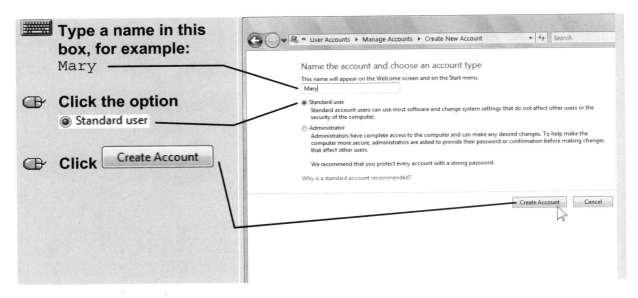

You see that a new account has been added:

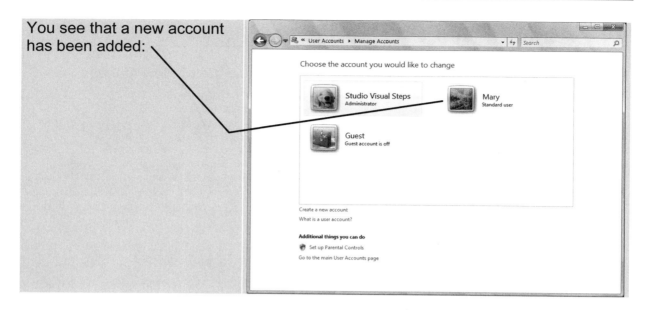

6.5 Deleting a User Account

If one of the users no longer uses the computer, you can remove his account. To be able to delete a user account, you must have an administrator account or the administrator password.

⇨ Please note:

When you remove a user account, the *Windows Mail* settings associated with this account are lost, as well as any saved e-mails, or files in the folders *Documents*, *Favorites*, *Music*, *Pictures*, *Videos* and *Music* and the files on the desktop.
Before you permanently delete the account, *Windows Vista* will ask if you want to save this information.

You can remove the new user account you just created like this:

In the window you see now, you can specify what you want to do with this account.

Windows Vista now asks what should be done with the files from this user. You can choose to save or delete the files in the folders *Documents, Favorites, Music, Pictures, Videos* and *Music* and the files on the desktop. If you choose to save the files, they will be placed on your desktop in a folder with the name of the deleted user account.

In this case you choose to delete the files:

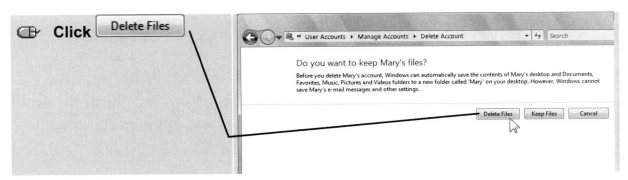

Finally, you are asked if you are sure you want to delete the account:

The user account has now been removed.

HELP! Do you see this window?

Windows Vista warns you that data may be lost when you delete an account while the user is still logged on.

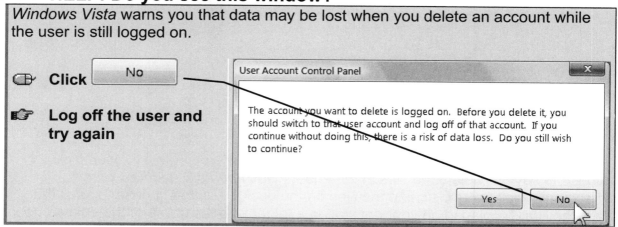

☞ **Click** No

☞ **Log off the user and try again**

6.6 Creating a Password for a User Account

Every user account can be protected with a password. If you want to make sure nobody can change your settings, you should create a password for your user account. You can do that like this:

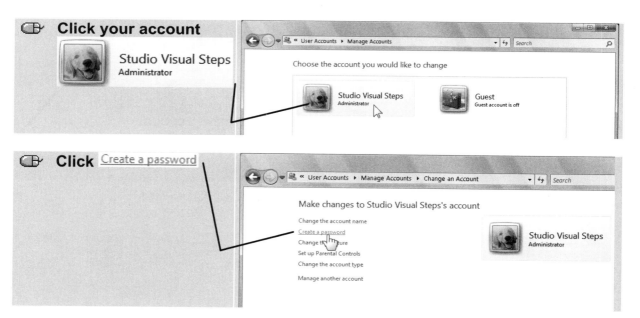

☞ **Click your account**

Studio Visual Steps
Administrator

☞ **Click** Create a password

In the next window you can type your password and a password hint. The password hint helps you when you have forgotten your password. Remember that passwords are case sensitive: if you type a capital letter in your password now, you have to do that every time you type your password.

Please note:

A password is only useful when others can not easily guess it. Use at least seven characters, combining letters and digits. Keep in mind that every user on your computer can see your password hint on the *Welcome Screen*. Keep your hint vague enough so that others can not guess your password. For example, 'first dog' or 'mother's maiden name'.

Type your password here

Type your password again here

Type your password hint here

☞ **Before you continue, write down your password**

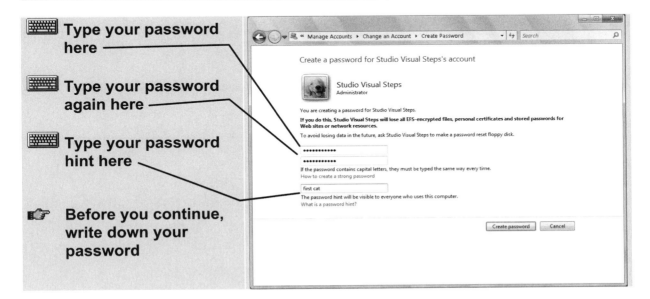

When you have entered your password and password hint, and you have written down your password, you can let *Windows Vista* activate the password:

Click Create password

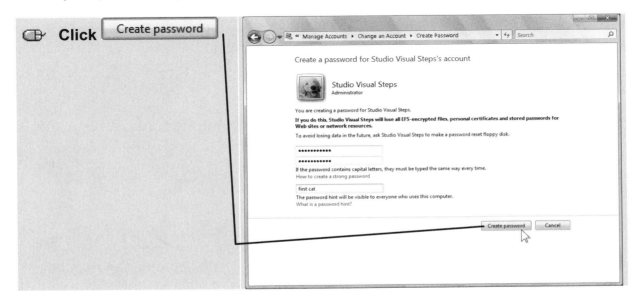

HELP! Do you see this window?

Then you have entered two different passwords.

> **User Account Control Panel**
>
> The passwords you typed do not match. Please retype the new password in both boxes.
>
> OK

⌨ **Type your password in both boxes again**

⇨ **Please note:**

Your password only protects your user account; other users can not log on to the computer using your name.

When another user tries to open your *Personal Folder*, he sees this window:

When a user with a standard user account clicks [Continue], he is prompted to enter the administrator password.

When an administrator clicks [Continue], he can access the *Personal Folder* of the other user!

You see why it is better to give the other users on your computer a standard user account instead of an administrator account.

Suppose you created a folder *C:\Letters* on the hard disk of your computer. This folder can be opened by all other users. Using the window *Computer* or *Windows Explorer* they can view what is stored on the hard disk of the computer and open this folder. So always keep your personal files and folders in (a subfolder of) your *Personal Folder*!

Tip

Shared documents
Even if all users have a standard user account that is protected with a password, it is still possible to share documents. You use the folder *Public Documents* for this. Every user can open this folder. This is how you save a document to the *Public Documents* folder in the window *Save*:

👆 **Click** 🔽 Browse Folders

👆 **Click** 📁 Public

👆 **Double-click** 📁 Public Documents

👆 **Click** Save

6.7 Changing a Password

When you protect your user account with a password, it is a good idea to change this password regularly. Like this:

👆 **Click** Change the password

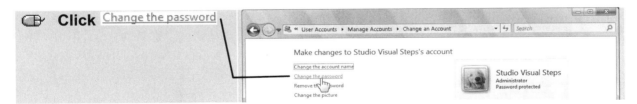

In the next window you have to enter your current password first. This is to make sure that you really are the user that is allowed to change the password. Then you can enter your new password and password hint:

⌨ **Type your current password**

⌨ **Type your new password**

⌨ **Type your new password again**

⌨ **Type a password hint for your new password**

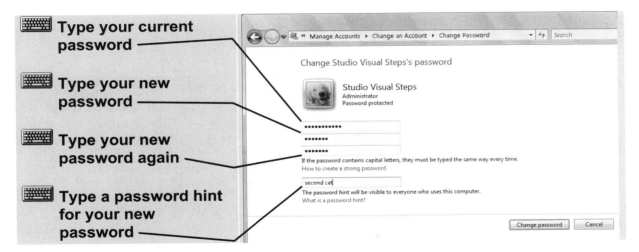

☞ **Write down your new password**

Now you can change the password:

👆 **Click**

Change password

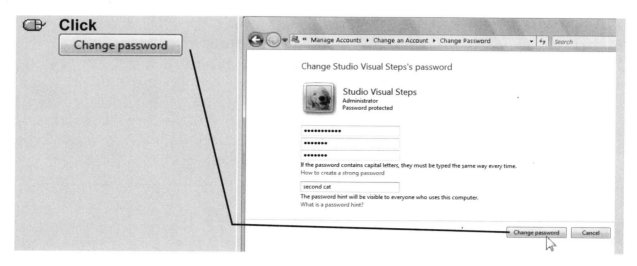

The password has been changed. Next time you log on to the computer, you have to enter the new password.

☞ **Close the** *User Accounts* **window** 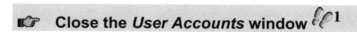¹

6.8 Creating a Password Reset Disk

It is possible that you forget your password in the future. If even the password hint does not help you remember the password, it is good to have something to fall back on. You can create a *password reset disk* that you can use to log on to *Windows Vista.* Then you can create a new password. You only have to create this disk once, no matter how often you change your password later.

⇨ **Please note:**

Although the term 'disk' is used in the windows, you will probably want to use some other kind of portable media, such as a USB stick. A USB stick is also called USB memory stick or USB flash drive. Most new *Vista* PCs will probably not even have a floppy disk drive as diskette are gradually being replaced by other storage media.

To go to the window where you can find the option to create a password reset disk:

☞ **Open the** *Control Panel* 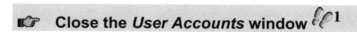¹⁸

Click
User Accounts and Family Safety

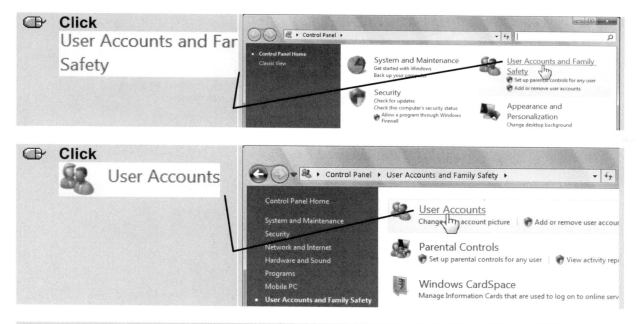

Click   User Accounts

☞ **Insert an empty, formatted diskette in the diskette drive**

or:

☞ **Insert a USB stick in the USB port of the computer**

When you choose this option, you will have to wait a moment before the USB stick is recognized by *Windows Vista*.

You will see a message in the lower right corner of your screen:

☞ **If necessary, close the *AutoPlay* window** 🐾¹

Click
Create a password reset disk

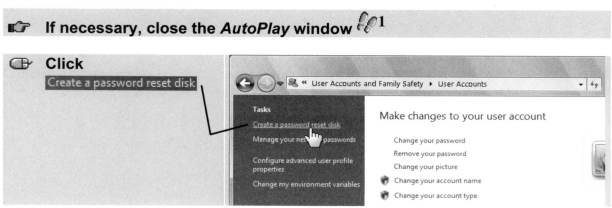

The *Forgotten Password Wizard* opens:

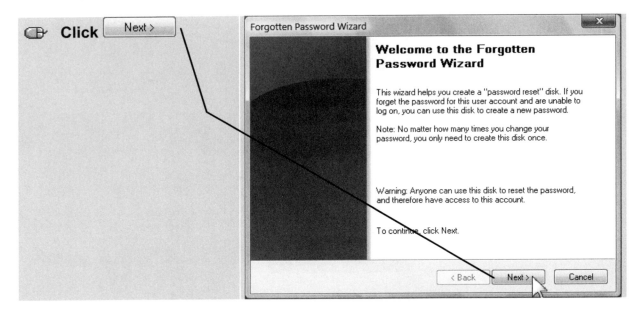

Now you can choose the drive where the password reset disk has to be created:

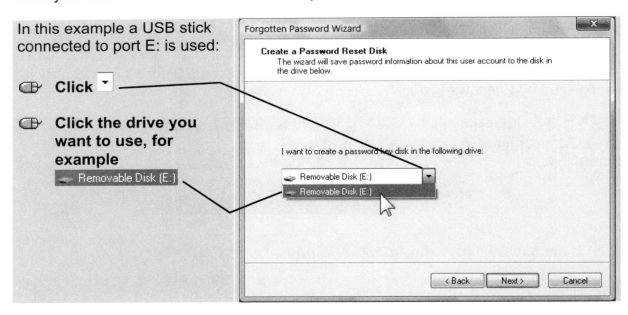

🖱️ **Click** [Next >]

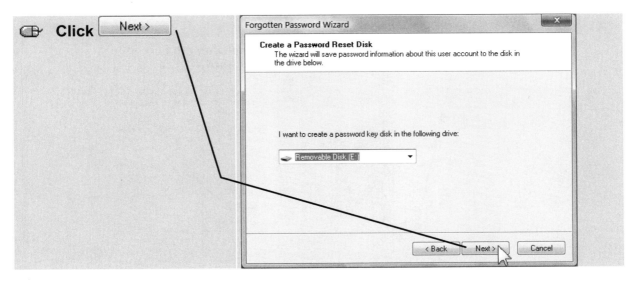

⌨️ **Type your current password here**

🖱️ **Click** [Next >]

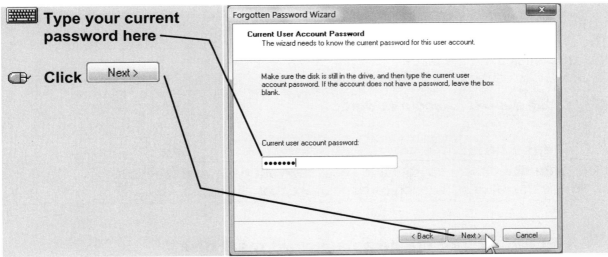

Now the *Forgotten Password Wizard* writes the reset information to the USB stick:

🖱️ **Click** [Next >]

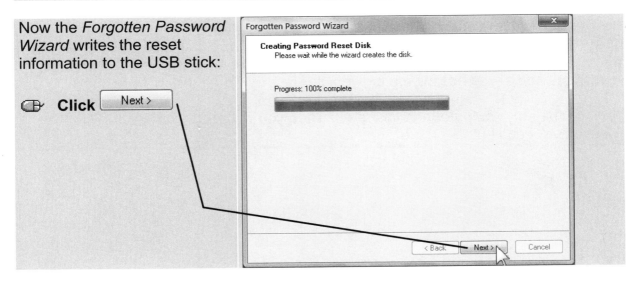

Click [Finish]

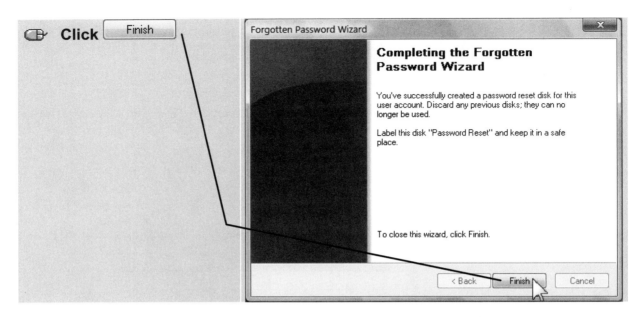

The password reset disk (your USB stick) is now ready for use. Make sure to keep this USB stick in a safe place.

 Close the *User Accounts* window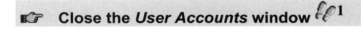

⇨ **Please note:**

Make sure other users do not have access to your password reset disk. Anyone could use this USB stick to log on to your account.

❄ **HELP! I did not create a password reset disk.**

When you lose your password and you did not create a password reset disk, you can no longer log on to your computer.
The (other) administrator can set a new password for you. In this procedure you will permanently lose part of your settings: your personal certificates, access to e-mail messages and saved passwords for websites.

Are you the only computer administrator? Then you will need to reinstall *Windows Vista* on your computer.

Tip

Using the password reset disk
When you lose your password, you can no longer log on in the *Welcome Screen*. The password reset disk allows you to create a new password outside your own account. You can use this new password to log on. Like this:

☞ **Click your user name**

Now you have to enter your password, but you do not.

☞ **Click** ➡

You see the message that your user name or password is invalid.

☞ **Click** [OK] **to leave this window**

☞ **Click *Reset password***

Now you see the first window of the *Password Reset Wizard.*

☞ **Insert the password reset disk or connect the USB stick to your computer and click** [Next >]

In the window you see now, you can choose the drive you placed the password reset disk in:

☞ **Click** ▾ **and then the drive you want to use, for example** [Removable Disk (E:)]

☞ **Click** [Next >]

Now you can enter your new password and password hint.

⌨ **Type your new password**

⌨ **Type your new password again**

⌨ **Type a new password hint**

☞ **Click** [Next >]

In the next window:

☞ **Click** [Finish]

Now you can log on using your new password.

6.9 Using the Guest Account

It is not necessary to create a user account for every user that occasionally uses your computer. When someone only needs to check his e-mail or look up something quickly on the Internet from time to time, it is a better idea to turn on the *Guest* account. People who do not have a user account, can use the *Guest* account to log on to the computer. The *Guest* account is a standard user account.

 Please note:

You can only activate the *Guest* account if you have an *Administrator* account yourself.

You turn on the *Guest* account as follows:

☞ **Open the *Manage Accounts* window** *ℓℓ³⁶*

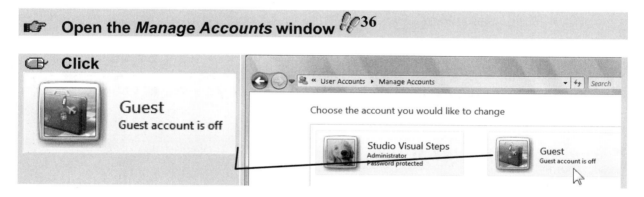

Click
Guest
Guest account is off

In this window you choose to turn on the *Guest* account:

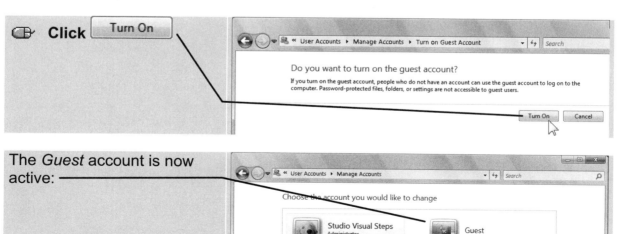

Click Turn On

The *Guest* account is now active:

Now you also see the user *Guest* in the *Windows Vista Welcome Screen.*

6.10 Fast User Switching

Windows Vista offers the option to quickly switch between users. This is very useful if you are working on the computer and another user wants to check his e-mail. You do not have to close all your programs and log off. In *Windows Vista* you can switch to another user account and then return to your account.

You can switch to the *Guest* account like this:

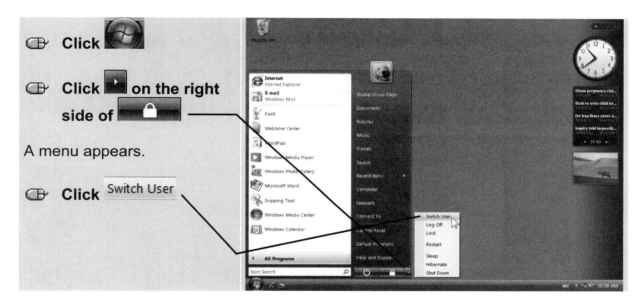

Now you see the *Windows Vista Welcome Screen.* Here you can choose the user account you want to switch to:

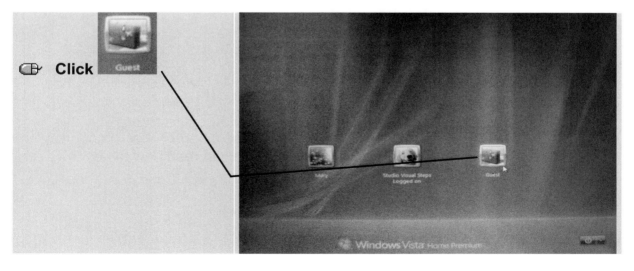

The *Guest* account now opens.

You can return to your own account from the *Guest* account. First you log off the *Guest* account:

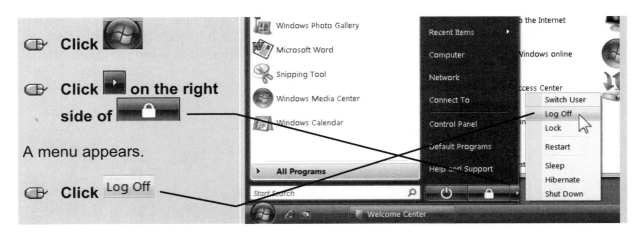

In the *Welcome Screen* you select your own account:

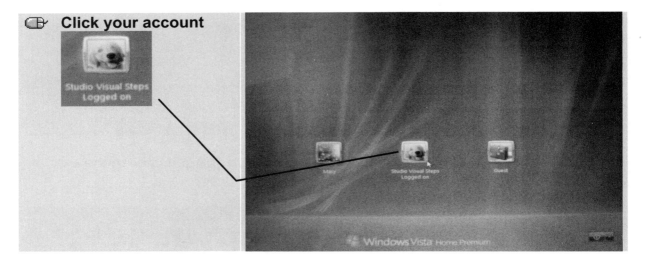

After entering your password, the user account is opened. Any programs you had opened are still active.

Up to this point you have learned how to create and use different user accounts, with or without password protection. In the next section you can read how to use the user accounts to protect your computer better.

Tip

Is it necessary to type a password each time?
By default, the screen saver is activated when you do not use your computer for over ten minutes. When you do not use your computer for over an hour, your computer is put to sleep.

According to the default settings you:
- do not have to type your password again when you interrupt the screen saver (by moving the mouse or pressing any key)
- must type your password again when you wake your computer from sleep (by pressing the power button on your computer's system case)

You can adjust these settings to your own preferences. Like this:

☞ **Right-click the desktop**

☞ **Click** Personalize

☞ **Click** Screen Saver

You see the window *Screen Saver Settings*:

Here you can choose which screen saver to use, and how many minutes of inactivity is allowed before it is activated:

By default, the option
☐ On resume, display logon screen
is **not** check marked:

This means you can continue working when you interrupt the screen saver.

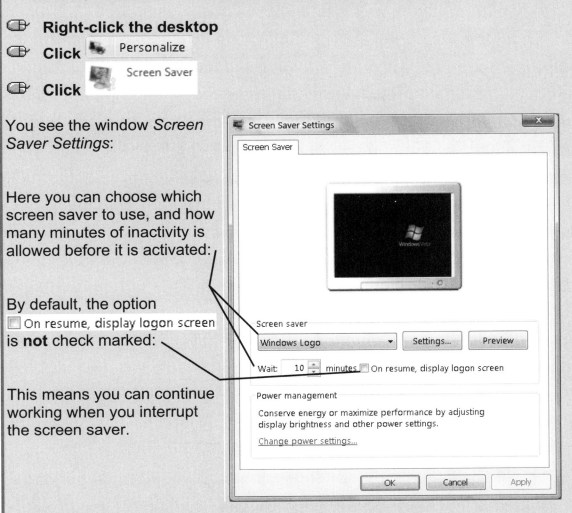

- Continue reading on the next page -

If you check mark this option, you will see the *Welcome Screen* when you interrupt the screen saver. You will then need to enter your password to log on.

You find the sleep settings in another window:

☞ **Click** Change power settings...

In the window *Power Options*:

☞ **Click** Require a password on wakeup

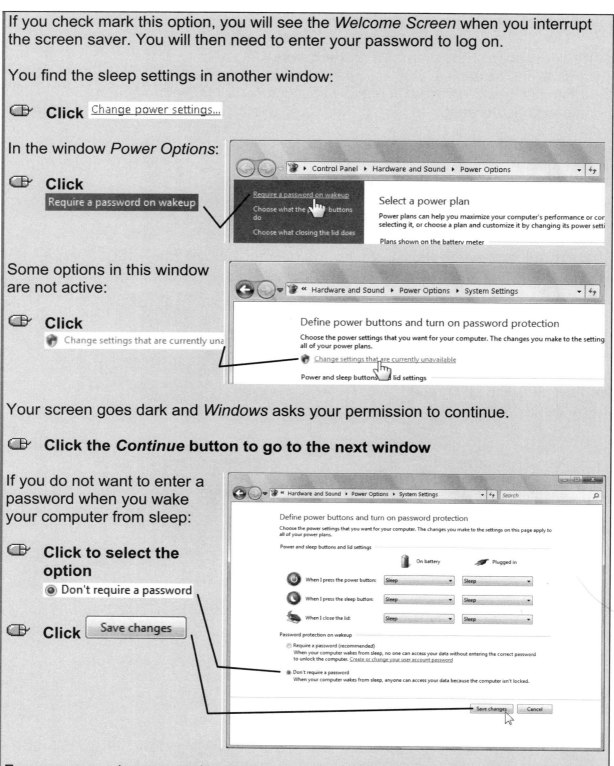

Some options in this window are not active:

☞ **Click** 🛡 Change settings that are currently una

Your screen goes dark and *Windows* asks your permission to continue.

☞ **Click the *Continue* button to go to the next window**

If you do not want to enter a password when you wake your computer from sleep:

☞ **Click to select the option**
    ⦿ Don't require a password

☞ **Click** Save changes

From now on, when you wake your computer from sleep, you will not have to type your password again.

6.11 User Account Control

You have already been introduced to *User Account Control* in *Windows Vista*. This feature causes your screen to darken and you must give permission to continue. This will prevent changes being made to your computer by users who do not have permission to do so. When you see a message from *User Account Control*, read through it carefully. Make sure that the name that is displayed corresponds to the task you want to perform or the program you want to open.

In a darkened screen you can see several different messages from *User Account Control*:

Windows needs your permission to continue
You see this message when you start a *Windows* function or program that can affect other users of this computer.

A program needs your permission to continue
This message is displayed when you open a program that is not part of *Windows*, but does have a valid digital signature (electronic security). This means you can assume this program is legitimate.

An unidentified program wants access to your computer
This message is displayed when you open an unknown program that does not have a valid digital signature from its publisher. This means that you are unable to check if the program is legitimate. It does not necessarily indicate danger, as many older, legitimate programs do not have signatures. However, you should use extra caution and only allow this program to run if you obtained it from a trusted source, such as the original CD or a publisher's website.

This program has been blocked
When your computer is connected to a network, the network administrator can block programs from running on your computer. To run this program, you can contact your administrator and ask to have the program unblocked.

If you want to use the full potential of *User Account Control*, you should create a standard user account for each user of the computer (including yourself). With this type of account you have sufficient rights to send e-mails, edit photos or surf the Internet.

You keep one administrator account that you protect with a password. It is advisable to (have the other users) do the same for the standard user accounts.

When a user who has a standard user account tries to install software for example, the screen will go dark. *Windows* will ask for the password of the administrator account. This way software can not be installed without your knowledge and permission.

The user with the standard user account has to enter the administrator password to be able to continue with this task:

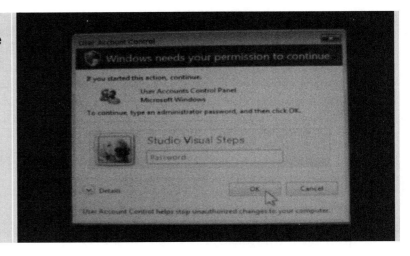

The administrator password must be entered each time before tasks can be performed that might:
- affect the settings of the computer or
- change the settings of other users.

For example, to set up *Parental Controls* you also need to enter the administrator password. In the next section you can read more about *Parental Controls*.

6.12 Parental Controls

You can use *Parental Controls* to control how other users, for example your (grand)children, use the computer. You can set limits on the hours they can use the computer, the types of games they can play, the websites they can visit, and the programs they can run.

 Please note:

Before you get started, make sure that the (grand)child for which you want to set *Parental Controls* has a standard user account. Like the other accounts, this account must be password protected. If there are user accounts that are not password protected, the *Parental Controls* might be bypassed.

In **sections 6.4** and **6.6** of this chapter you can read how to create a user account and protect it with a password.

You can set up *Parental Controls* through the *Control Panel*:

☞ **Open the *Control Panel* 🔌 18**

⊞ **Click**
  🔘 Set up parental controls for an

Your screen goes dark and you need to give permission to continue. If you are using a standard user account yourself, you must enter the administrator password.

⊞ **Click the *Continue* button**

You see all user accounts on your computer.

⊞ **Click the account you want to set up *Parental Controls* for**

Next, turn on *Parental Controls*:

⊞ **Click the option**
  ◉ On, enforce current settings

As soon as you turn on *Parental Controls*, the rest of this window becomes active.

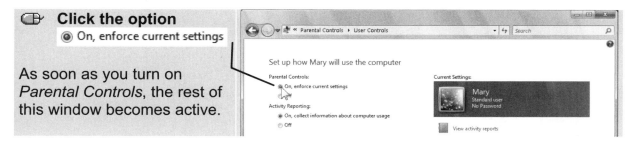

Now you can adjust the separate settings for each component of *Parental Controls*.

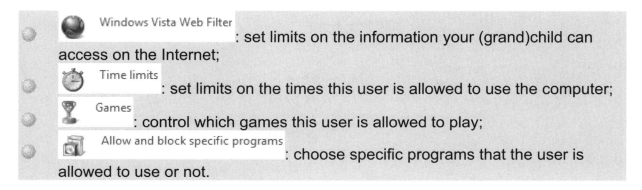

○ 🌐 Windows Vista Web Filter : set limits on the information your (grand)child can access on the Internet;

○ ⏱ Time limits : set limits on the times this user is allowed to use the computer;

○ 🏆 Games : control which games this user is allowed to play;

○ 🗃 Allow and block specific programs : choose specific programs that the user is allowed to use or not.

As an example you are going to adjust the settings for Time limits :

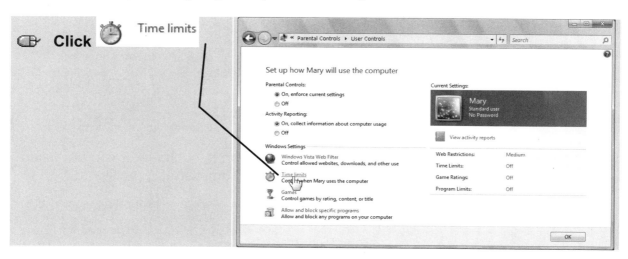

☞ **Click** Time limits

In this window you can choose which hours this user is allowed to use the computer. Outside these hours he or she will not be able to log on.

By default all hours are ☐ Allowed . By clicking or dragging the blocks, you can change this to ■ Blocked .

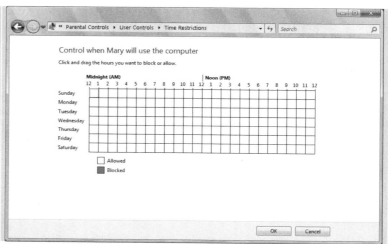

☞ **Click the hours you want to block**

In this example the hours between 8:00 PM and 8:00 AM are blocked. You can choose the hours you want to block yourself. When you are done:

☞ **Click** OK

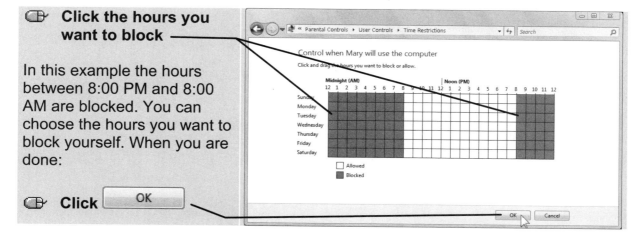

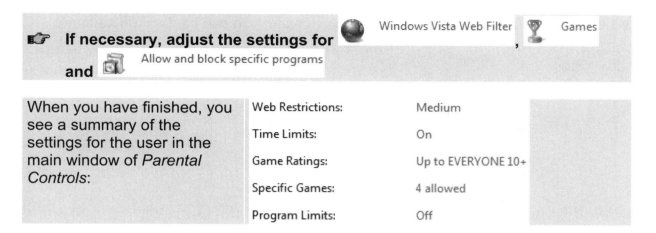

☞ **If necessary, adjust the settings for** Windows Vista Web Filter , Games **and** Allow and block specific programs

When you have finished, you see a summary of the settings for the user in the main window of *Parental Controls*:

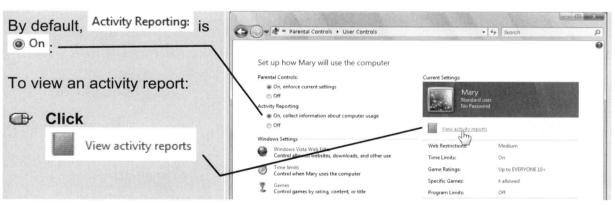

Web Restrictions:	Medium
Time Limits:	On
Game Ratings:	Up to EVERYONE 10+
Specific Games:	4 allowed
Program Limits:	Off

Once you have set up *Parental Controls*, you can use *Activity Reporting* to keep a record of the computer activity of the user of this account.

By default, Activity Reporting: is ⦿ On .

To view an activity report:

🖰 **Click** View activity reports

Here you see the layout of an activity report:

From time to time a message will appear at the bottom of your screen, to remind you to read the activity report. Clicking this message will open the report.

🖰 **Click** ⬅

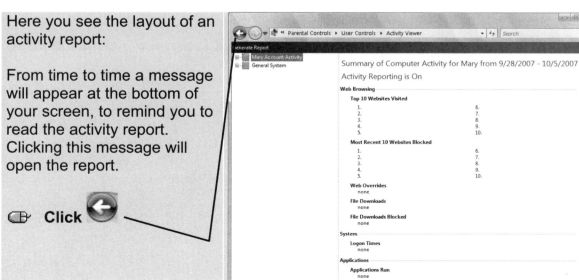

When you are satisfied with the changes you made, you can confirm the settings:

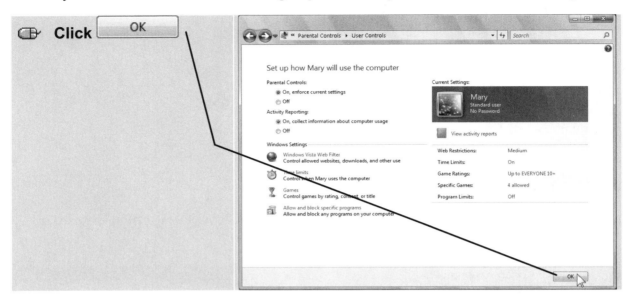

☞ **Click** OK

6.13 Removing a Password

If you decide you do not need to protect your user account with a password, you can remove the password.

⇨ **Please note:**

When you have set up *Parental Controls*, it is better to keep the password. When there are user accounts that are not password protected, the *Parental Controls* might be bypassed.

You can remove your password like this:

☞ **Open the *Manage Accounts* window** $\ell\ell^{36}$

☞ **Click your account**

☞ **Click** Remove the password

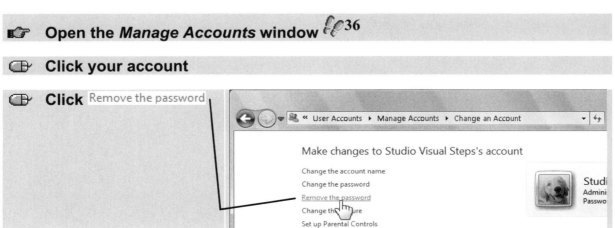

Windows Vista checks if you are really the user that is allowed to remove the password. That is why you have to type your password first:

 Type your password

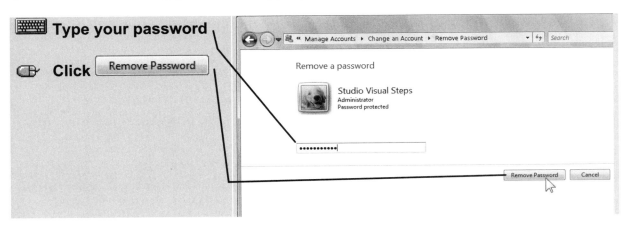

Now your password has been removed.

 **Close all windows** ℓℓ¹

⇨ **Please note:**

If you decide later on to set a password for your account, do not forget to create a new password reset disk!

In this chapter you have learned how to work with user accounts. In the following exercises you can repeat what you have learned.

6.14 Exercises

Have you forgotten how to do something? Use the number beside the footsteps to look it up in *Appendix B How Do I Do That Again?*

Exercise: A New User Account

In this exercise you create a new user account. This is only possible if you have an administrator account yourself.

✔ Open the *Manage Accounts* window. *ℓℓ*³⁶

✔ Create a new standard user account named *Exercise*. *ℓℓ*³⁷

Exercise: Changing the User Account

In this exercise you apply some changes to the new user account.

✔ Change the account picture to the picture of the fish. *ℓℓ*³⁸

✔ Change the account name to *Delete*. *ℓℓ*³⁹

✔ Close all windows. *ℓℓ*¹

Exercise: Deleting an Account

In this exercise you delete the new user account. You need an administrator account for this.

✔ Open the *Manage Accounts* window. *ℓℓ*³⁶

✔ Click the account named *Delete*.

✔ Delete the user account and do not save the files that belong to this account. *ℓℓ*⁴⁰

✔ Close all windows. *ℓℓ*¹

6.15 Background Information

Glossary	
Activity report	Feature in *Parental Controls* that you can activate to keep a record of the computer activity of your (grand)child.
Administrator account	User account that lets you make changes that will affect other users. Administrators can change security settings, install software and hardware, and access all files on the computer. Administrators can also make changes to other user accounts.
CD-Recordable	Type of CD you can write (burn) files to. These files can not be deleted or replaced.
Guest account	An account for users who do not have a permanent account on your computer. With a *Guest* account users can access the computer, but not your personal files. Users with a *Guest* account can not install programs of hardware, change settings or create a password.
Parental Controls	Use this feature to control how other users, for example your (grand)children, use the computer. You can set limits on the hours they can use the computer, the types of games they can play, the websites they can visit, and the programs they can run.
Password	A secret string of characters that lets users log on to a computer and access files, programs, and other resources. Passwords help ensure that unauthorized users do not access the computer.
Password hint	Hint to help you remember your password that appears when you type the wrong password.
Password reset disk	Use this to set a new password when you have forgotten your old password. Although the name indicates otherwise, you can also create a password reset disk on a USB stick.

- Continue reading on the next page -

Screen saver	A moving picture or pattern that appears on a computer screen when the mouse or keyboard has not been used for a specified period of time.
Sleep	Sleep is a power-saving state. Sleep saves all open documents and programs, and allows the computer to quickly resume full-power operation (typically within several seconds) when you want to start working again.
Standard user account	This type of account lets you use most of the capabilities of the computer, but permission from an administrator is required if you want to make changes that affect other users or the security of the computer.
Time limits	Part of *Parental Controls* you can use to control when children are allowed to log on to the computer. Time limits prevent children from logging on during specified hours. You can set different log on hours for every day of the week. If they are logged on when their allotted time ends, they will be automatically logged off.
USB port	A narrow, rectangular connection point on a computer where you can connect a USB (Universal Serial Bus) device.
USB stick / USB memory stick	A small device used to store information. A USB sticks plugs into the USB port of your computer. *Windows Vista* shows a USB stick as a removable disk.
User account	A user account is a collection of information that tells *Windows* what files and folders you can access, what changes you can make to the computer, and your personal preferences, such as your desktop background or color theme. User accounts make it possible that you can share a computer with several people, but still have your own files and settings.
User Account Control	This feature helps prevent unauthorized changes to your computer. Before performing actions that could potentially affect your computer's operation or that change settings that affect other users, your screen goes dark. You are asked for your permission (if you use an administrator account) or you are asked for the administrator password (if you use a standard user account).
Windows Vista Web Filter	Part of *Parental Controls* that you can use to limit the number of websites that can be visited.

Source: Windows Help and Support

6.16 Tips

Tip

Windows Vista demos

Windows Help and Support contains a narrated video demonstration about the subjects of this chapter: Demo: Understanding user accounts .

☞ **Open *Windows Help and Support*** 🦶13

In the *Search Box*:

⌨ **Type:** demo

🖱 **Click** 🔍

You see a list of demos.

🖱 **For example, click** Demo: Understanding user accounts

In the next window:

🖱 **Click** ▶ Watch the demo

The program *Windows Media Player* opens and the demo starts playing automatically:

☞ **Watch the demo**

When the demo is finished, you can close *Windows Media Player*.

🖱 **Click** X

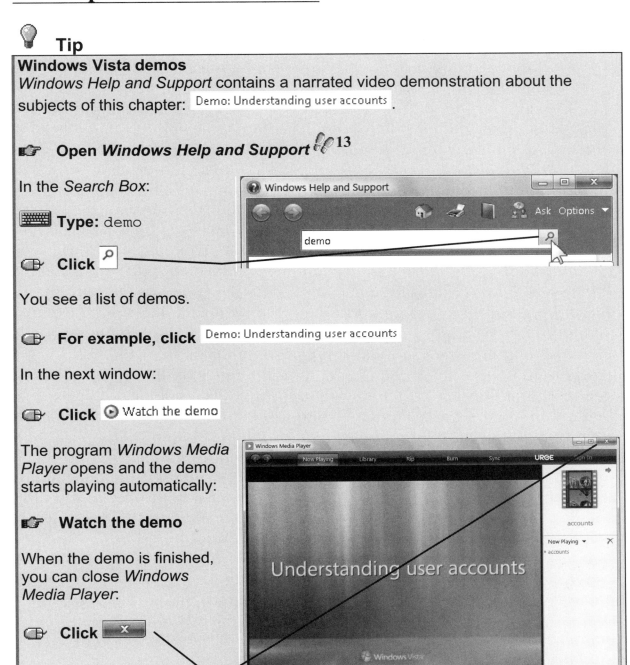

Notes

Write down your notes here.

7. Backup and System Restore

Making backups (copies) of files has become increasingly important for computer users. More and more people store crucial information on their computer. Not only business projects or financial records, but also photos and videos. These days, most cherished memories and unforgettable moments are recorded with digital photo and video cameras.

Important advice: be sure to make regular backups of your files, because some day your computer may stop working. Maybe it will happen soon, because of a short-circuit in your computer or an aggressive virus attack. It may not happen until years from now, but eventually normal wear and tear will takes it toll. When this happens, it is always unexpected. You probably will have no time left to rescue your data.

Microsoft recognizes the importance of good backup procedures. That is why *Windows Vista* has been equipped with new features to enable easy backups of large amounts of data. In this chapter you will be introduced to the various possibilities *Windows Vista* offers to secure your data.

In this chapter you will learn:

- what the *Backup and Restore Center* is;
- what a complete PC backup and a recovery CD are;
- how to create a complete PC backup;
- how to create a full backup;
- how to select the necessary files;
- how to set up an automatic backup;
- what an incremental or additional backup is;
- how to restore a backup;
- how an automatic backup works;
- how to create a new full backup;
- how to create and restore a system restore point.

 Please note:

To be able to do the exercises in this chapter you need one or more recordable CDs or DVDs.

7.1 Backup and Restore Center

Windows Vista has a central location where you can create backups: *the Backup and Restore Center*. Here you can set what kind of backup you want to create, and when. You open the *Backup and Restore Center* like this:

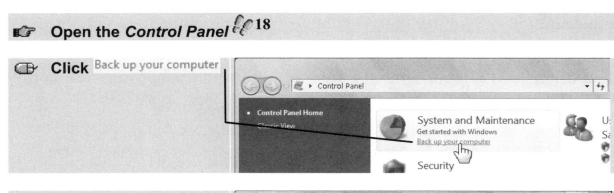

In this example you see the window *Backup and Restore Center* of *Windows Vista Home Premium*:

In *Windows Vista Home Basic* you see a similar window.

Did you create a backup before? Then the date of the last backup is displayed here:

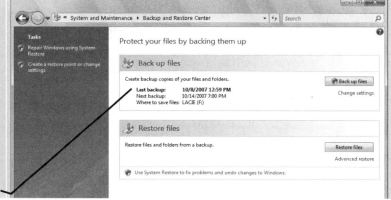

If you have *Windows Vista Ultimate*, you see this window with extra features for creating and restoring a *Complete PC Backup*:

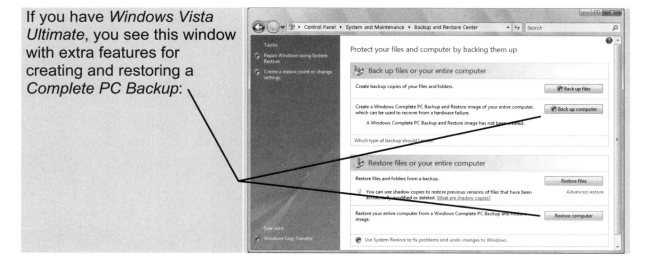

7.2 Windows Complete PC Backup

Windows Vista Ultimate contains the program *Windows Complete PC Backup*. You can use this program to create a complete backup of your computer. Do you have *Vista Home Basic* or *Home Premium*? Then you can just read through this section.

Windows Complete PC Backup creates a backup image, which contains copies of your programs, system settings, and files. You can use this backup image to restore the contents of your computer if your hard disk crashes or your computer suddenly stops working. A complete backup is also known as a *recovery CD.*

To be able to create a *Windows Complete PC Backup* image, your hard disk must be formatted to use the NTFS File System. In *Windows Help and Support* you can find more information on this subject.

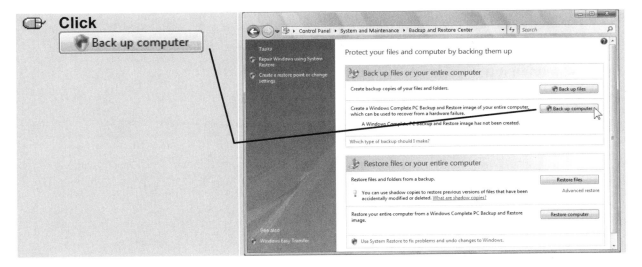

Your screen goes dark. You see the window *User Account Control* where you need to give your permission to continue.

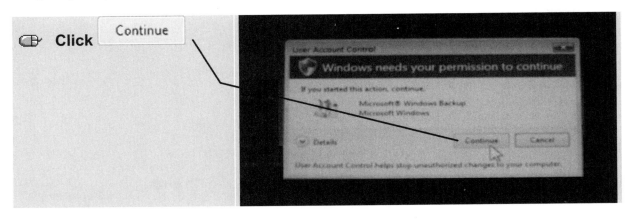

Then you see the next window:

In this window you can choose where you want to save the backup: on a (external) hard disk or DVD.

Please note: if you save the backup to an external hard disk, that disk must also be formatted to use the NTFS file system. If that is not the case, you will see a warning that the disk is not a valid location for a backup.

In this example the backup is saved to DVD:

When you have made your choice:

⮞ **Click** Next

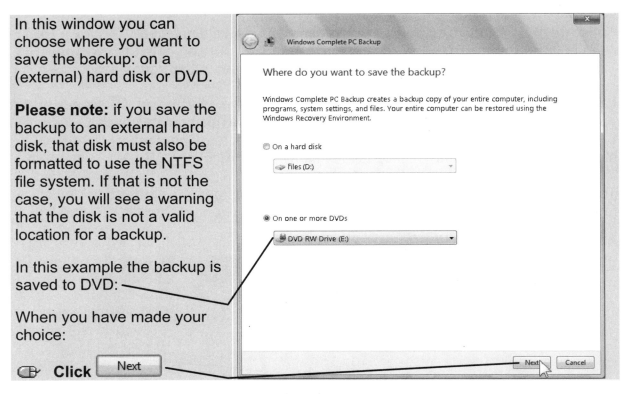

You see the disks in your computer that can be included in the backup. In this example there are two. You may see a different list on your PC.

⮞ **Click the disk(s) you want to include in the backup**

⮞ **Click** Next

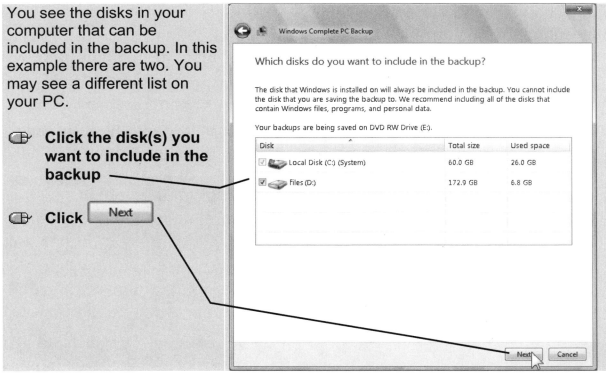

In the next window you see how many DVDs you need for the complete backup. In the example the backup will take five to nine DVDs:

If you want to start creating the backup, click Start backup.

If you want to cancel the backup, click Cancel:

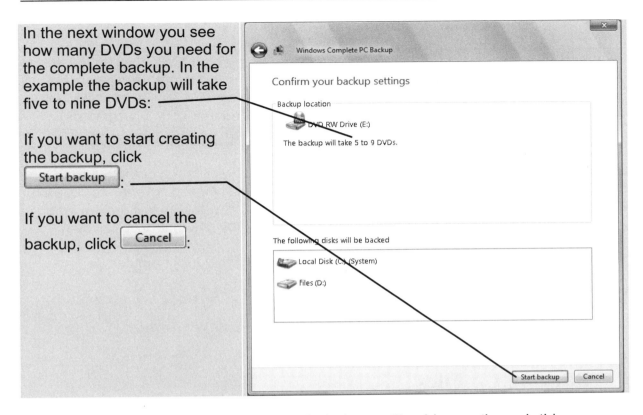

When you start the backup, a number of windows will guide you through this procedure. Follow the instructions in each window. At the end of the procedure you will have a number of DVDs or an external hard disk with a complete backup of your current system. Store this backup in a secure place.

If you ever need to restore the backup you can start the procedure from the *Backup and Restore Center*.

You can use the button Restore computer:

You will be guided through the procedure by a number of windows. Follow the instructions in each window.

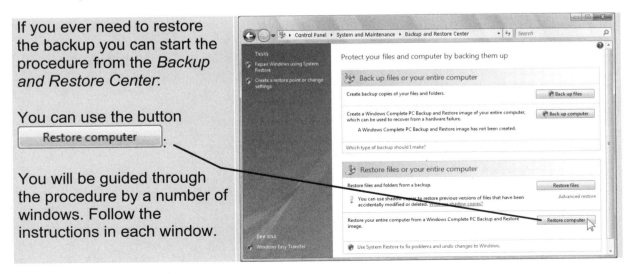

Please note:

When you restore your computer from a *Windows Complete PC Backup* image, it is a complete restoration. You can not select individual items to restore, and all of your current programs, system settings, and files will be replaced.
It is important to make regular backups to secure your recent work, your photos etcetera. In the next sections you can read how to do that.

Windows Vista Home Basic and *Home Premium* do not facilitate a complete PC backup. However in some cases this is done automatically using a separate program that has been added by the computer manufacturer. This program will appear when you start the computer for the first time. In that case follow the instructions in each window and store the backup in a secure place.
If necessary, refer to the documentation you received with your computer.

☞   **Close all windows until you see the *Backup and Restore Center* window again** 🦶¹

7.3 Backing Up Files

In the *Backup and Restore Center* of *Vista* you can create a backup of your own files. Backing up the files that are important for you helps to protect them from being permanently lost or changed in the event of accidental deletion, a short circuit, fire, theft, or a software or hardware failure. If any of those things occur and your files are backed up, you can easily restore those files.
You see the window *Backup and Restore Center*.

You are going to create a file backup:

🖰   **Click** Back up files

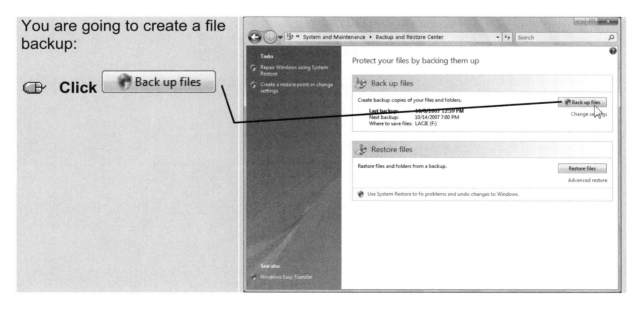

HELP! I see an error message.

Do you have a laptop or notebook and you see this window?

It is not possible to create a backup when your laptop is running on battery power. This is to prevent problems and unreliable backups when the battery runs out during the backup process.

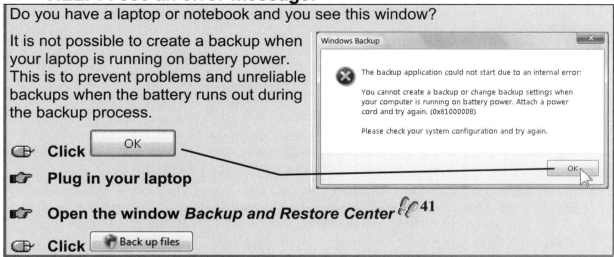

☞ **Click** `OK`

☞ **Plug in your laptop**

☞ **Open the window** *Backup and Restore Center* 🦶 **41**

☞ **Click** `Back up files`

Your screen goes dark. You see the window *User Account Control* where you need to give your permission to continue.

☞ **Click** `Continue`

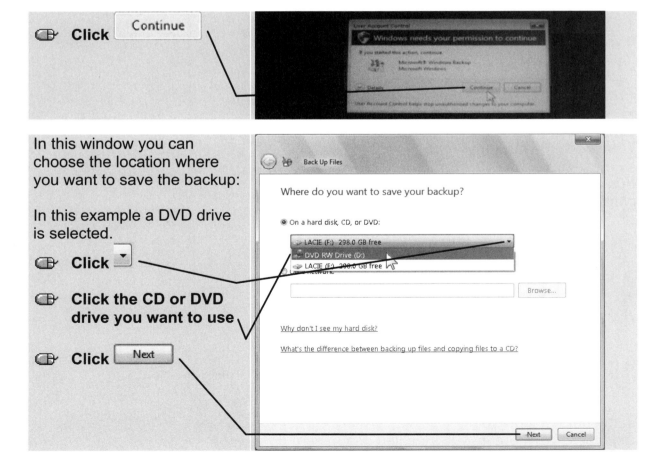

In this window you can choose the location where you want to save the backup:

In this example a DVD drive is selected.

☞ **Click** `▾`

☞ **Click the CD or DVD drive you want to use**

☞ **Click** `Next`

Which location?
The available locations to save a backup to depend on the setup of your computer. Take the following into account:

- It is not possible to save the backup to the same hard disk you are trying to back up. It is also not possible to save the backup to the hard disk *Windows Vista* is installed on. That makes sense, because in case of computer problems you will not be able to use both your original files and your backup.
- You can save a backup to another hard disk in your computer.
- If the hard disk has been divided in several partitions, it is possible to back up to another partition. It is not advisable to use this as your only backup, because it is still the same hard disk. In case of problems you will be unable to use this disk. Combine this method with regular backups on another location.
- You can not back up files to a USB stick. USB sticks are meant for temporary storage and are not suitable for backups.
- Backing up files to diskettes or tape drives is also not possible.

The most suitable storage media for backups are external hard disks, CDs or DVDs.

If you have multiple hard disks in your computer, you see this window:

Here you see the disks in the computer that can be included in the backup. In this example there are two. You may see a different list on your computer.

☞ **Click the disk(s) you want to include in the backup** ⎯⎯

☞ **Click** [Next]

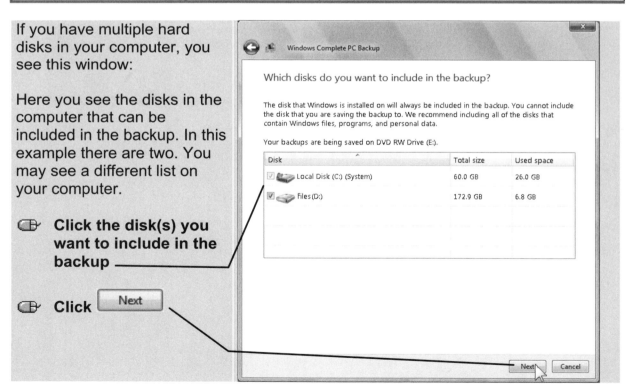

In the next window you can select which types of files to be included in the backup, regardless of where they are located on the hard disk.

To get more information about a file type that can be included in the backup, you point at the file type:

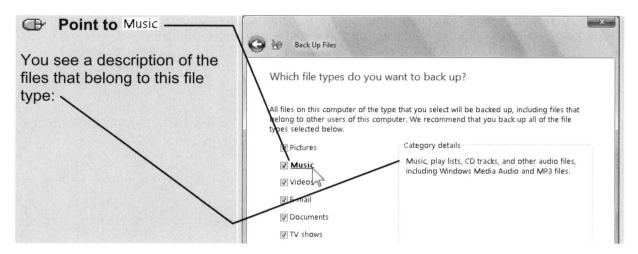

You may also decide not to back up certain categories. Perhaps you are already using another method to back up certain types of files, or maybe the files are no longer important to you.

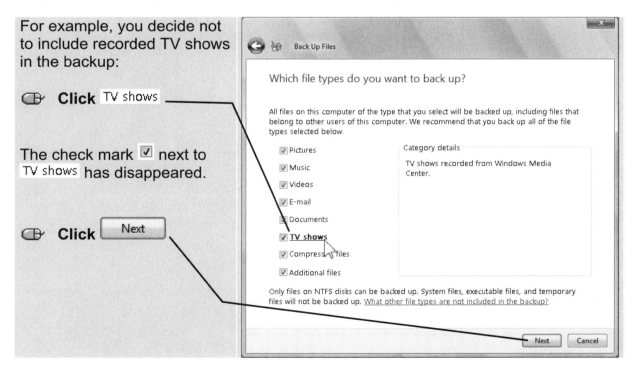

Backups should be created on a regular basis. In the next window you can select how often you want to create a backup. How often you should back up your files depends on how important they are and how often they change.

Please note:

Automatic backups are not available in *Windows Vista Home Basic*. The next window will not be shown in this edition. You will have to make the backup yourself using the *Backup and Restore Center*. *Windows Vista* will frequently remind you to create a backup.

You see the current settings:

Click
Sunday

Click Monday

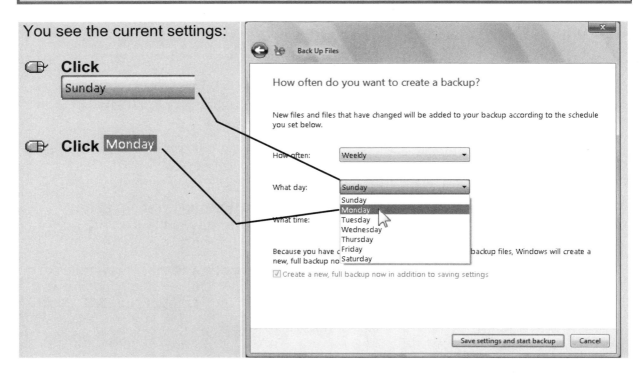

The backup will be created weekly on Mondays, at the time you specify. If the computer is not turned on at that time, the backup procedure will continue as soon as you turn on your computer.

A window will appear where you are asked to insert the CD or DVD that is to be used for the backup. If you have decided to use an external hard disk, the backup will be created automatically when the disk is connected to the computer.

☞ **Choose the desired settings**

If you want to create a backup of your files now:

👉 **Click**
Save settings and start backup

If you want to stop the backup process:

👉 **Click** Cancel

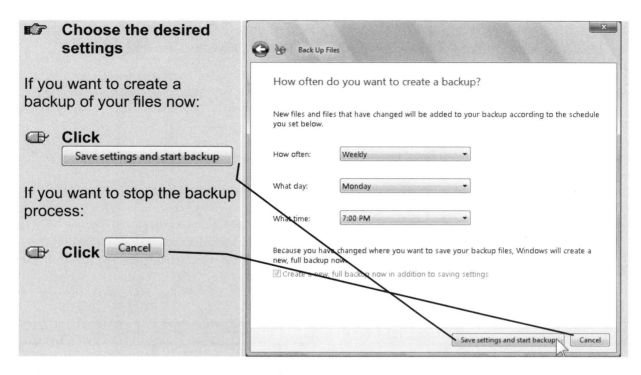

While the back up is in progress you can continue to work on the computer. Do not turn off the computer during the backup procedure.

If it is necessary to interrupt the backup process, click Stop backup . When you open the *Backup and Restore Center* again, you can continue the process at the point where it was interrupted the last time. This will also happen when you have to interrupt the backup process because you have run out of the amount of CDs or DVDs necessary to save the files.

When you start the backup, you will be guided through the procedure by a number of windows. Follow the instructions in each window.

You see that the backup is being prepared:

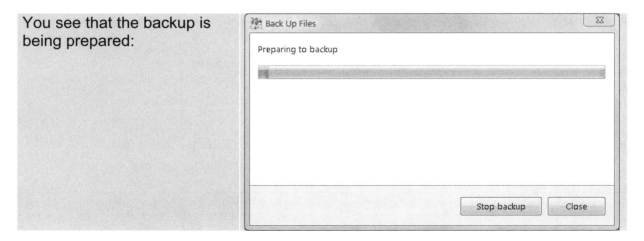

After a short while you are asked to insert a disc in your CD or DVD writer. In this window you see the label you should write on the disc. Always use a special CD marker to avoid damaging the disc.

☞ **Write the label on the CD or DVD**

☞ **Insert the CD or DVD in the writer**

👆 **Click**  OK

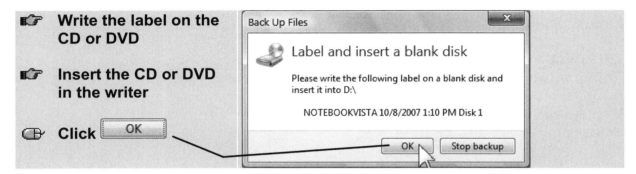

If necessary the disc is formatted first.

⇨ **Please note:**

When the disc is formatted, all data on the disc is erased.

👆 **Click** Format

During the formatting process you see this window:

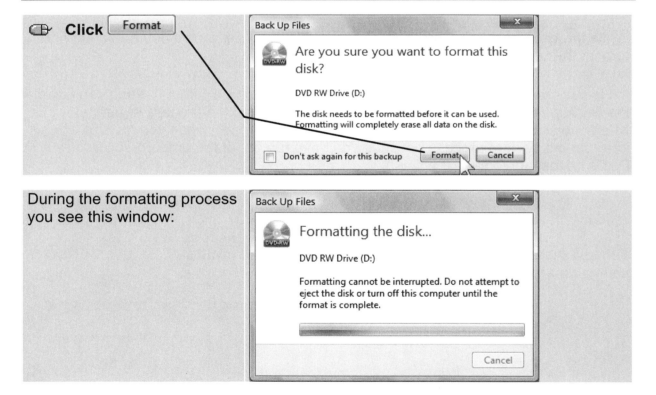

 Please note:

As you can read in the previous window, you can not interrupt the formatting process.

When the disc is formatted, the backup starts automatically. You can follow the progress in this window:

 Please note:

If you need more discs for your backup, the backup program will ask you to insert the next disc. Follow the instructions in the window and write the correct label on each disc. This way you will be able to restore the backup in the right order later.

When the backup is finished, you see the status window:

You see when the last backup was made and (possibly) when the next one will be made: ——

<img> **Click** ⬜×

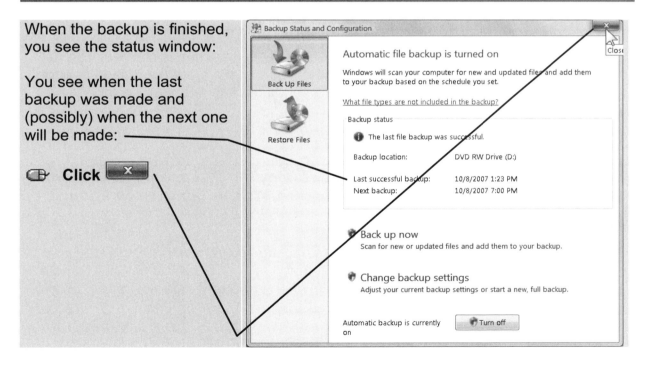

You see the *Backup and Restore Center* again:

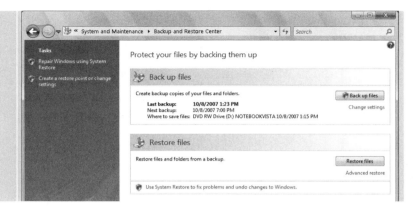

 Tip

If you want to change the backup schedule or the settings for file types to include in the backup, click Change settings in this window.

7.4 Incremental Backup

The first time you start the backup procedure a new, full backup is created. The next time you can choose to limit the backup to the files that have been modified or added since the last backup. This is called an incremental backup and saves a lot of time and disk space.

 Please note:

A full backup is **not** the same as the *Windows Complete PC Backup* that was described in the previous section. In a full backup, *Windows* and all programs and settings are not backed up.

After the first full backup, the *Windows Vista* backup program will only create incremental (additional) backups of the data that has changed. You can also create an incremental backup yourself, for example when important data has changed on your computer.

The settings for file types that are included in the backup can remain unchanged. You do the following:

 If necessary, open the *Backup and Restore Center* $\ell\ell$ 41

⬚ **Click** `Back up files`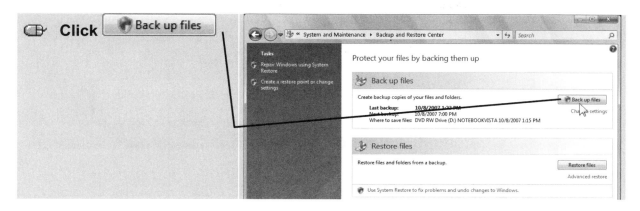

The screen goes dark. You see the window *User Account Control* where you need to give your permission to continue.

⬚ **Click** `Continue`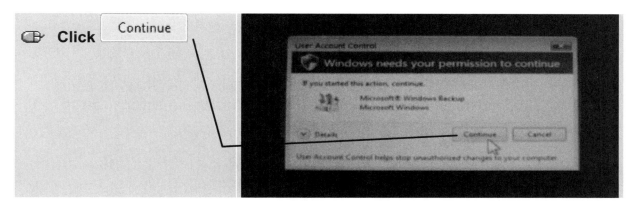

If you have not yet inserted a disc for your backup in the writer, *Windows Vista* will ask you to do that now.

During the backup process you see a small window just above the notification area on the right side of the taskbar:

 HELP! I do not have enough discs.

If you do not have enough discs to complete the backup, you can interrupt the backup process and continue later.

During this backup you can also continue working. Because this is not a full backup, it can be done very quickly.

When the backup has completed, you see this message in the notification area:

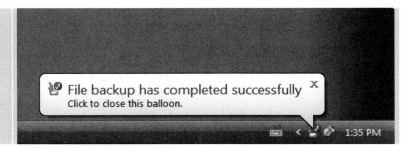

 Please note:

When you use incremental backups, you also need to keep the discs with the previous backups. Together these discs are a full backup. Do not throw away or overwrite these discs, otherwise you will no longer have a complete backup.

7.5 Restoring a Backup

Whenever you need to restore a backup you use the *Backup and Restore Center*. It is best to just read through this paragraph. Do not follow these actions unless you really want to restore a backup, for example after data loss.

☞ **If necessary, open the *Backup and Restore Center*** 🐾41

🖱️ **Click** `Restore files`

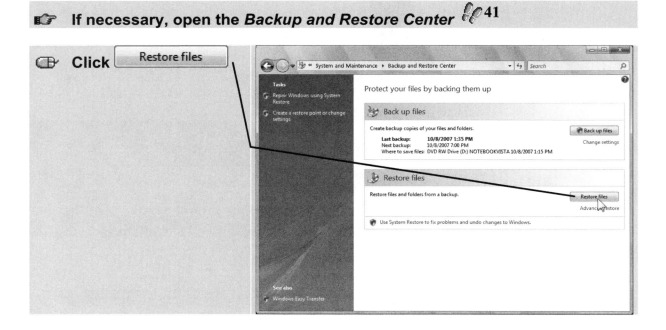

Usually you want to restore the most recent backup. If you want to solve a problem that was present for a longer period, it may be necessary to restore an older backup. This means you will lose the changes that you have made after that backup was made.

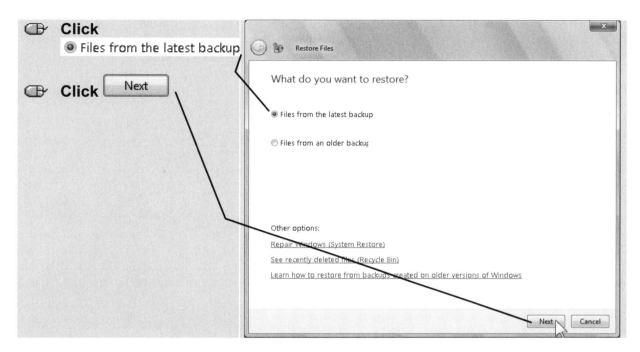

Now you can choose which files or folders you want to restore. To restore your music files, you do the following:

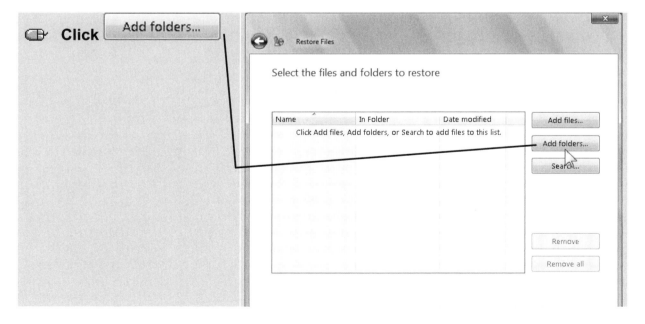

☞ **Click** Music

☞ **Click** Add

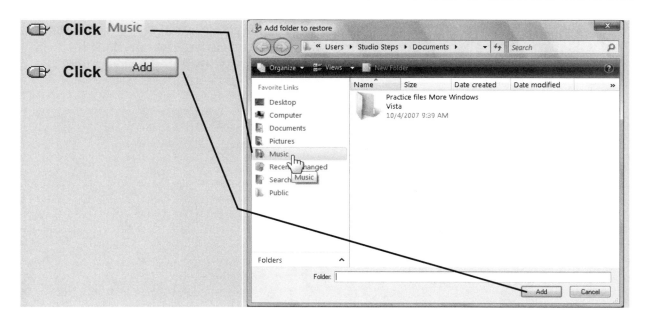

💡 **Tip**

If you want to restore all the files on a disk, click Computer and then click the disk you want to restore, for example C: .
Repeat these actions if you want to restore more disks. Keep in mind that only data files are restored, not program files or parts of *Windows Vista*.

The folder Music has been added and will be restored:

☞ **Repeat these steps for each folder you want to restore**

☞ **Click** Next

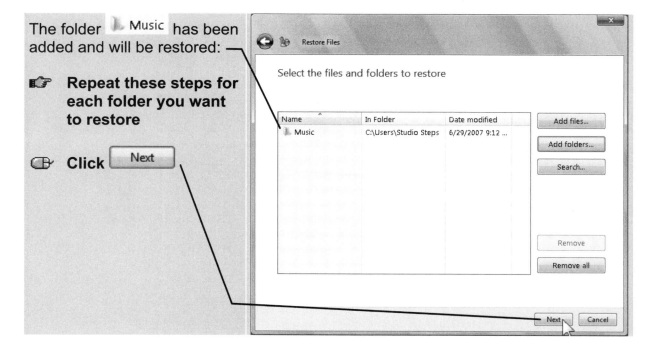

In most cases, the files you restore have to replace the original files on the disk. However, it is possible to restore the files to another location, for example when the original hard disk is damaged.

In this example the files are restored to the original location:

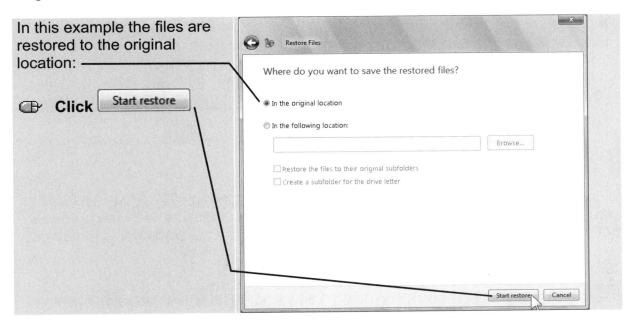

Click Start restore

⇨ **Please note:**

If your backup consists of more than one disc, you will be prompted to insert the other discs during the procedure. Make sure to insert the correct disc. You will see the label of the necessary disc in the window.

When the restore process has completed, you see this window:

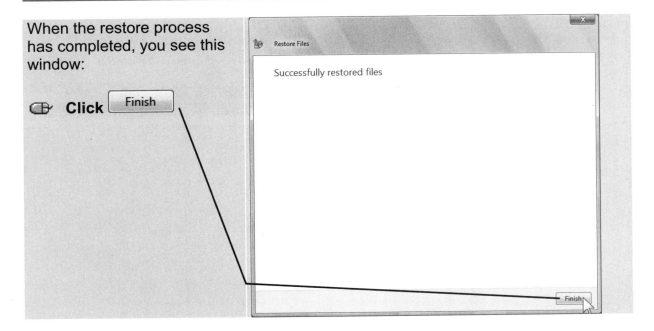

Click Finish

Now you see the *Backup and Restore Center* again.

 HELP! Restoring the files went very quickly.

The length of the restoration process depends on the amount of data. If it went very quickly, it does not mean that nothing happened. There were probably very few music files that had to be restored.
You will see that the restoration process takes longer next time, for example when you restore photo or video files.

7.6 Automatic File Backup

When you have set an automatic file backup for a specific time, *Windows Vista* will create the backup automatically if the computer is on at that time. If the computer is not on at that time, the backup will be created as soon as the computer is turned on.

 Please note:

Just read through this section, so you will know what to do when the automatic file backup starts.

As soon as *Windows Vista* wants to create an automatic file backup, you are notified in the lower right corner of your desktop:

If you want to create the backup:

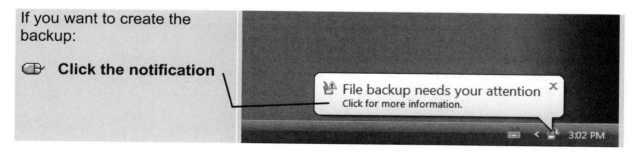

☞ **Click the notification**

You see this window:

Click Back up now

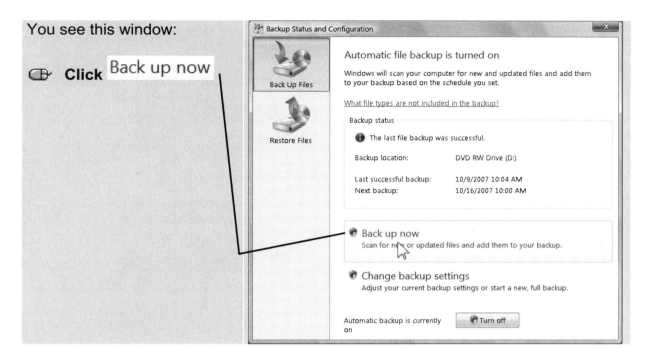

Tip

You can still change the settings for your backup, for example the file types to include in the backup. To do so, click Change backup settings.

The screen goes dark and you need to give your permission to continue:

Click Continue

Because the necessary backup disc is probably not in the writer yet, you are asked to insert the (first) backup disc:

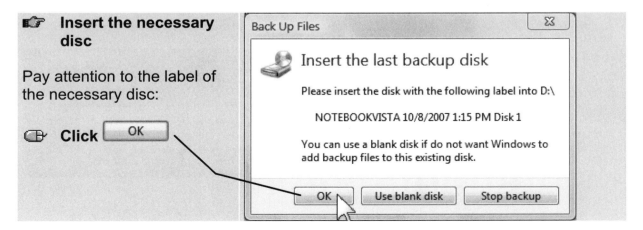

Insert the necessary disc

Pay attention to the label of the necessary disc:

Click OK

HELP! I can not find the necessary disc.

If you do not have the necessary disc right now, you can also use a blank disc.

Then:

 Click Use blank disk

If necessary, the disc will be formatted.

HELP! I have lost a disc.

If you have lost one or more backup discs, the backup is no longer usable. In that case you will need to create a new full backup.

Now the additions and changes are written to the disc.

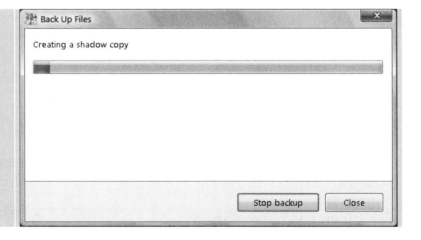

When the process has finished, you see this message in the lower right corner of your desktop:

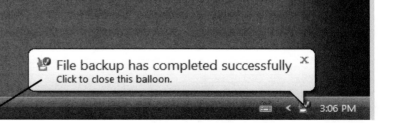

Click the notification

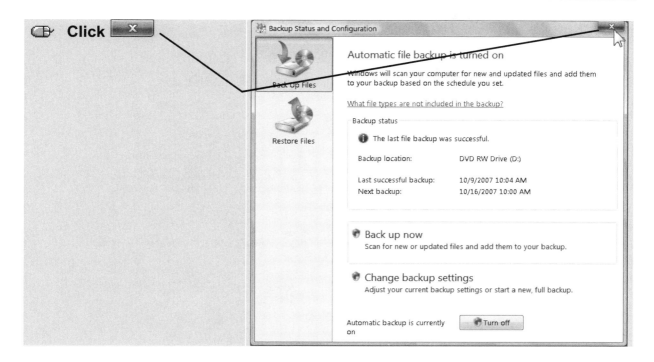

7.7 New Full Backup

To avoid having to store a lot of backup discs (the full backup and the incremental backups) it is advisable to create a full backup on a regular basis. For example monthly. When you create a new, full backup you have a new, more recent version.

⇨ **Please note:**

Do not use your old backup discs yet, use other discs to create the new full backup instead. If something goes wrong when the new backup is made, you may need your previous backup. Do not reuse your old discs until the new backup is completed successfully.

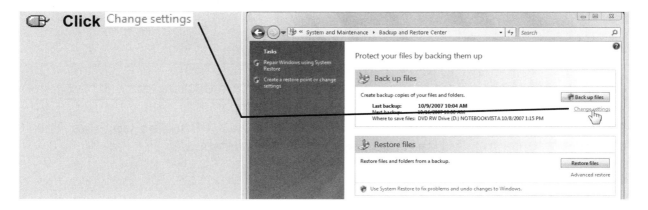

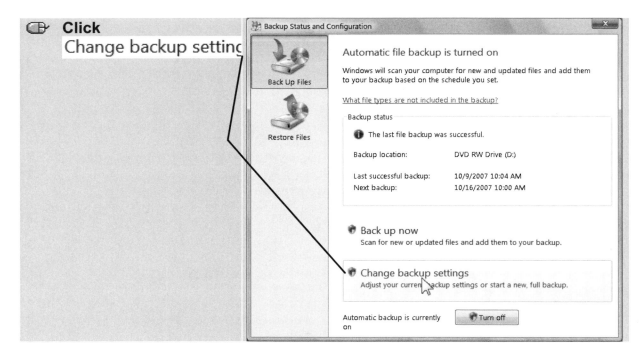

Click Change backup settings

Your screen goes dark and you need to give your permission to continue:

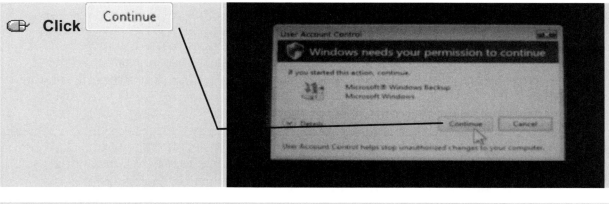

Click Continue

 Close the window *Backup Status and Configuration* 1

💡 **Tip**

If you do not want to create automatic full backups anymore, click 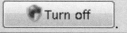.

This starts the wizard you were introduced to in **section 7.3 Backing Up Files**. The settings you enter in this wizard replace your previous settings.

7.8 System Restore

Backing up your files helps to protect them from being lost or changed in the event of computer problems or accidental deletion. Sometimes, the installation of a program or a driver can cause an unexpected change to your computer or cause *Windows* to behave unpredictably. In that case your files are still intact, but *Windows* is not reliable anymore.

Restoring a backup of your files does not solve that problem. Restoring a complete PC backup or recovery CD will make your computer work properly again, but you will lose all of your personal files and any programs that were recently installed.

System Restore creates automatic restore points to help you restore your computer's system files to an earlier point in time. These restore points contain information about registry settings and other system information that *Windows* uses. When *Windows Vista* no longer works properly, you can try restoring your computer's system to an earlier date when everything did work correctly. Usually this solves the problems.

7.9 Creating Restore Points

Windows Vista creates automatic restore points every day and also at important moments, for example, when you install new programs or devices. At crucial moments you can also create restore points manually if necessary.

In the top left corner of the window:

Click Create a restore point or change settings

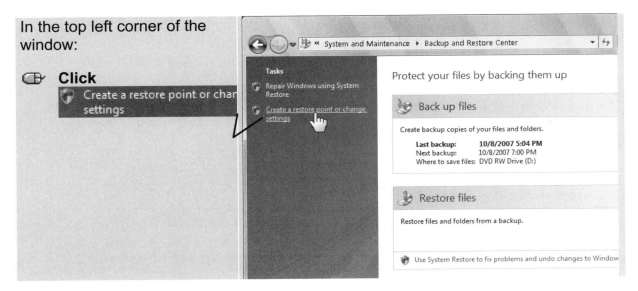

Your screen goes dark. You see the window *User Account Control* where you need to give your permission to continue.

Click Continue

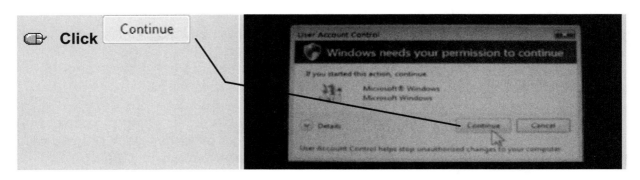

You see when the last restore point was created:

Click
Local Disk (C:) (System)

Usually this is the disk where *Vista* is installed.

Click Create...

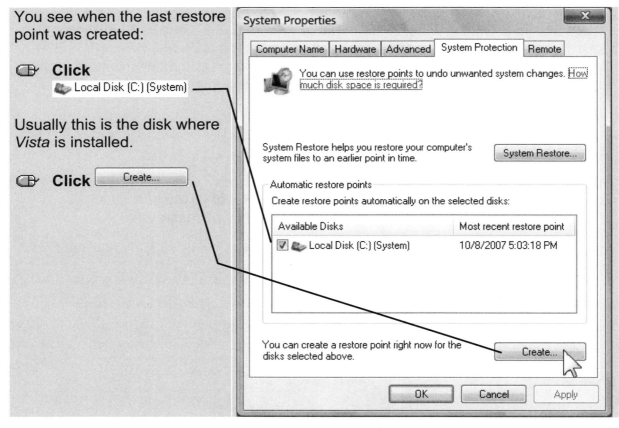

Type a name for the restore point

Click Create

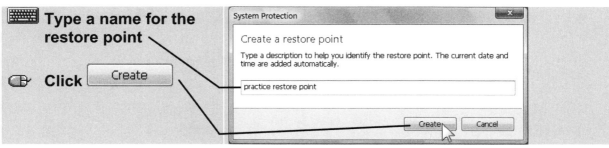

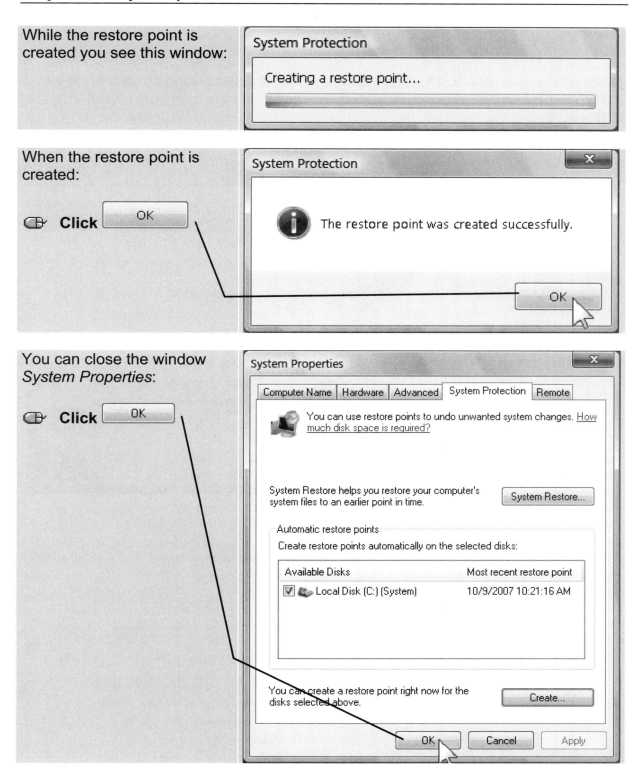

While the restore point is created you see this window:

When the restore point is created:

⏴ **Click** [OK]

You can close the window *System Properties*:

⏴ **Click** [OK]

You see the window *Backup and Restore Center* again.

7.10 Restoring Restore Points

In the *Backup and Restore Center* you can repair *Windows* using *System Restore*.

 **Please note:**

When you use *System Restore* your computer will be restarted:

☞ **Close all programs and save your work before you start *System Restore*.**

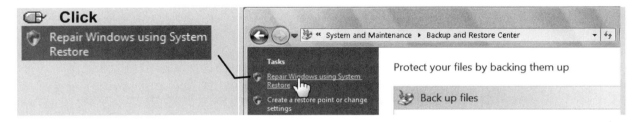

Your screen goes dark. You see the window *User Account Control* where you need to give your permission to continue.

After a few moments the *Wizard System Restore* starts:

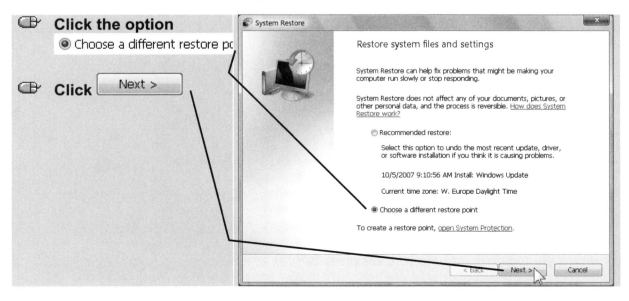

Click the restore point you want to use ──

Click **Next >**

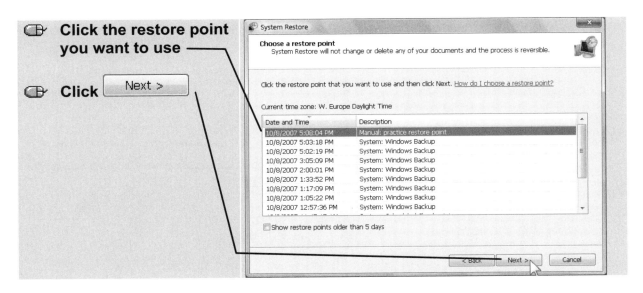

⇨ Please note:

By default, only the restore points created in the last five days are displayed. If your problem started before that, for example since you installed a new printer a week ago, click ☐ Show restore points older than 5 days to see the older restore points as well.

If you have several hard disks in your computer, you can select the disks you want to restore in the next window. You always have to restore the disk that contains *Windows Vista* . In most cases that will be the (C:) disk. Restoring any other disk is optional.

In this example there is only one hard disk. You are taken to the window where you can confirm your restore point.

Click **Finish**

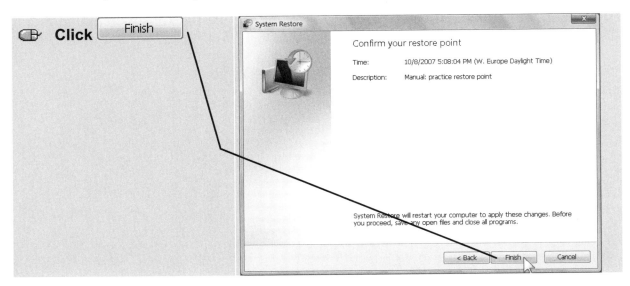

System Restore prompts you for a confirmation:

Click Yes

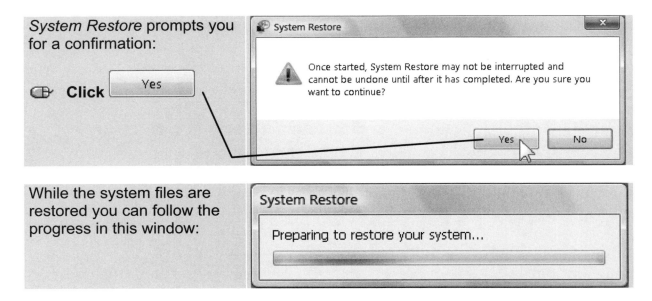

While the system files are restored you can follow the progress in this window:

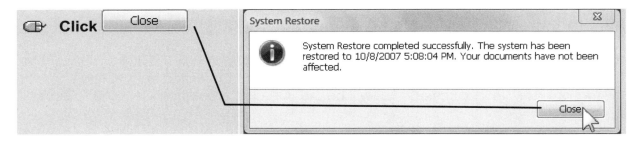

When *System Restore* has completed, *Windows Vista* is shut down and restarted. When you see the desktop again, you see this message:

Click Close

In most cases *Windows* will now function normally again.

In this chapter you have learned how to create and restore backups of your important files. You have also practiced *System Restore*.

In the following exercises you repeat a few of the tasks you have practiced in this chapter.

7.11 Exercises

Have you forgotten how to do something? Use the number beside the footsteps to look it up in *Appendix B How Do I Do That Again?*

Exercise: Adjusting Backup Settings

In this exercise you change the day the automatic backup is made. You can not do this exercise if you use *Windows Vista Basic*.

✓ Open the *Backup and Restore Center*. 𝓁𝓁 **41**

✓ Click `Change settings`.

✓ Click Change backup settings.

✓ Click `Next >` until you see the window with the day and time of the automatic backup.

✓ Change the day the backup is made and save the change. 𝓁𝓁 **42**

✓ Close the windows *Backup Status and Configuration* and *Backup and Restore Center*. 𝓁𝓁 **1**

Exercise: Creating System Restore Points

In this exercise you create a system restore point yourself.

✓ Open the *Backup and Restore Center*. 𝓁𝓁 **41**

✓ Create a system restore point for the (C:) disk. 𝓁𝓁 **43**

✓ Close the *Backup and Restore Center*. 𝓁𝓁 **1**

7.12 Background Information

Glossary	
Backup	A backup is a copy of files, programs and/or settings. Preferably, a backup is stored in a separate location from the original. You can have multiple backups of a file if you want to keep track of changes.
Complete PC Backup	Backup image, which contains copies of your programs, system settings, and files. The backup image is stored in a separate location from the original programs, settings, and files. You can use this backup image to restore the contents of your computer if your hard disk or entire computer ever stops working. *Windows Complete PC Backup* is not included in *Windows Vista Home Basic* and *Windows Vista Home Premium*.
Full backup	Backup of user files, like documents, images, music etcetera. Programs and *Windows Vista* files are not copied when a full backup is created.
Incremental backup	Additional backup that only stores files that were added or changed since the last full or incremental backup.
NTFS	A file system used by a computer to organize files on the hard disk. If you install a new hard disk, it must be partitioned and formatted using a file system before you can store files or data on this disk. In *Windows Vista* you can choose between the file systems NTFS and FAT32.
Partition	Part of a computer hard disk that functions like a separate disk. Separate, formatted partitions share your computer's memory and storage space. Partitions allow you to install and use more than one operating system on the computer.

- Continue reading on the next page -

Restore Point	A representation of a stored state of your computer's system files. Restore points are created by *System Restore* at specific intervals and when *System Restore* detects the beginning of a change to your computer. Also, you can create a restore point manually at any time.
System Restore	*System Restore* helps you to restore your computer's system files to an earlier point in time using a *restore point*. It is a way to undo system changes to your computer without affecting your personal files, such as e-mail, documents, or photos.
Wizard	Program that guides you through a procedure in a sequence of windows. In each window you get instructions on what to do next.

Source: Windows Help and Support

Grandfather - father - son backups

Even if you create backups on a regular basis things can go wrong. You can end up being unable to use your original data as well as your backup. For example when a malfunction occurs during the backup process. Or when you infect the backup with a virus that has not yet been discovered on your computer. Then both your original files as well as the backup will be infected.

To warrant the reliability of your backups, you can save different generations of backups on rewritable discs. This is done as follows:

- You start by making a full backup you call the *grandfather*.
- Some time later, for example a week or a month, you create another full backup on a new set of discs you call the *father*. You also keep the *grandfather*.
- The next time you create a new full backup you call the *son*. You also keep the *grandfather* and *father*.
- Then the next time you create a full backup on the *grandfather* discs, then on the *father* discs and finally on the *son* discs.

When something goes wrong during the backup process, or the backup contains an error or a virus, you can always go back two generations. This increases the chance of having a reliable backup. Do not make the interval between the generations too short, for example use intervals of a week or a month. In between these full backups you create the regular incremental backups.

Store your backups in a safe place
You can also lose your data as a result of fire or theft. Always keep one set of backup discs outside your own home when you keep important data on your computer. And make sure to renew that backup regularly as well.

Creating a backup or copying files yourself
You can secure your data by creating backups or by copying files to another disc yourself. What is best in your situation depends on the type of data and the things you want to do with the data:

- If you want to create a safety copy of (all) your data that you can restore to your computer if necessary, it is best to create a backup. A backup file is always compressed and takes up less space.

- If you want to copy data so you can use it on another computer, it is best to copy it to a separate CD or DVD. A backup CD or DVD is not always readable on another computer, especially when that computer works with another version of *Windows*.

- If you want to put a couple of files or folders on a disc, for example to be able to show your holiday photos at work, you need to collect these files yourself and copy them to a CD or DVD.

- It is best to copy data you want to keep for a longer time, like wedding pictures, your bookkeeping or important documents, to a separate CD or DVD. That way these files are easily accessible on any computer you might want to use.

To summarize: backups are made for security reasons. If you want to use the files for activities other than restoring your computer (share, show etcetera) it is better to write a separate CD or DVD.

You can find more information about copying files to CDs and DVDs in **chapter 8 Writing Files to CD or DVD**.

Backups, recovery CD of restore points?

Creating backups and creating recovery points are both methods to make sure you can keep working after something has gone wrong. In some cases you need the backup, in other cases you use *System Restore* or your recovery CD.

In the next summary you can read which one to use in different situations:

- In case you have lost (or are unable to use) part of your personal files (documents, photos, music, etcetera), you can restore these files using your (full or incremental) backup. During the restore process you can choose which files you want to restore.

- When a program does not work properly or no longer works properly, you have to reinstall the program from the original discs or download it again from the Internet. This is also a reason not to sell or give a program you bought to another person. It is best to remove the program completely using the *Control Panel* before you reinstall it.

- If your computer functions, but you get error messages from *Windows Vista*, then you can use *System Restore* to try to restore your system to a point in time when *Windows Vista* still worked properly. Usually, this will be right before the moment you installed a new program or device, or before a *Windows Vista* update. Also read the next tip about going back to the *Last Known Good Configuration*.

- If your computer does not function at all, or shows very serious problems, you can restore your complete PC backup (recovery CD or image). If you do this, you will lose all your files and data and also the programs you installed. Then you need the original program discs to reinstall the programs and the full backup to restore your personal files. Very often you will need additional CDs with drivers or other programs to be able to install the devices you use with your computer, like a printer or a modem.

Make sure to keep your recovery CD, backups and original program discs in a safe place, allowing you to find them easily in case of problems.

7.13 Tips

 Tip

Last Known Good Configuration
This is a *Windows Vista* startup option that uses the most recent system settings that worked correctly. Every time you turn your computer off and *Windows Vista* shuts down successfully, important system settings are saved in the registry. You can use those settings to start your computer if a problem occurs. For example, if a new driver for your graphics card is causing problems, or an incorrect registry setting is preventing *Windows Vista* from starting correctly, you can restart your computer using *Last Known Good Configuration*.

Follow these steps:

☞ **Remove all diskettes, CDs and DVDs from the computer**

👆 **Click**

👆 **Click** [▶] **next to** **, and click** Restart **in the menu that appears**

Do one of the following:
1. If your computer has a single operating system installed, press the F8 key repeatedly as your computer restarts. You need to press F8 before the *Windows* logo appears. If the *Windows* logo appears, you will need to try again by waiting until the *Windows* logon prompt appears, and then shutting down and restarting your computer.
   In the *Advanced Boot Options* screen, use the arrow keys to highlight **Last Known Good Configuration**, and then press the Enter key.

2. If your computer has more than one operating system, use the arrow keys to highlight the operating system you want to start, and then press F8.
   In the *Advanced Boot Options* screen, use the arrow keys to highlight **Last Known Good Configuration**, and then press the Enter key

Windows Vista will then resume starting normally.

Last Known Good Configuration only affects system settings. It does not change your e-mail, photos, or other personal data on your computer. It will not help you recover a deleted file or a corrupted driver. To do that, you need to have previously backed up the data, or you need to reinstall the driver from the original source.

Source: Windows Help and Support

8. Writing Files to CD or DVD

Windows Vista includes simple software that allows you to burn (write data to) CDs and DVDs. You can choose between two file systems: *Live File System* and *Mastered.*

In this chapter you can read how to write files from your hard disk to CD or DVD. You will learn which file system is the most appropriate one for different needs.

You can use this feature to quickly make a safety copy of your important files, such as photo files or text files. You can use the CD or DVD to transfer files to another computer or share them with others.

If the hard disk of your computer is nearly full, you can gain extra space by copying larger files like music or video files to a CD or a DVD. You can then remove the original files from your hard disk and still be assured your files are safe and secure.

In this chapter you learn:

- which file systems are available for CDs and DVDs;
- how to create a *Live File System* disc;
- how to write data to a disc and erase it again;
- how to create a disc using the *Mastered* file system;
- how to add or remove files from a queue;
- how to change *AutoPlay* settings for CDs and DVDs.

⇨ **Please note:**

To be able to work through this chapter without any difficulty, it may **sometimes** be necessary to remove other disc writing software from your computer. Some programs automatically take over the write function from *Windows Vista.*

First try to work through this chapter. When the windows look very different from what you see in this chapter, then the *Windows Vista* write function has been disabled. Remove your other disc writing software only if you still have the original CD-ROM or DVD that contains this program. Then you can install the program later if you want to use the more advanced features of that program.

8.1 What Do You Need?

In *Windows Vista* you can write CDs as well as DVDs. Your computer needs a *writer* (also called *burner*) for that. New computers usually have a built-in disc writer. Most writers are capable of writing CDs as well as DVDs.

 Please note:

The process of transferring data to a CD or DVD disc is called *writing* a disc. Sometimes other terms are used to describe the same process: *burning* or *copying* data to a disc. The device you use for writing a disc is called a *writer* or *burner.*

 Please note:

Some computers both have a CD/DVD player as well as a writer. In that case make sure to insert the disc in the correct drive. Usually the writer is marked with the text *writer* or *RW* (Read/Write).

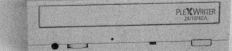

 HELP! Do I have a CD/DVD writer?

Are you unable to find the writer in the *Computer* window?

Do you see Cd-rom-station or DVD-station ? Then most likely your computer does not have a CD or DVD writer, but only a CD-ROM player or a CD/DVD-ROM player.

Sometimes these icons do represent a writer. Check the documentation you received with your computer to find out what type of CD or DVD drive you have. It is also possible that your writer was not installed correctly. Please refer to the user's guide that accompanied your CD/DVD writer to learn how to correctly install the writer.

You also need to have at least one **new writable CD or DVD** at hand. Choose a disc of the type **rewritable** so you can use it in all exercises. In the exercises in this chapter a DVD-Rewritable is used. You can save, erase and replace files on a rewritable disc. The sleeve of such a disc is marked CD-RW, DVD-RW or DVD+RW.

 Please note:

To be able to see the same windows as in this book, use a new and unused CD or DVD-Rewritable. When you use a disc that was used before, the windows you see may look different than in this book.

Tip

There are different types of writable CDs and DVDs. When you choose to save files to CD or DVD later on, you can choose a different type of CD or DVD than the rewritable disc used in this chapter. A summary of available types of CDs and DVDs can be found in the *Background Information* at the end of this chapter.

8.2 Choosing Between Two File Systems

Windows Vista allows you to write CDs as well as DVDs. Before you can do that, you need to format the rewritable disc you are going to use for the exercises. Formatting the disc prepares it for use with *Windows Vista.* You can choose between two file systems when you format the disc:

- *Mastered*
  The CD or DVD you write using this file system can also be read in computers with older versions of *Windows* (before *Windows XP*) and devices like CD and DVD players that are able to read digital music and video files. When you create a disc using this file system you need to write all files to the disc at once. If you already have experience with *Windows XP*: the *Mastered* file system works the same way as writing a disc in *Windows XP*.

- *Live File System*
  This file system is only compatible with *Windows Vista* and *Windows XP*. Writing files on CD or DVD is also called 'copying' in this system. You can keep adding files to a *Live File System* disc and deleting them again, just like you can on a USB stick or diskette.

By default *Windows Vista* selects the *Live File System*, but you will see that you can make your own choice when you format the disc.

It is necessary to format the disc first, even later on when you work with other types of discs such as recordable discs. Recordables can only be formatted once, but rewritables can be formatted over and over again.

 Tip

You can find an extensive comparison of the two file systems in the *Background Information* at the end of this chapter. There you will also find tips on the best choice of file system for a specific purpose.

8.3 Formatting a Disc

When you insert a new, unformatted writable CD or DVD in the writer, you will first need to format it.

☞ **Insert a new CD or DVD-Rewritable in your writer**

In this example a DVD-Rewritable is used.

You see this window:

☞ **Click**
Burn files to disc
using Windows

Note that the term *burn* is used instead of write.
A laser *burns* your data to disc which is why the terms burning or burn to disc are frequently used.

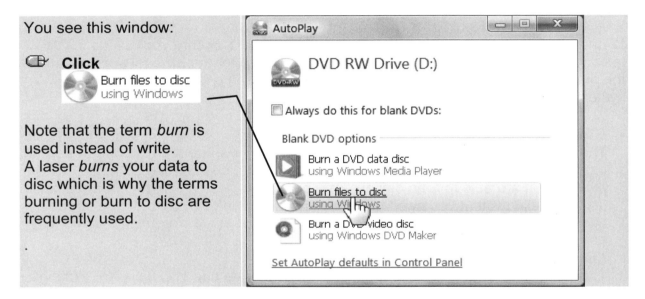

 HELP! I do not see this window.
Depending on the settings of your computer, the window may not appear. In that case, proceed as follows:

☞ **Click**

☞ **Click**
Computer

☞ **Double-click your writer**

Then you see the window that is shown next.

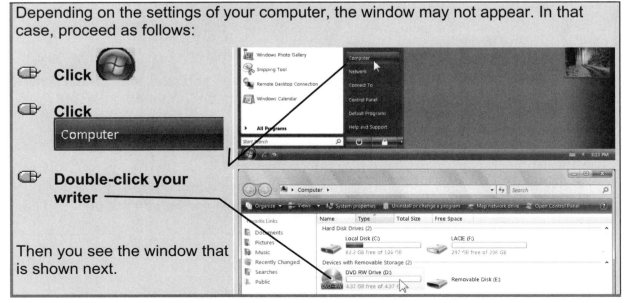

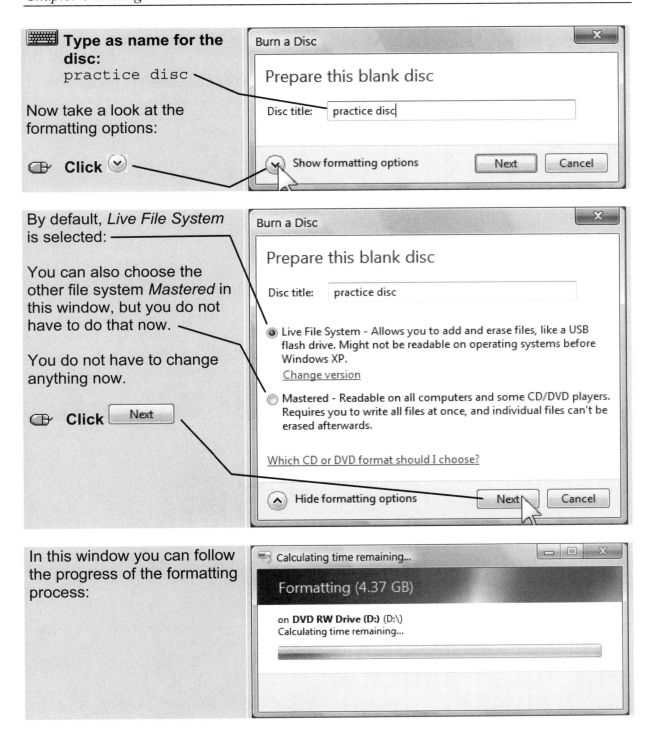

⌨ **Type as name for the disc:**
`practice disc`

Now take a look at the formatting options:

☞ **Click** ⌄

By default, *Live File System* is selected:

You can also choose the other file system *Mastered* in this window, but you do not have to do that now.

You do not have to change anything now.

☞ **Click** Next

In this window you can follow the progress of the formatting process:

As soon as this window disappears, the formatting is done.

8.4 Compiling a Data Disc

The *Folder window* is opened. Here you can select the files you want to copy to the formatted disc:

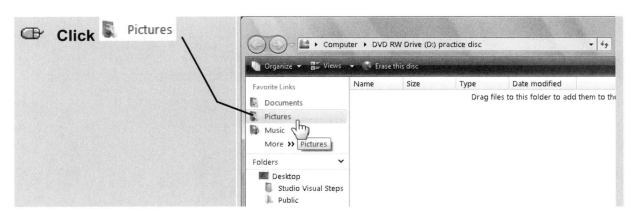

Click Pictures

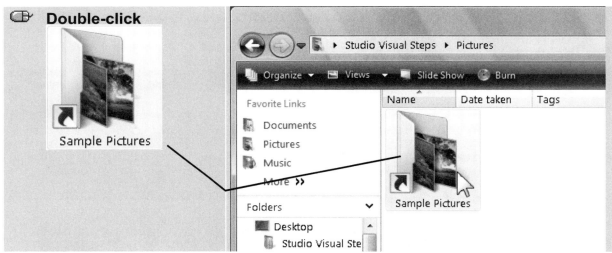

Double-click

Sample Pictures

➡️ **Please note:**

 This icon does not represent a folder containing images, it is a shortcut to the folder *Sample Pictures*. You can tell by the blue arrow 📷 on the folder. When you copy (write) this shortcut to the disc, the contents of the folder will not be copied.

You see the images in the folder *Sample Pictures*. Now you can select the files you want to copy to the disc:

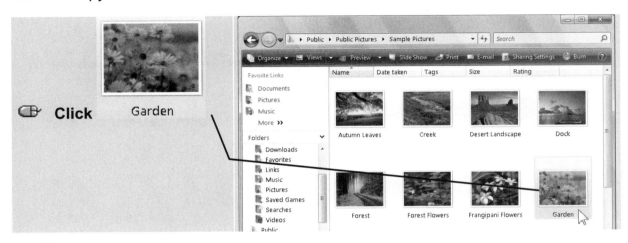

You can also select a consecutive group of files by holding the key down while you click:

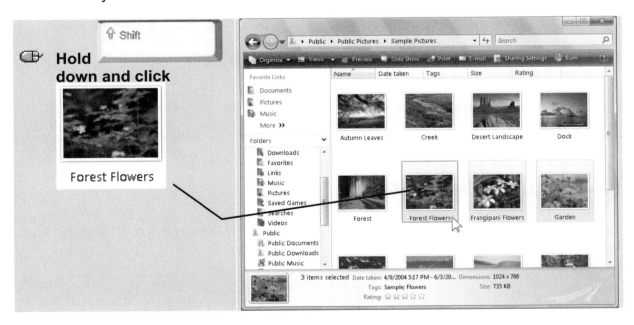

The images from *Garden* to *Forest Flowers* have now been selected.

In case you do not want to select all the images in between, you can select separate files using the Ctrl-key on your keyboard:

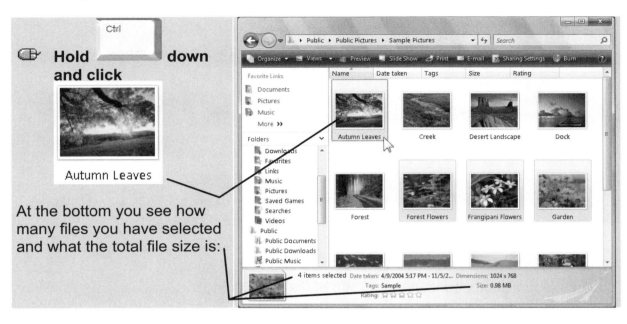

You have now selected the images from *Garden* to *Forest Flowers* and the image *Autumn Leaves*.

 Tip

If you activated the check box feature in the next chapter, you can also simply check mark the images you want to use instead.

8.5 Writing a Data Disc

Using the *Live File System* you write (burn) the selected files to the disc directly. The button you need to use is labeled *Burn*.

HELP! I do not see Burn.

Depending on the display settings of your computer it is possible that you do not see the button Burn when you have selected one or more files or folders. In that case you see the button » on the right side of the toolbar:

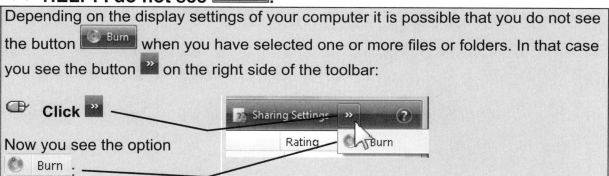

☞ **Click** »

Now you see the option

Burn :

The files are written to the disc immediately. You can write (copy) complete folders in this same manner. In that case you select folders instead of single files.

During the writing process you see this window:

Note that writing is called *copying* in this window:

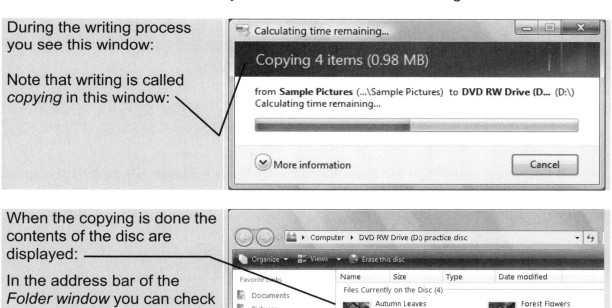

When the copying is done the contents of the disc are displayed:

In the address bar of the *Folder window* you can check the location of these contents:

▸ Computer ▸ DVD RW Drive (D:) p

8.6 Adding Files to a Live File System Disc

You can add more files to a *Live File System* disc later. You can do that like this:

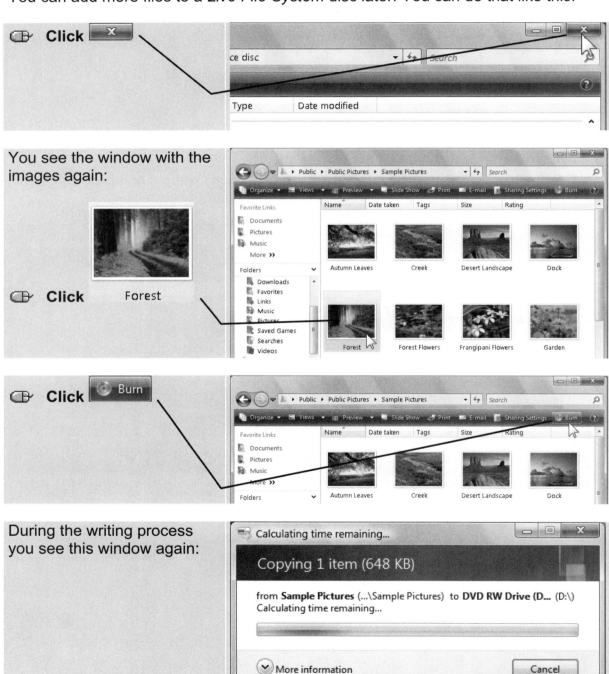

When the writing process has finished, you return to the window with the images. If you want to, you can write more files to the disc. That is not necessary now.

☞ Close the window 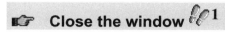¹

Close or finalize a CD or DVD

Before you can use a recordable disc formatted in the *Live File System* format in other computers and devices, you need to close the current disc session to prepare the disc for use. By default, *Windows* closes your disc automatically when it is ejected by pressing the eject button on the disc drive. Closing the disc can take a few minutes and requires 20 MB of disc space. After you close a disc session, you can still add additional files to the disc. But you must close each additional session to be able to use the disc on another computer.

Since closing a session takes up about 20 MB of disc space, it is recommended not to take the disc out of the drive after every file you write. It is better to write as many files as possible in one session. One session is defined as the period of time the disc is in the writer before taking the disc out.

In some programs you can **finalize** your disc instead of closing the current session. Usually this is necessary to have the disc function properly in that program. Once a disc is finalized, you can no longer add any additional files to it.

8.7 Deleting Data from a Live File System Disc

Files you have written to a *Live File System* disc can later be deleted from the disc. You can do that like this:

☞ Open the *Computer* window ⁱⁿᵍ¹⁹

Double-click your writer

DVD RW Drive (D:) Practic File

The writer may have a different drive letter on your computer.

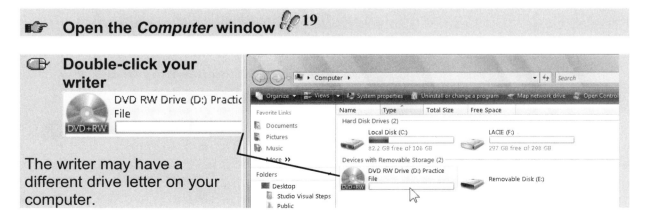

To be able to delete a file you have to select it first:

Click Garden JPG File 504 KB

Delete

Press

💡 **Tip**

Deleting more files

To delete more files at once, you can select the files using ⇧ Shift and Ctrl like you did in the previous section.

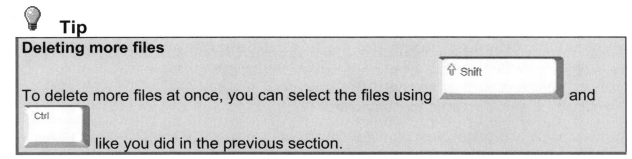

You must confirm that you want to permanently delete this file:

Click Yes

The file is being deleted:

The file has been deleted from the disc:

8.8 Erasing a Live File System Rewritable Disc

You can delete all files on a rewritable disc at once. Then you can reuse and format the disc again, and choose the other file system. To erase the rewritable disc, you do the following:

Click

➡ **Please note:**

Recordable discs can not be erased the same way. CD-Recordables (CD-R) and DVD-Recordables (DVD-R/DVD+R) can only be formatted once. When you insert one of those discs in the CD/DVD drive, you do not see the button on the toolbar.

Click Next

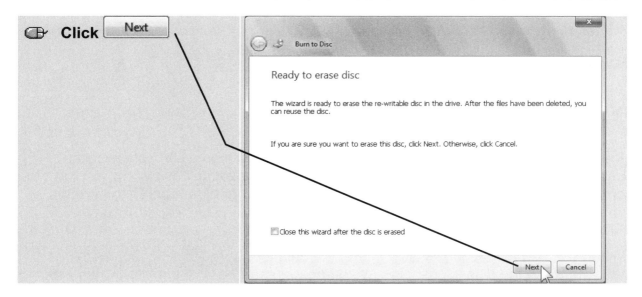

You see the progress of the erase process:

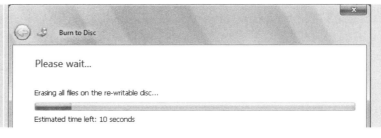

After some time you see the message that the erase was completed successfully:

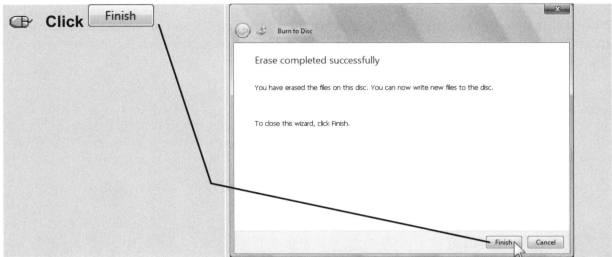

Click Finish

You see the desktop again.

When you erase a rewritable disc this way, it will be formatted again the next time you use it. Then you can choose the other file system if you want.
This is not possible with recordable discs. These discs can only be formatted and written to once and cannot be erased.

☞ **Remove the disc from the writer**

8.9 Mastered File System

If you want to use the CD or DVD in another device such as a DVD player, you usually need to use the *Mastered* file system. This is also the case when you want to create a disc that can be used in computers with other or older operating systems.

⇨ **Please note:**

When you use the *Mastered* file system, the data are stored in a temporary folder until you write the disc. Consequently you need extra free space on your hard disk when you use this file system, varying between 650 MB for a CD and 8.5 GB for a dual layer DVD.

☞ **Insert the rewritable disc you just erased in your writer**

Or - if you do not have it:

☞ **Insert a new blank recordable disc in your writer**

In this example the same DVD-Rewritable is used.

You see this window:

⊕ **Click**

Burn files to disc
using Windows

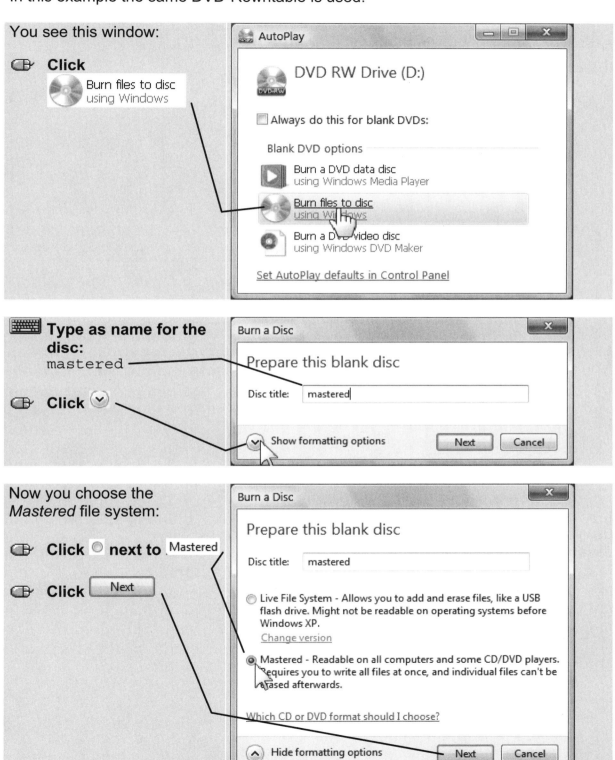

⌨ **Type as name for the disc:**
mastered

⊕ **Click** ⌄

Now you choose the *Mastered* file system:

⊕ **Click** ○ **next to** Mastered

⊕ **Click** [Next]

You see the contents of the disc right away:

There are no files on the disc yet:

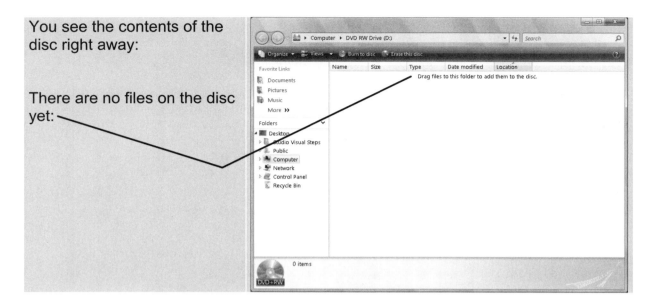

8.10 Adding Files to the Queue

In this file system the files are placed in a queue before they are written to the disc. You can add files to the queue like this:

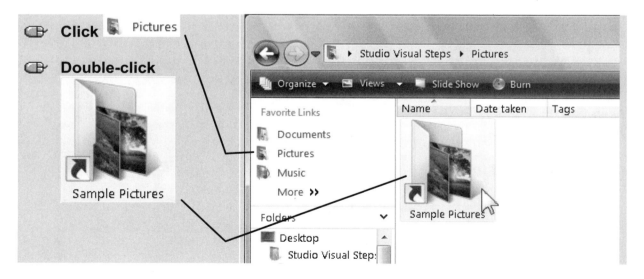

Now the files in between are also selected.

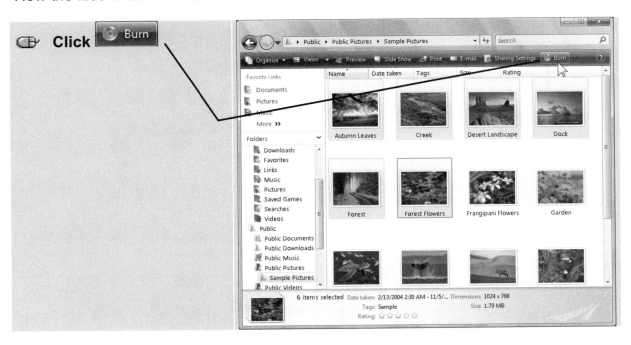

Using the *Mastered* file system the files are not written to the disc right away, they are placed in a queue first. The complete list of selected files has to be written to the disc at once.

The queue appears in a new window:

You also see the message that you have files waiting to be written to the disc: ⟶

Note that in this message the term *burned* is used instead of *copying*.

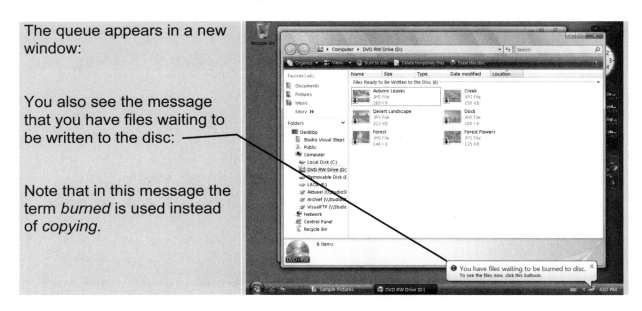

You can always add files to a queue. First you minimize the *queue* window:

🖱 **Click** ⬜

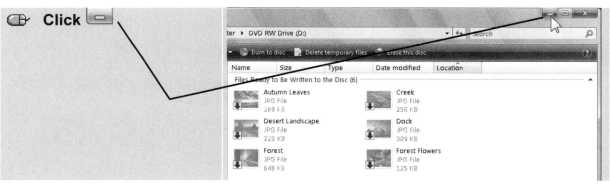

🖱 **Click**   Garden

🖱 **Click**   Burn

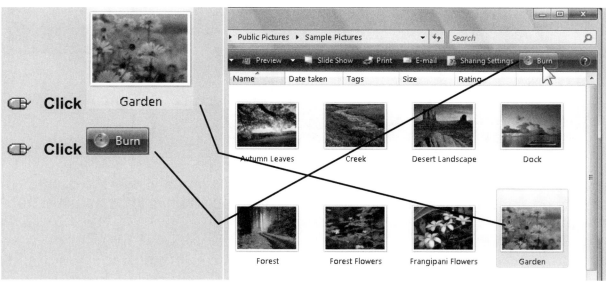

Again, you see the message that you have files waiting to be written to the disc:

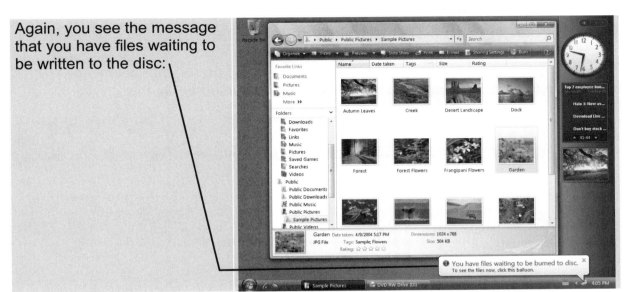

You are going to restore the minimized window with the queue. You use the taskbar button of this window for that:

☞ **Click**

    DVD RW Drive (D:)

You see the queue again:

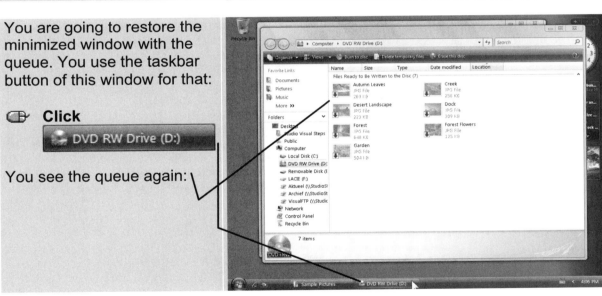

8.11 Deleting Files from the Queue

You can remove files from a queue, for example when you decide not to write a certain file to disc. Deleting a file from the queue can be done like this:

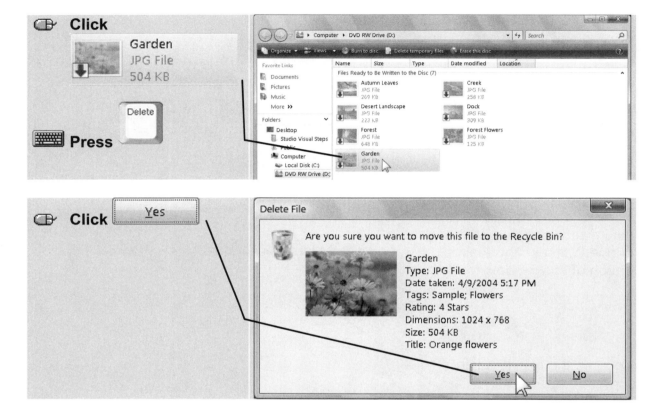

8.12 Writing the Queue to Disc

When you are satisfied with the queue, you can write the files to the disc:

You see the window *Prepare This Disc*:

The recording speed is selected automatically:

Click Next

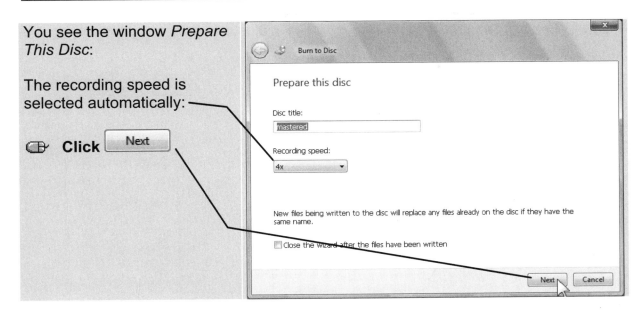

Because you can not add files to this disc when the writing process is finished, you may see this warning:

Click Yes

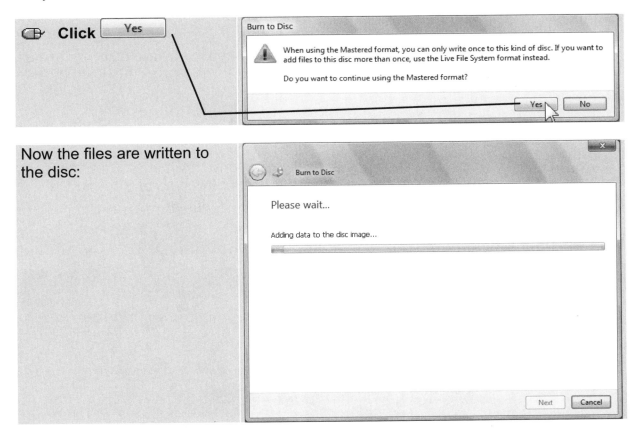

Now the files are written to the disc:

When the writing process is completed, the disc is ejected and you see this window:

In this window you can
choose to write the same
queue to another disc:

That is not necessary
for this exercise:

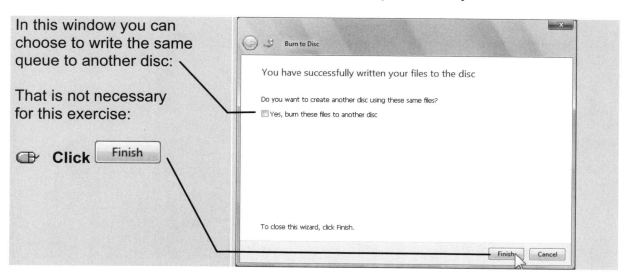

Click Finish

☞ **Remove the disc from the writer**

☞ **Close the *Sample Pictures* window** 1

The images have been written to the disc. In the next section you are going to take a look at them.

8.13 Viewing the Contents of the Disc Using Photo Gallery

When you insert a disc with a certain type of file in the drive, *Windows Vista* can automatically open the program that you prefer to use for this type of file. You are going to check the preferred setting for images on your computer:

☞ **Open the *Control Panel*** 18

You see the *Control Panel*:

Click
Play CDs or other media automati
below
Hardware and Sound

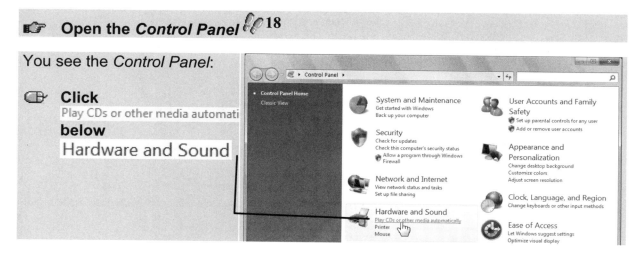

You see the window *AutoPlay*, where you can choose to start *Windows Photo Gallery* automatically when you insert a disc containing images in the drive:

☞ **Check if the setting**

    🖼 View pictures using Windo

is displayed next to

    📄 Pictures

If this is <u>not</u> the case on your computer:

☞ **Click the current setting next to**

    📄 Pictures

☞ **Click**

    🖼 View pictures using Windows

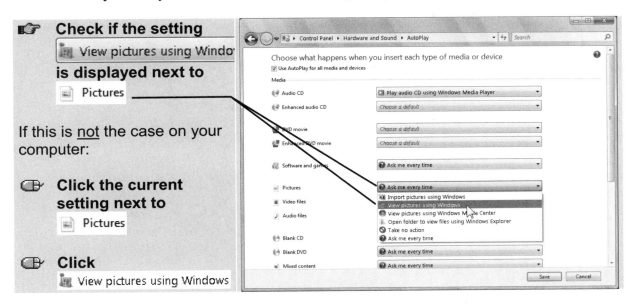

You see the correct setting: ⎯

☞ **Click** ⎢ Save ⎥

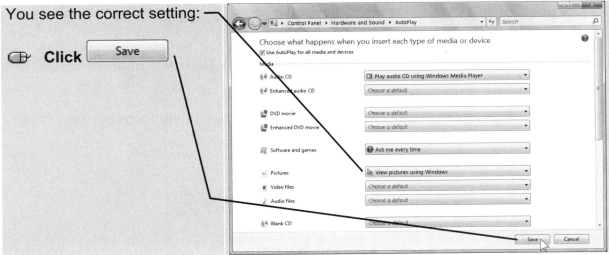

☞ **Close the *Control Panel* 🚶¹**

From now on, *Windows Photo Gallery* will be started automatically when you insert a disc containing images. You can try that:

☞ **Insert the disc containing images in your CD/DVD drive**

After a few moments *Windows Photo Gallery* opens and you see the first image:

To view the next image:

☞ **Click** ▶❙

You can view all images on the disc like this.

☞ **Close the *Windows Photo Gallery* window** ℓℓ¹

☞ **Remove the disc from the CD/DVD drive**

You can read more about working with *Windows Photo Gallery* in **chapter 10 Useful Vista Programs**.

In this chapter you have learned how to write files to disc. In the following exercises you can repeat these tasks.

8.14 Exercises

Have you forgotten how to do something? Use the number beside the footsteps to look it up in *Appendix B How Do I Do That Again?*

Exercise: Live File System

In this exercise you write files to a CD or DVD using the *Live File System.*

✓   Insert a new or erased CD/DVD-RW in the writer.

✓   Click Burn files to disc using Windows .

✓   Format the disc using the *Live File System.* ℓℓ44

✓   Click the folder *Music*.

✓   Double-click the folder *Sample Music*.

✓   Select three files. ℓℓ45

✓   Write the files to the disc. ℓℓ46

✓   Delete one of the files. ℓℓ47

✓   Erase all files from the disc (only possible with a rewritable disc). ℓℓ48

✓   Remove the disc from the writer.

Exercise: Mastered

In this exercise you write files to a CD or DVD using the file system *Mastered*.

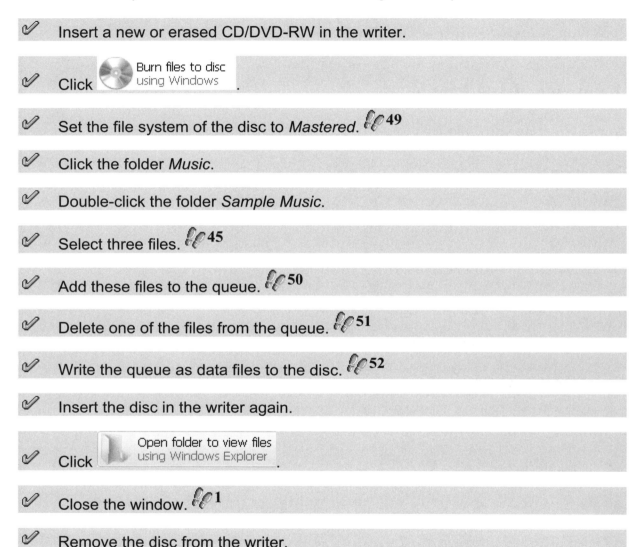

Insert a new or erased CD/DVD-RW in the writer.

Click Burn files to disc using Windows.

Set the file system of the disc to *Mastered*. $\ell\ell$ **49**

Click the folder *Music*.

Double-click the folder *Sample Music*.

Select three files. $\ell\ell$ **45**

Add these files to the queue. $\ell\ell$ **50**

Delete one of the files from the queue. $\ell\ell$ **51**

Write the queue as data files to the disc. $\ell\ell$ **52**

Insert the disc in the writer again.

Click Open folder to view files using Windows Explorer.

Close the window. $\ell\ell$ **1**

Remove the disc from the writer.

8.15 Background Information

Glossary	
Close disc	The process that enables you to use a CD or DVD in another computer or device. As long as you have free space on the disc, additional files can be added to the disc after it is closed. Closing a disc uses about 20 MB per session.
Data	Files like documents, photos, music files and videos that are stored on the computer.
Finalize disc	A process used by disc writing programs that occurs after files are written (burned) to a CD or DVD. After a disk is finalized, it is ready to be played in another computer or device, but you can no longer add files to it.
Formatting	Before you can store data on a disc, the disc must be formatted. This means the disc is prepared for use according to the requirements of *Windows Vista*.
Mastered	File system used to create CDs and DVDs. Discs created using the *Mastered* file system can be used on older computers, but an extra step is required to write the collection of files to the disc.
Live File System	File system used to create CDs and DVDs. You can copy files to a *Live File System* disc whenever you want, you do not need to write (burn) all files at the same time. Can be used on *Vista* and *Windows XP* PCs. May not be compatible with other devices.
Queue	List of files that are waiting to be written to a CD or DVD formatted using the *Mastered* file system.
Writer/burner	A device you can use to copy files to recordable CDs and DVDs.

Source: Windows Help and Support

How a writer / burner works

Data is stored on a CD or DVD digitally, in a series of ones and zeros. Irregularities like tiny raised bumps are created on the reflective surface of the disc in a long spiral. When you play the disc in a CD/DVD player, the disc spins around and its reflecting surface is scanned by a laser beam. The reflected light is measured by a sensor. At places where there is a bump, the laser beam is not reflected correctly. Based on this information, the sensor sends a tiny burst of electrical current to the computer or does not. The computer processes this information and translates it to a form you can use.

On audio CDs and movie DVDs you buy in the store, the information is stored on the disc as tiny holes. The writer in your computer uses tiny holes (CD/DVD-Recordables) or spots (CD/DVD-Rewritables). The laser beam heats tiny areas on the recording surface. This creates dark spots on the recording surface of the rewritable disc. These can be removed again by heating the surface. When a rewritable disc is used for the second time, the old information is removed at the same time the new information is stored. This process takes more time than just writing a disc.

To read a disc, it is important that the holes or spots are burned at regular intervals. That is why you have to choose the writing speed beforehand, you can not adjust it during the writing process.

If any glitches occur during the writing process, the disc will be unusable. A glitch can occur when the steady current of data to the writer is disrupted. The introduction of the *burnproof* option on the writer ensures that the writing process can be resumed at the right place if the stream of data to the writer is temporarily disrupted.

Audio or video CDs / DVDs

To be able to play music and movies in a CD or DVD player, the disc and the files should have a special format. It is best to use programs especially designed for working with audio or video to create these discs. This way you can create CDs and DVDs that are suitable for use in a regular standalone CD or DVD player.

For example, in *Windows Photo Gallery* you can create a slide show using your own pictures and write it to a video DVD. With *Windows Movie Maker* you can create a movie using your own video files and write it to a video DVD. With *Windows Media Player* you can write audio CDs using music files you have stored on your computer.

Choosing between Live File System or Mastered

What choice to make depends on what you want to do with the burned CD or DVD disc.

***Live File System* discs:**
- You can write (copy) files straight to the disc.
- Are convenient if you want to leave a disc in your computer's writer and copy files to it at your convenience.
- Are convenient because there is no time-consuming queuing and burning process like you have with *Mastered* discs. Each file is copied to the disc as soon as you drag it to the disc folder.
- When you use a rewritable disc like a CD-RW, DVD-RW or DVD-RAM you can delete separate files or format the disc to free disc space.
- Possibly need to be **closed*** before they can be used on other computers.
- Are only compatible with *Windows XP* and newer versions of *Windows*.

* Before you can use a recordable disc (such as CD-R, DVD-R, or DVD+R) formatted with the *Live File System* format in other computers and devices, you need to **close** the current disc session to prepare the disc for use. By default, *Windows* closes your disc automatically when it is ejected by pressing the eject button on the disc drive. Closing the disc can take a few minutes and requires 20 MB disc space.

- Continue reading on the next page -

Mastered discs:
- You need to select the entire collection of files that you want to copy to the disc, and then write them all at once.
- Are convenient if you want to write a large collection of files, such as an audio CD.
- Are compatible with older computers and devices such as CD and DVD players.
- You need a large amount of hard disk space to be able to write a *Mastered* disc (as much as the capacity of the disc you are going to write).

You see this text balloon in the lower right corner of your screen:

After you close a disc session, you can still add additional files to the disc. But you must close each additional session to be able to use the disc on another computer.

Please note: some programs might **finalize** your disc instead of closing the current session. You can not add any additional files to a disc once it has been finalized.

Source: *Windows Help and Support*

Types of CDs and DVDs

There are many types of CDs and DVDs. Here follows a short overview with the most important properties:

Type	Properties	Cap.	Compatible with
CD-ROM	Read only	650 MB	Most computers and devices (CD and DVD players)
DVD-ROM	Read only	4,7 GB	Most computers and devices (DVD players)
CD-R	Can be written to once only. Nothing can be erased.	650 MB or 700 MB	After closing compatible with most computers and devices (CD and DVD players)
DVD-R or DVD+R	Can be written to once only. Nothing can be erased.	4,7 GB	After closing compatible with most computers and devices . (DVD players)
CD-RW	Can be written to multiple times. Files can be deleted, disc can be erased.	650 MB	Compatible with many computers and devices, but not all. Especially older devices cause problems.
DVD-RW or DVD+RW	Can be written to multiple times. Files can be deleted, disc can be erased.	4,7 GB	Compatible with many Computers and devices, but not all. Especially older devices cause problems.
Dual layer DVD DVD DL	DVD with double storage capacity	8,5 GB	Only suitable for the newest devices. Not yet supported by all programs.

Comments:

- **R** stands for *recordable*. Data can be written to the disc, but not erased. **RW** stands for *rewritable*. Data can be written and erased again multiple times.

- The + and - versions indicate a different type. Most devices can handle both types. Refer to the technical specifications of your device to see which type is supported.

Writing speed

When you read the product descriptions for CD/DVD writers, you always see numbers like *4x*, *16x* or *48x*. The *x* here means 'times'. The term *4x* for example indicates the speed of the writer. It means that the writer can write data to a disc four times faster than the base speed. The base speed is 150 KB per second for CD writers and 1.13 MB per second for DVD writers. But writing a disc will always take longer, because the writer needs time to get up to full speed and time to open and close the disc. This makes the writing process take longer than just the time needed to write the data.

On writers that can handle rewritables, you see three or four numbers. These numbers indicate the speed for reading, writing recordable discs and writing rewritable discs. These speeds are also different for each disc type, such as CD, DVD or DVD-DL (dual layer). Based on these numbers, you can roughly compare the speeds of different writers.

The writing speed you can use for writing a CD also depends on the maximum speed of the used CD. This speed can vary between brands and types of CDs. You can find these speeds on the CD case. If the maximum speed of the CD is lower than that of the writer, the CD will be written at that lower speed.

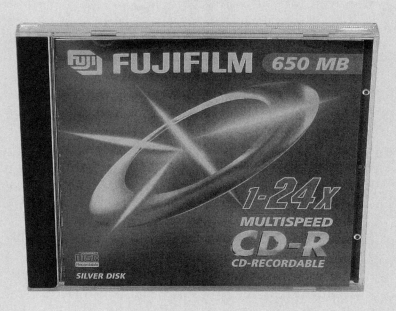

8.16 Tips

 Tip

During the writing process the data must be delivered to the writer in a steady, uninterrupted stream. If that is not the case, the writing process may fail. *Burnproof* writers automatically compensate for this problem. Refer to the manual of your writer to find out if your writer is burnproof.

Do you regularly have problems writing discs in *Windows Vista*? Then try the following:

- close all other programs;
- turn off the screen saver;
- temporarily break the Internet connection;
- turn off scan programs that scan your hard disk for viruses etcetera;
- make sure there is enough free space on the hard disk;
- make sure the recordable discs and the writer are clean;
- write the disc at a lower recording speed (see the tip about this subject);
- try recordable CDs or DVDs of another brand;
- defrag the hard disk.

 Tip

UPS (Uninterruptible Power Supply)
Voltage surges and sags can disrupt the way your computer and writer work. A small flickering of lights can indicate a voltage sag. You can prevent this yourself by not turning on or off any heavy-duty equipment in the nearby vicinity of your computer during the writing process. However, sometimes these fluctuations are caused outside your house. In that case it may be worth the trouble to buy a UPS (uninterruptable power supply).

A UPS is a device that is installed between your computer and its power supply. It contains a battery that ensures the computer keeps working for a certain amount of time in case of a power failure. UPS devices will usually also protect the computer against voltage surges and sags and frequency differences.

Tip

Lowering the recording speed
When you write a disc using the *Mastered* file system, you can choose the recording speed. Usually you will choose the highest possible speed. But when discs are not written correctly, you can choose a lower speed. You can adjust the recording speed in the following window:

 Click `4x`

 Click the speed you want to use

You may see other speeds on your computer.

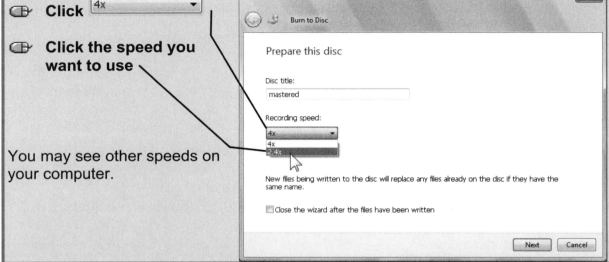

 Tip

Check important discs regularly
Contrary to popular belief, data on CDs and DVDs can not be kept forever. Tests have shown that sometimes even after a few years, the data has become unusable.

It is advisable to store important data on high quality discs. The quality of a written disc depends on (among others):
- the production process of the disc;
- the type of writer used to write the disc;
- the way the disc was written (in multiple sessions or at once);
- the way the disc is treated and stored;
- the type of disc.

More expensive discs are not always better. To make a good choice, you can refer to tests performed by independent organizations like computer magazines, consumer organizations etcetera.
Now that important data is stored on CD or DVD very often, it is advisable to regularly check discs containing important data. This will decrease the chance that you can no longer view your wedding video or photo collection after a couple of years.

Tip

Write the contents on your CDs and DVDs

Has this happened to you? You are sure you stored your holiday photos on a CD, but which disc is it? When you regularly create backups and copies, you will soon have a large number of discs. Then it becomes very important to write the contents on the disc. You can do that in a couple of ways:

- when your discs are stored in the original jewel case, you write the contents on the sleeve. This is advisable for audio CDs and DVDs, because you can also list the separate tracks. But discs in a jewel case are more expensive than discs on a *spindle* and take up a lot of storage space.

- you can use a special pen or marker to write the contents on the printed side of the disc. Make sure to use suitable markers, others may damage the surface. Make sure you only write on the printed side, that is where you see the brand and type of the disc. Since the space is limited, you can not write too much. Tip: you can also mark the disc with a number and keep a list (on the computer or manually) of the contents of each disc.

- there are special labels you can stick to CDs and DVDs. These labels have exactly the right size and contain a layer of glue that does not damage the surface. Use a special label applicator to put the label exactly in the center of the disc. When the label is not centered exactly, the disc may lose its balance in your writer/player. Then it no longer functions properly. You can write on the labels, or print them using *label* software.

- modern writers include the *lightscribe* technology, enabling you to print on discs that are suitable for that. Your label is 'burned' onto your disc with the same laser used to burn its data. First you write the data on one side of the disc, then you turn the disc and print the label.

There are also special programs you can use to write your (photo/music) collection and create a table of contents at the same time. Using the search function you can quickly find out which disc a certain item is stored on. However, first you need to make sure you can identify the discs by a name or number.

Tip

Dragging files to the CD/DVD
You can also write files to a *Live File System* disc by dragging them to the writer.

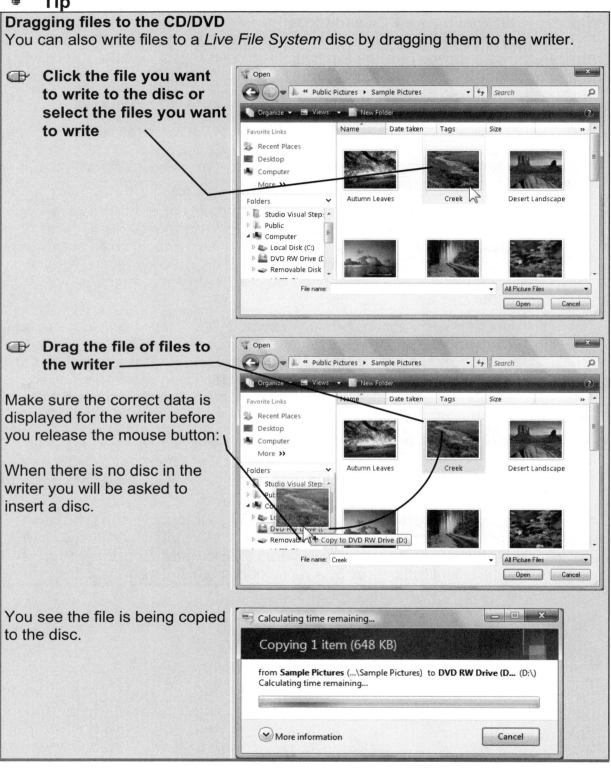

Click the file you want to write to the disc or select the files you want to write

Drag the file of files to the writer

Make sure the correct data is displayed for the writer before you release the mouse button:

When there is no disc in the writer you will be asked to insert a disc.

You see the file is being copied to the disc.

9. Advanced Features of the Folder Windows

The folder windows in *Windows Vista* contain a number of useful features. There are various ways to navigate through your files and folders. For example using the *Folder list* in the *Navigation Pane*. In the *Preview Pane* you can preview files without having to open them first. In the *Details Pane* you can quickly view and edit the properties associated with files.

Windows Vista also contains an excellent search feature. In this chapter you will get to know the advanced possibilities of *Search Box* in the *Folder window*. To be able to find a file quickly, the search results can be filtered in various ways. A search you might want to use again, can be saved.

In the Visual Steps book **Windows Vista for SENIORS** (ISBN 978 90 5905 274 1) you have acquired some basic knowledge about the *Folder window*. You have learned how to move, copy and delete files and folders in the *Folder window*. In this chapter you will expand your knowledge and learn more about the *Folder window*.

In this chapter you will learn how to:

- open your *Personal Folder*;
- change the folder view;
- work with the *Navigation Pane*;
- display and hide the menu bar;
- preview a file in the *Preview Pane*;
- change the file properties in the *Details Pane*;
- use the *Search Box*;
- filter search results;
- search the entire computer;
- save a search;
- find and open a saved search;
- work with the changing buttons on the toolbar.

9.1 Opening Your Personal Folder

Your *Personal Folder* is the folder containing your folders *Documents*, *Pictures*, *Music*, *Contacts* and other folders. The *Personal Folder* is labeled with the same name as your user account in *Windows Vista.* The button you use to open your *Personal Folder*, is located in the top right corner of the *Start menu*. Take a look:

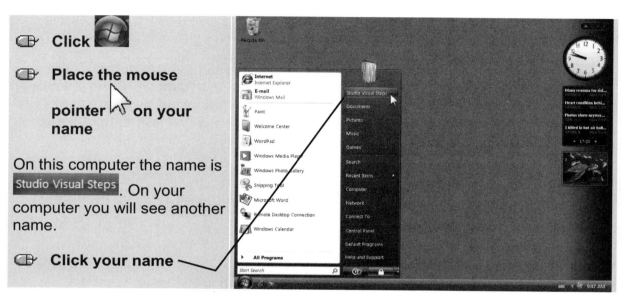

☞ **Click**

☞ **Place the mouse**

   pointer on your
   name

On this computer the name is
Studio Visual Steps . On your
computer you will see another
name.

☞ **Click your name**

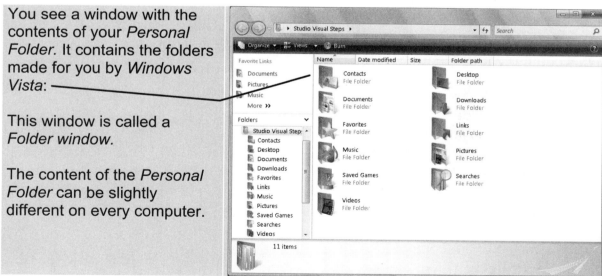

You see a window with the
contents of your *Personal
Folder*. It contains the folders
made for you by *Windows
Vista*:

This window is called a
Folder window.

The content of the *Personal
Folder* can be slightly
different on every computer.

HELP! I do not see all the folders in the left pane.

If the left pane of your window does not show folders like those in the previous figure:

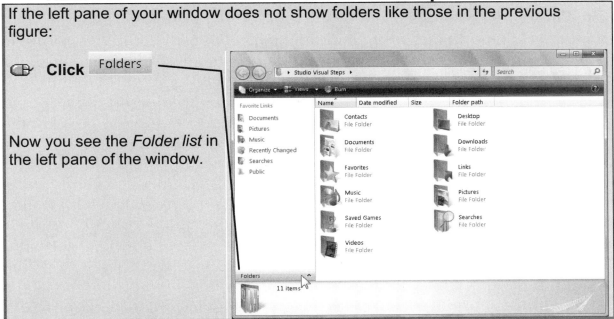

 Click Folders

Now you see the *Folder list* in the left pane of the window.

9.2 Changing the Display of the Folder Window

There are several ways to display your folders in the *Folder window*. Maybe the window looks different on your screen. You can check the settings like this:

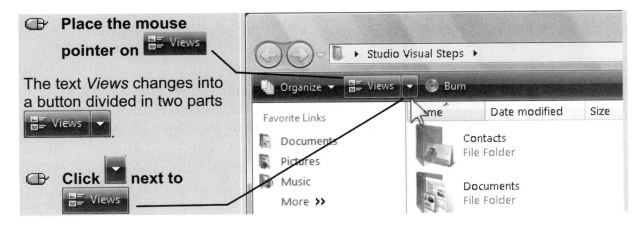

 Place the mouse pointer on Views

The text *Views* changes into a button divided in two parts Views .

 Click next to Views

A menu appears:

Click

The files and folders will now be displayed as 'tiles'.

There are more settings you can use to change the display of the *Folder window*:

Click

A menu appears:

Click

A submenu appears:
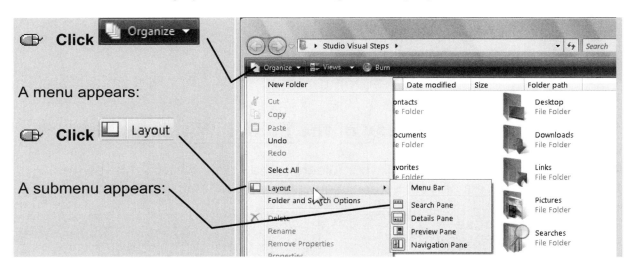

In this second menu only the options Details Pane and Navigation Pane are active. If an option is active, it is highlighted with a light blue box around the icon. If the icon is not highlighted, you can activate the option by clicking it.

Click (if necessary)
Details Pane

Repeat these actions (if necessary) to activate the Preview Pane and Navigation Pane
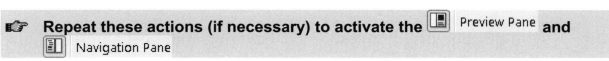

Deactivating an option is done the same way, by clicking the highlighted option in the list.

☞ **Repeat these actions (if necessary) to deactivate the option**
        ▦ Search Pane

Now the *Folder window* on your computer looks the same as the figure shown in this example:

☞ **If necessary, drag the vertical scroll bar down**

☞ **Double-click**

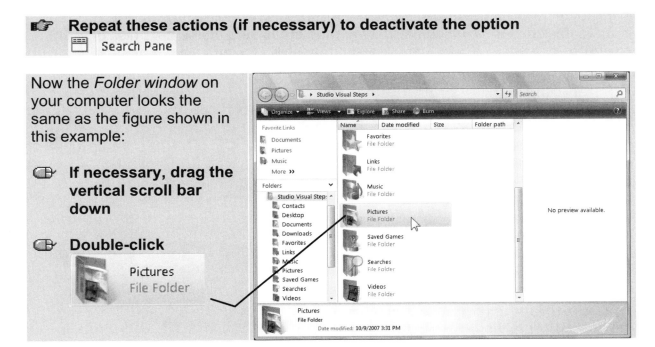

Pictures
File Folder

You see the content of your *Pictures* folder. It is possible that you have already stored some photos in there. This folder contains a shortcut to the folder *Sample Pictures* that *Vista* has placed on your computer:

☞ **Double-click**

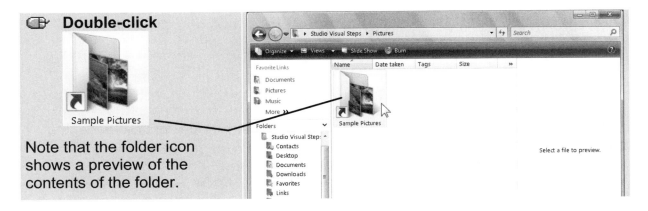

Sample Pictures

Note that the folder icon shows a preview of the contents of the folder.

🩹 **HELP! My files and folders are displayed differently.**

If your files and folders are displayed differently in the window:

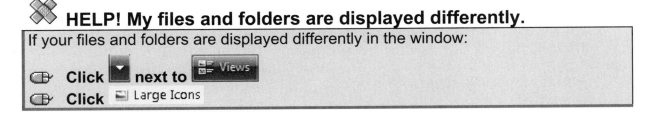

☞ **Click** ⯆ **next to** ▤ Views

☞ **Click** ⊟ Large Icons

9.3 The Parts of the Folder Window

A *Folder window* shows you more than the contents of a folder. It has specific areas that are designed to help you navigate around the folders on the hard disk of your computer, or work with files and folders more easily. To refresh your memory, the parts of the *Folder window* are identified in the next example:

The *Navigation Pane* shows all files and folders on the hard disk of your computer:

Notice how the address bar

📁 ▸ Public ▸ Public Pictures ▸ Sample Pictures

identifies the folder you are in:

The files contained in this folder are shown as icons in the *File list*:

The *Details Pane* shows information about the selected file:

In the *Preview Pane* a preview of the selected file is displayed:

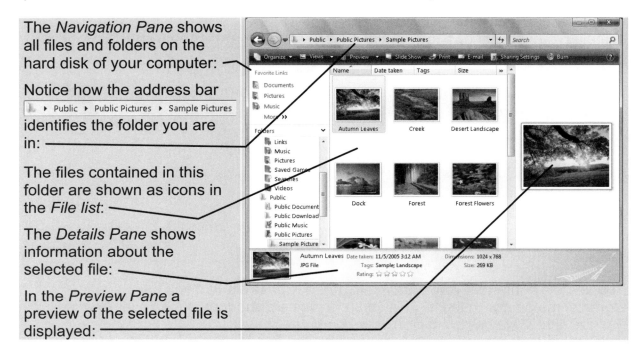

In the next sections you will take a closer look at the different parts of the *Folder window*.

9.4 Favorite Links

The *Navigation Pane* on the left hand side of the *Folder window* has two parts: the *Favorite Links* and the *Folders list*.

Here you see the *Favorite Links*:

It is possible that you do not see the same links on your PC, but the hyperlink More ❯❯ instead.
When you click this link, other links will appear.

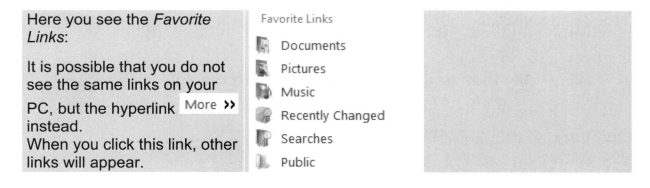

When you click one of these links, the contents of the corresponding folder are displayed in the *File list*.

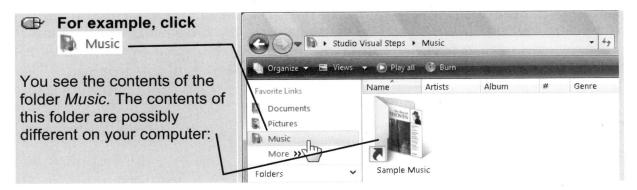

☞ **For example, click**

You see the contents of the folder *Music.* The contents of this folder are possibly different on your computer:

The buttons can be used to quickly navigate between previously opened folders. To return to the previous folder:

☞ **Click**

The folder *Sample Pictures* is opened again.

The button can be used to return to the folder you opened after the current folder. If you opened multiple folders in a row, there is a quicker way to switch between these folders:

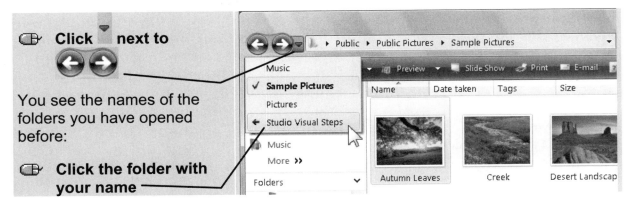

☞ **Click** next to

You see the names of the folders you have opened before:

☞ **Click the folder with your name**

You see the contents of your *Personal Folder* again.

9.5 Working with the Folder List

In the *Folder list* in the *Navigation Pane* you see all folders on the hard disk of your computer. You can use the *Folder list* to navigate directly to each folder or subfolder.

The *Folder list* is the bottom part of the *Navigation Pane*.

Just click a folder name to display the contents of the folder in the *File list*:

Here you see the contents of the *Personal Folder*
Studio Visual Steps :

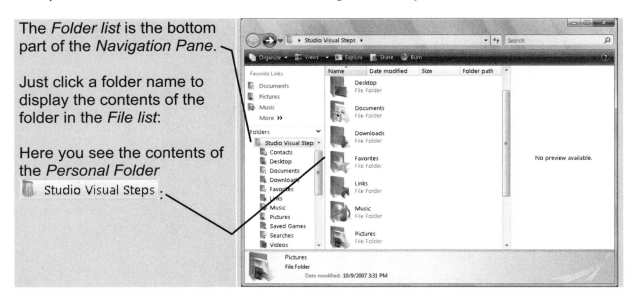

On your computer, the *Personal Folder* Studio Visual Steps of course has the name of your user account. In the following exercises, select your own user name every time you are asked to click on or next to Studio Visual Steps .

☞ Place the mouse pointer on the folders in the *Folder list*

Next to some folders you see arrow icons appear.

▷ means the folder is collapsed. The available subfolders are not visible.

◢ means the folder is expanded. All subfolders are visible.

☞ Click ◢ next to
◢ Studio Visual Steps

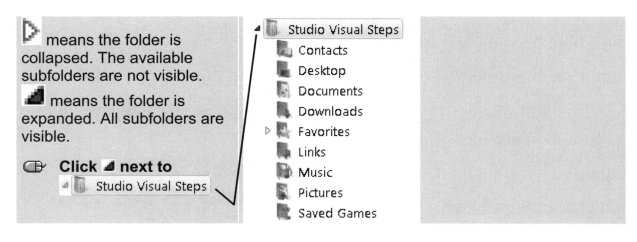

The black arrow has now changed into a white arrow.

☞ **Click** ▷ **next to**
  ▷ 📁 Studio Visual Steps

All subfolders of your *Personal Folder* are visible again.

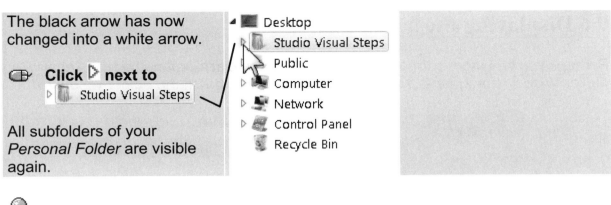

💡 **Tip**

Navigate using the address bar
The address bar shows which folder is opened. When your *Personal Folder* is opened, you see the name of your user account. In this example it is
📁 ▸ Studio Visual Steps ▸ . Every time you read *Studio Visual Steps*, replace this name with your own user account name.
You can use the address bar to quickly navigate to another folder. To open one of the subfolders of your *Personal Folder*:

☞ **Click** ▸ **on the right side of**
  📁 ▸ Studio Visual Steps

You see a list of all the folders in your *Personal Folder*.

☞ **Click** 🖼 Pictures

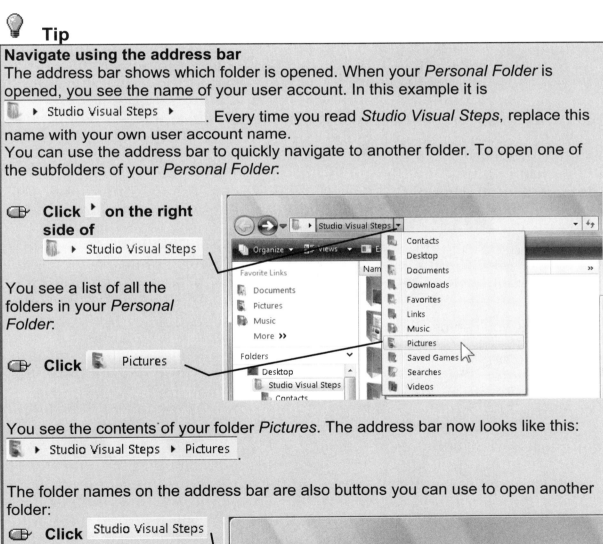

You see the contents of your folder *Pictures*. The address bar now looks like this:
🖼 ▸ Studio Visual Steps ▸ Pictures

The folder names on the address bar are also buttons you can use to open another folder:

☞ **Click** Studio Visual Steps

The *Personal Folder* Studio Visual Steps is opened again.

9.6 Displaying the Menu Bar

Perhaps you feel more comfortable working with the classic menu bar you knew with earlier *Windows* programs. You can display this menu bar in the *Folder window*:

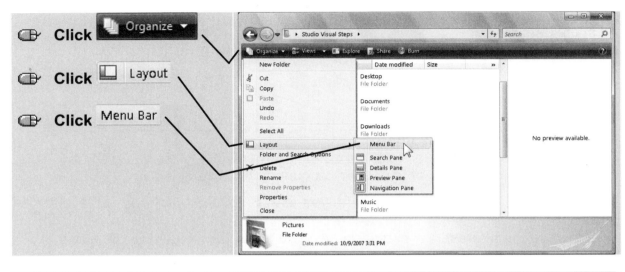

Click Organize ▾

Click Layout

Click Menu Bar

The menu bar is displayed below the address bar:

For example, you can use the menu bar to navigate to another folder:

Click View

Click Go To

Click Sample Pictures

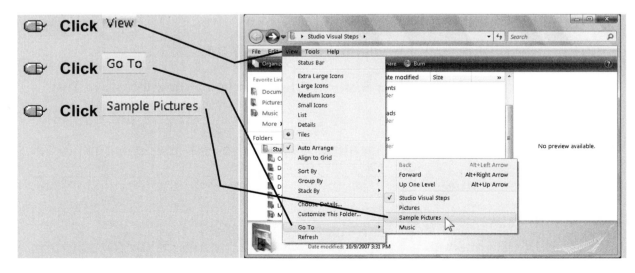

You see the *Sample Pictures* folder again. Now you can hide the menu bar:

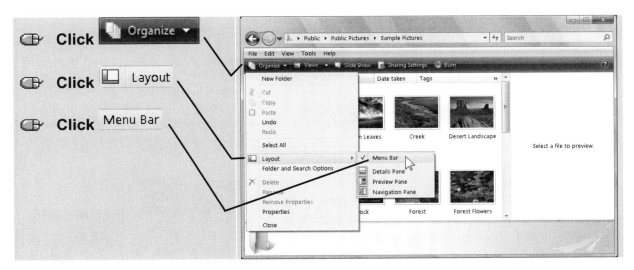

9.7 Previewing a File in the Preview Pane

In the *Preview Pane* you can display a preview of a selected file:

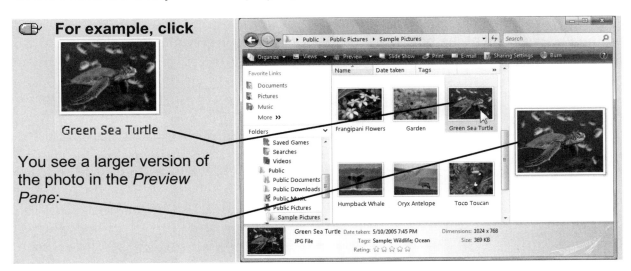

HELP! I no longer see the Preview Pane.

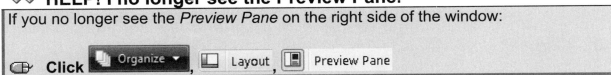

Tip

Previewing files in the Preview Pane
The *Preview Pane* can be used to preview many types of files. If you select a text file or e-mail message for example, you can view the contents of the file without opening it in a program.

When you select a video file, the first frame of the video clip is shown in the *Preview Pane*.

Use the button 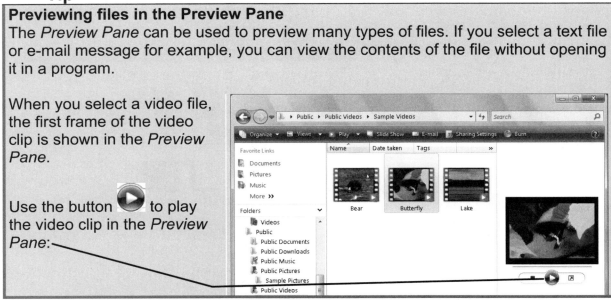 to play the video clip in the *Preview Pane*:

9.8 Changing File Properties in the Details Pane

In the *Details Pane* at the bottom of the *Folder window* you see the properties associated with the selected file:

You see for example when the photo was taken and the dimensions of the photo:

In the *Details Pane* you can change several items. For example, this is how you change the date:

👆 **Click the date**
5/10/2005 7:45 PM

Now you can type a new date, or even open a small calendar:

👆 **Click** ⊞▾

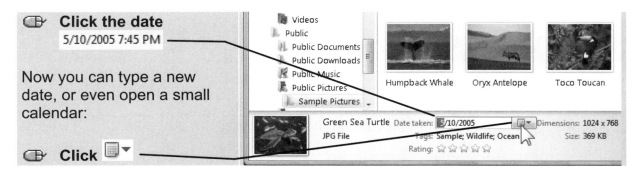

In the calendar you can select a new date by clicking it. For example, select the next day:

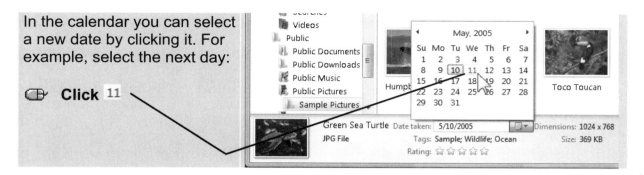

👆 **Click** 11

Now you have to save the change you made:

👆 **Click** Save

9.9 Ratings and Tags

You can also change the *rating* and *tags* of a file. Rating means that you show your appreciation for a file by giving it a certain number of stars. This is how you give this photo a high five-star rating:

👆 **Click the fifth star** ☆

👆 **Click** Save

This is a useful way to make a distinction between your favorite and not so favorite photos.

Another way to organize your photos is by using *tags*. A tag is a word or short phrase you add to a photo. The photo of the tree in this example has the tags Sample; Wildlife;. It is possible that you do not see any tags on your PC, but just the text Add a tag.

You can add a tag to a photo yourself:

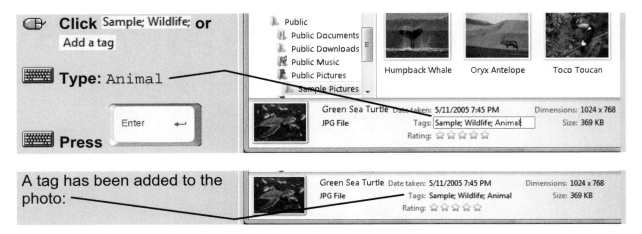

A tag has been added to the photo: —————

You will encounter the ratings and tags again in the next section where you get to know the search feature of the *Folder window*.

9.10 Using the Search Box

Windows Vista includes excellent search possibilities.

In the *Folder window* you find a *Search Box* in the top right corner: ————

You can use this *Search Box* to filter the files and subfolders that are displayed in the *File list*.

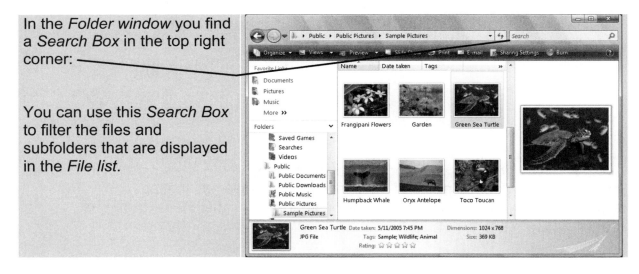

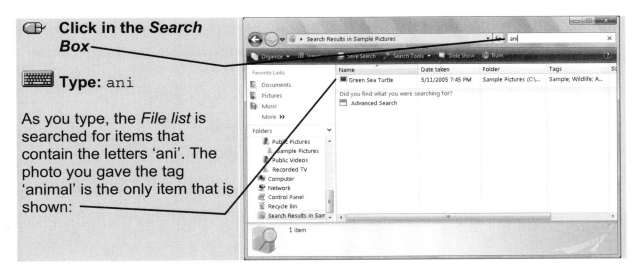

🖱 **Click in the *Search Box***

⌨ **Type:** ani

As you type, the *File list* is searched for items that contain the letters 'ani'. The photo you gave the tag 'animal' is the only item that is shown:

You see that the search feature not only looks for file names. Other file properties like tags are also searched.

HELP! My search results are displayed differently.

Do you see a large icon instead of the detailed view in the example? Then you can adjust the view like this:

🖱 **Click** ▼ **next to** ▦ Views

🖱 **Click** ▦ Details

When you shorten the search term, the search result changes right away:

⌨ **Press** ← Backspace

Now the search feature looks for files containing the letters **an** in the name or tags. The search result now consists of three files:

Depending on the tags used on your computer you will see more or less files in the search result.

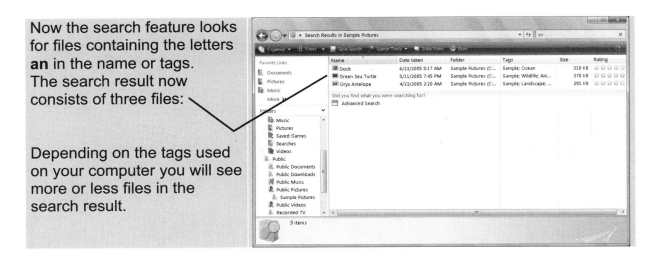

9.11 Filtering Search Results Using the Column Headers

When your search has resulted in a long list of files, you can filter it. You can do that by using the *column headers*. This is how you can filter all photos with the tag 'animal' and 'sample' from the search result:

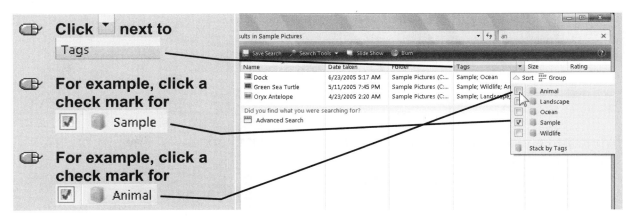

☞ **Click ▼ next to**
   Tags

☞ **For example, click a check mark for**
   ☑ Sample

☞ **For example, click a check mark for**
   ☑ Animal

When these tags are not available:

☞ **Choose other tags**

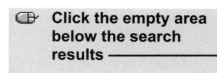 **Click the empty area below the search results** ——————

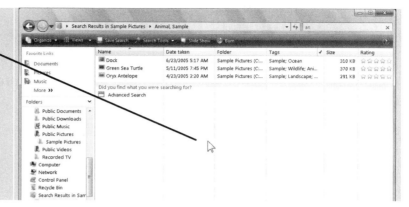

The menu is closed.
You see the filtered search results:

The search results on your computer may be different from those in the example.

 Tip

Filter, stack, group and sort
In addition to using the column headers to filter the contents of the *File list*, they can also be used to *stack*, *group*, and *sort* the files
You can read more about this in the tips at the end of this chapter.

 Tip

Other filter options
You can filter the search results even further using the other column headers:

- **Name**: here you can select the first letter of the file name A - E, F - L, M - R and S - Z.
- **Date taken**: here you can select a specific date, or the photos without a date instead.
- **Folder**: if the search results are found in several subfolders, you can choose which folder(s) to display in the search results.
- **Size**: here you can choose photos with a file size between 10 KB - 100 KB and 100 KB - 1 MB.
- **Rating**: here you can choose the number of stars.

 Tip

Tags
When you have a large collection of digital photos, you can use tags to organize your photos. Each photo can contain several tags. For example, you can give a photo you took of a nice tree during your holiday in France the tags 'holiday France' and 'nature'. A photo you took of your grandchild during the same holiday, can be given the tags 'holiday France' and 'grandchildren'. If you do this consistently for all your photos, it will be very easy to locate and display a series of photos with matching tags using the *Search Box*.

9.12 Searching the Entire Computer

You can also use the *Search Box* to filter the contents of the entire computer. This is very helpful when you can not remember anymore where you stored a file. First you select the entire computer in the *Folder list*:

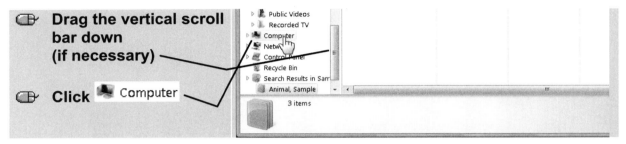

☞ **Drag the vertical scroll bar down (if necessary)**

☞ **Click Computer**

The contents of your computer are displayed:

There may be different drives and devices displayed on your screen than in this example.

☞ **Click the *Search Box***

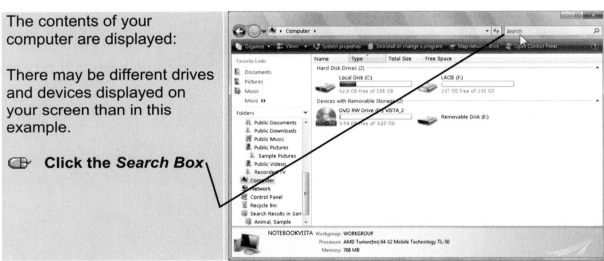

⌨ **Type:** bear

A video file is found (if things go according to plan):

This is a sample video that came with *Windows Vista*.

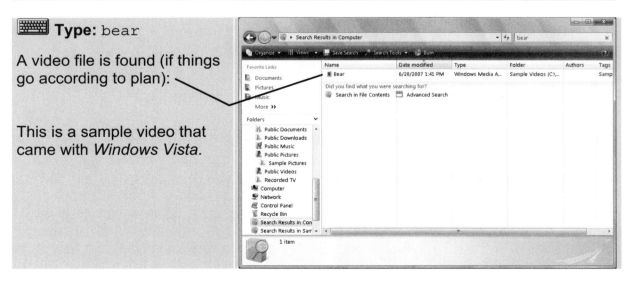

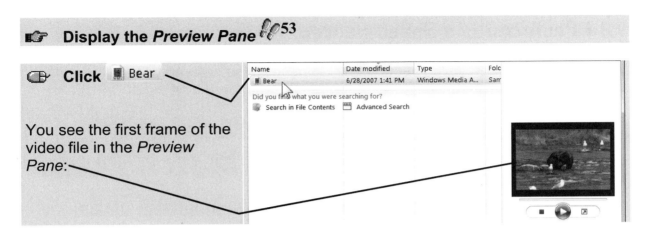

☞ **Display the *Preview Pane*** 🖰53

🖱 **Click** 🎬 Bear

You see the first frame of the video file in the *Preview Pane*:

9.13 Saving a Search

Windows Vista gives you the opportunity to save a search. This way you can perform the same search without having to re-enter your search criteria. Try that with the current search:

🖱 **Click** 🖥 Save Search

A window appears where you can give the search a name.

⌨ **Type:**
video with bear

🖱 **Click** Save

The search has been added to the subfolder *Searches* in your *Personal Folder*. The search is performed again and the address bar now looks like this:

🔵 ▸ Studio Visual Steps ▸ Searches ▸ video with bear

On your computer you see the name of your own *Personal Folder* (your user account name instead of 🔵 ▸ Studio Visual Steps).

9.14 Performing a Saved Search

Your search has been saved in the folder *Searches.* You can verify this:

 Click Searches

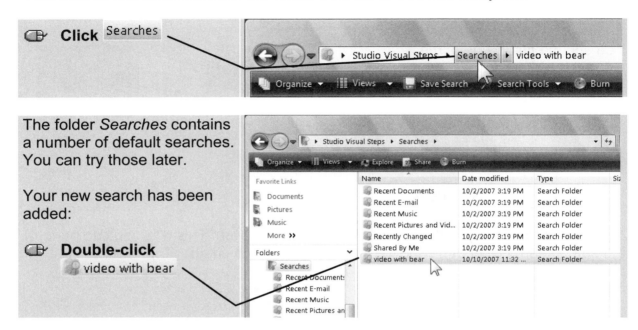

The folder *Searches* contains a number of default searches. You can try those later.

Your new search has been added:

 Double-click video with bear

HELP! My search results look different.

If you can not see the detailed display like in the example:

Click ▼ **next to** Views

Click Details

⇒ Please note:

A saved search can be opened whenever you want. When you add or remove files and folders that correspond to the search criteria, the search result will change.

You see the search result again. The saved search video with bear has been added to the search result:

9.15 The Changing Buttons on the Toolbar

Perhaps you have noticed that in *Windows Vista* the toolbar in the *Folder window* changes its appearance. After your last search the toolbar looks like this:

When you click the video file that was found, the toolbar changes:

Now the toolbar looks like this:

The contents of the toolbar are constantly adapted to the most obvious tasks for the selected file or folder.

For example, the video file can be played right away with the  button.

As soon as you open a folder containing photos the toolbar changes again:

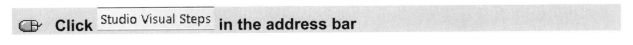

In this example Studio Visual Steps is the name of the *Personal Folder*. On your computer you will see a different name. Select your own *Personal Folder*.

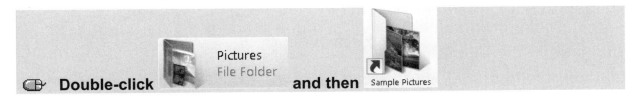

Now the toolbar looks like this:

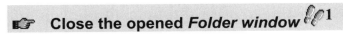

With the button Slide Show you can view the photos that are listed in the opened folder as a full-screen slide show.

☞ **Close the opened *Folder window*** 𝒷𝓁1

In this chapter you have been introduced to the advanced features of the *Folder window* in *Windows Vista*. Use the following exercises to practice what you have learned.

9.16 Exercises

Have you forgotten how to do something? Use the number beside the footsteps to look it up in *Appendix B How Do I Do That Again?*

Exercise: Opening a Folder Window

In this exercise you will practice navigating between folders, previewing a file and changing file properties.

✔ Open your *Personal Folder.* 🐾 54

✔ Open the folder *Pictures* using the *Favorite links.* 🐾 55

✔ Open the folder *Sample Pictures.* 🐾 20

✔ Open the folder *Pictures* using the *Folder list* in the *Navigation Pane.* 🐾 56

✔ Go back to the folder *Sample Pictures.* 🐾 28

✔ If necessary, open the *Preview Pane.* 🐾 53

✔ View the file *Waterfall* in the *Preview Pane.* 🐾 57

✔ Give the file a five-star rating. 🐾 58

✔ Add the tag 'nature' to the file. 🐾 59

✔ Close the *Folder window.* 🐾 1

Exercise: Searching

In this exercise you practice searching for files and saving searches.

✓ Open your *Personal Folder*. ✍ **54**

✓ Display the parts of your computer in the *Folder list* using the *Navigation Pane*. ✍ **56**

✓ Search for the word *nature* using the *Search Box*. ✍ **60**

✓ View the search results.

✓ Save the search with the name *nature photos*. ✍ **61**

✓ Open the folder *Searches* using the address bar. ✍ **62**

✓ Run the search *nature photos* again. ✍ **63**

✓ View the search results.

✓ Close the *Folder window*. ✍ **1**

9.17 Background Information

Glossary	
Address bar	The address bar appears at the top of every *Folder window*. Using the address bar, you can see which folder is opened in the *Folder window*. The address bar displays the exact location of the folder on the hard disk of your computer.
Details Pane	Shows the most common properties associated with the selected file. File properties contain information about a file, such as the author, the date you last changed the file, and any descriptive tags you might have added to the file.
File	The generic name for everything saved on the computer. A file can be a program, a data file with names, text you have written or a photo. Actually, everything that is on the hard disk of your computer is called a file.
File list	This is where the contents of the current folder are displayed.
Filtering	Displaying files that meet certain criteria. For example, you can filter photo files by a certain tag, so that you only see the photos that have that tag. Filtering does not delete files, it simply changes the view so that you only see the files that meet your criteria.
Folder	A folder is a container that helps you organize your files. Every file on your computer is stored in a folder. A folder may also contain other folders (subfolders).
Folder list	List of folders in the *Navigation Pane*. Using the *Folder list* in the *Navigation Pane* you can navigate directly to the folder you are interested in by clicking this folder.
Folder window	When you open a folder using the *Start menu*, a *Folder window* appears that shows the contents of this folder. A *Folder window* has specific areas that are designed to help you navigate around the folders on the hard disk of your computer. You can also move, copy and delete files and folders in this window.

- Continue reading on the next page -

Menu bar	Bar containing titles of menus, found below the title bar of the program. Every menu contains a list of options. The menus are hidden until you click their titles in the menu bar.
Navigation Pane	Shows the list of folders that can be opened in the *Folder window*.
Personal Folder	A folder containing your most frequently used folders (such as *Documents*, *Pictures*, *Music*, *Favorites*, *Contacts*, and other folders that are specific to your user account). The *Personal Folder* is labeled with the name of your user account. The button you can use to open your *Personal Folder* is located at the top of the *Start menu*.
Preview Pane	Part of the *Folder window* you can use to preview the contents of a file. If you select an e-mail message, text file, or picture, you can see its contents without opening it in a program.
Rating	Five-star rating system that can be applied to a file, indicating how much you like it. One being the lowest and five being the highest.
Search Box	Box in the top right corner of the *Folder window*. As you type in the *Search Box*, the contents of the folder are immediately filtered to show only the files that match what you typed. The *Search Box* searches only the current folder and any of its subfolders, not the entire computer.
Tag	Word or short phrase you add to the properties of a file. Tags can help you organize your photo collection and help you find a particular photo more easily.
Toolbar	The toolbar in the *Folder window* enables you to perform a range of common tasks. The buttons on the toolbar are constantly adapted to the relevant tasks for the selected file or folder. When you click an image file, you see different buttons on the toolbar than when you click an audio file.

Source: Windows Help and Support

9.18 Tips

 Tip

Selecting files and folders using check boxes
Windows Vista contains a useful feature that allows you to quickly select multiple
folders and/or files by using check boxes:

If this feature has not been activated on your computer, you can turn it on like this:

☞ **Open the folder *Pictures***

🖱 **Click** [Organize ▼], Folder and Search Options

🖱 **Click the tab** [View]

🖱 **Drag the vertical scroll
bar down**

🖱 **Click to check mark**
☐ Use check boxes to select items

🖱 **Click** [OK]

The feature is now active.

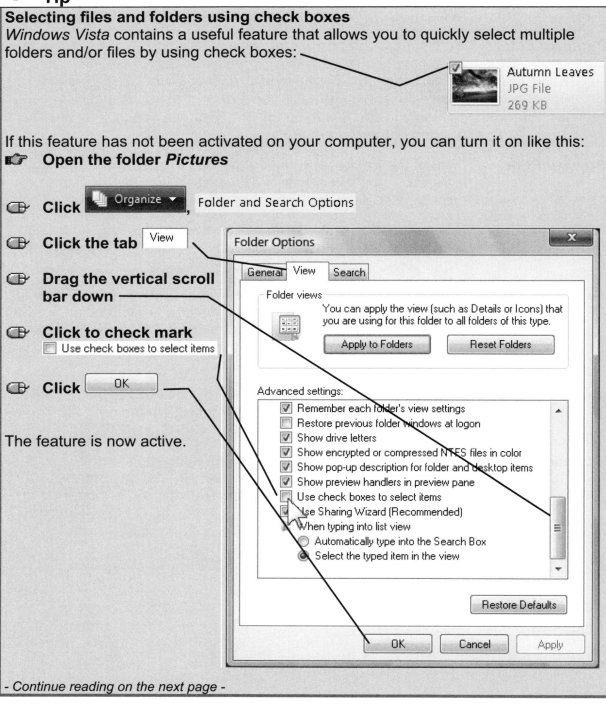

- Continue reading on the next page -

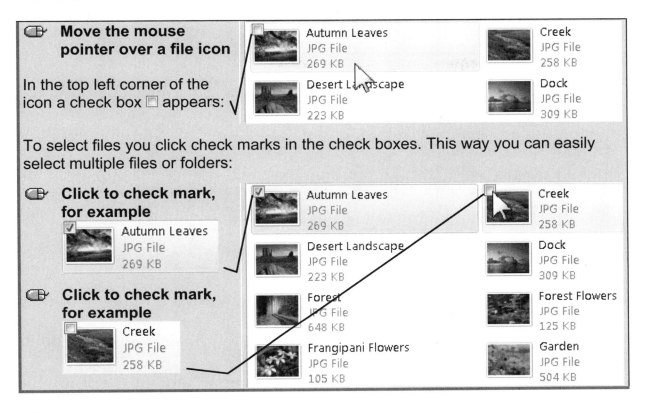

To select files you click check marks in the check boxes. This way you can easily select multiple files or folders:

Click to check mark, for example

 Autumn Leaves
JPG File
269 KB

Click to check mark, for example

Creek
JPG File
258 KB

💡 **Tip**

The Search Box in the Start menu
The *Folder window* is not the only place to perform a search. In the *Start menu* you also find a *Search Box*:

👆 **Click** ⊞

The *Start menu* with the *Search Box* appears. You do not need to click inside the box first.

⌨ **Start typing**

As you type, the search results appear above the *Search Box* in the left pane of the *Start menu*.

The *Search Box* will scour your programs and all of the folders in your *Personal Folder*. It will also search your e-mail messages, saved instant messages, appointments and contacts.

Tip

Displaying extra columns
By default, not all of the columns are visible in a *Folder window*. You can choose which columns you want to display. For example, you can display the *Authors* column. This column is very useful when you want to organize text files.

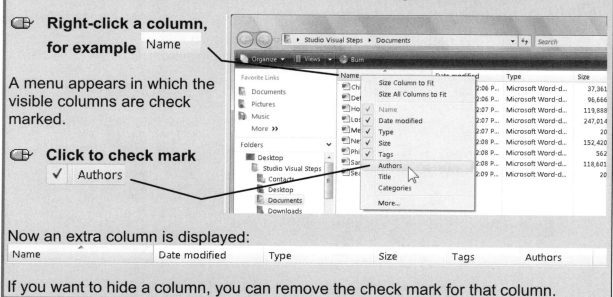

☞ **Right-click a column, for example** Name

A menu appears in which the visible columns are check marked.

☞ **Click to check mark** ✓ Authors

Now an extra column is displayed:

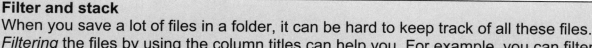

If you want to hide a column, you can remove the check mark for that column.

 Tip

Filter and stack
When you save a lot of files in a folder, it can be hard to keep track of all these files. *Filtering* the files by using the column titles can help you. For example, you can filter the files by the name of an author, so you only see the files written by that person:

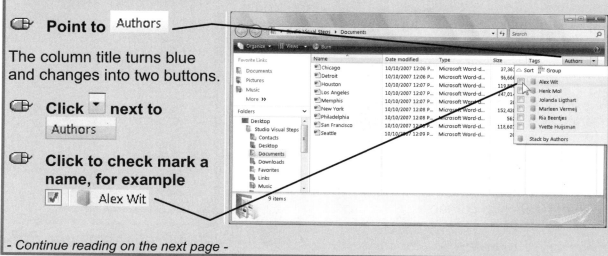

☞ **Point to** Authors

The column title turns blue and changes into two buttons.

☞ **Click** ▾ **next to** Authors

☞ **Click to check mark a name, for example** ☑ Alex Wit

- *Continue reading on the next page* -

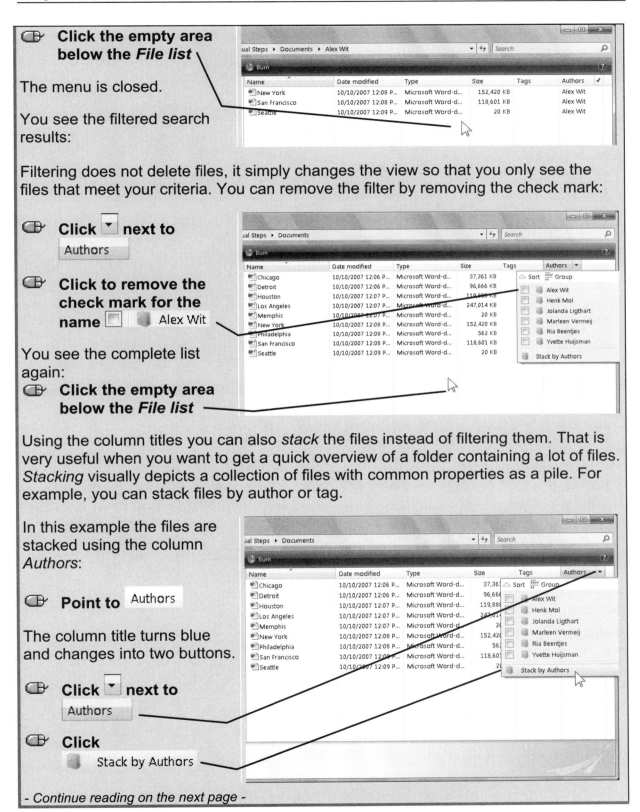

☞ **Click the empty area below the *File list***

The menu is closed.

You see the filtered search results:

Filtering does not delete files, it simply changes the view so that you only see the files that meet your criteria. You can remove the filter by removing the check mark:

☞ **Click** ▼ **next to** Authors

☞ **Click to remove the check mark for the name** ☐ 📦 Alex Wit

You see the complete list again:

☞ **Click the empty area below the *File list***

Using the column titles you can also *stack* the files instead of filtering them. That is very useful when you want to get a quick overview of a folder containing a lot of files. *Stacking* visually depicts a collection of files with common properties as a pile. For example, you can stack files by author or tag.

In this example the files are stacked using the column *Authors*:

☞ **Point to** Authors

The column title turns blue and changes into two buttons.

☞ **Click** ▼ **next to** Authors

☞ **Click** 📦 Stack by Authors

- Continue reading on the next page -

You see the result right away. For each author a stack icon is displayed. You can view the contents of a stack like this:

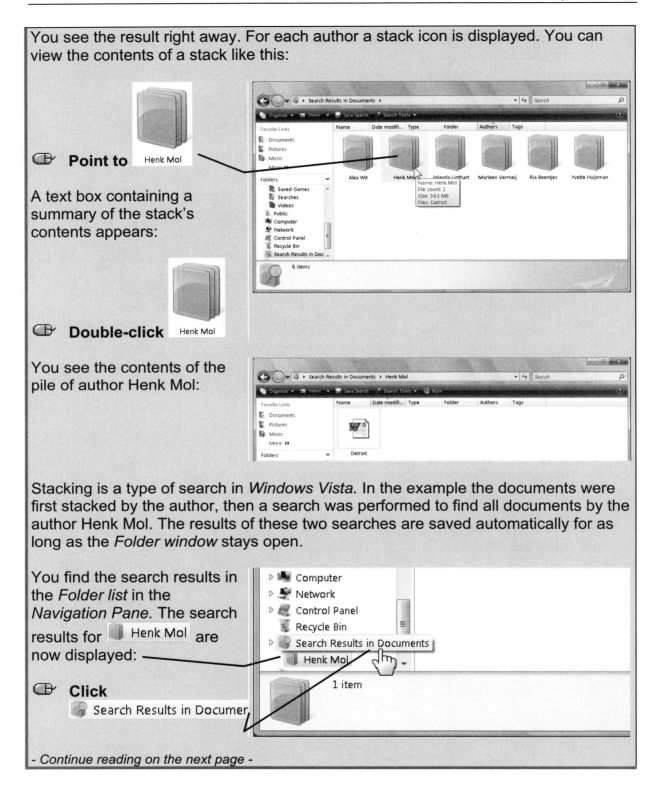

☞ **Point to** Henk Mol

A text box containing a summary of the stack's contents appears:

☞ **Double-click** Henk Mol

You see the contents of the pile of author Henk Mol:

Stacking is a type of search in *Windows Vista*. In the example the documents were first stacked by the author, then a search was performed to find all documents by the author Henk Mol. The results of these two searches are saved automatically for as long as the *Folder window* stays open.

You find the search results in the *Folder list* in the *Navigation Pane*. The search results for ▯ Henk Mol are now displayed:

☞ **Click** 🔍 Search Results in Documer

- Continue reading on the next page -

Now you see the results of the previous search, stacking the documents:

 Double-click another stack

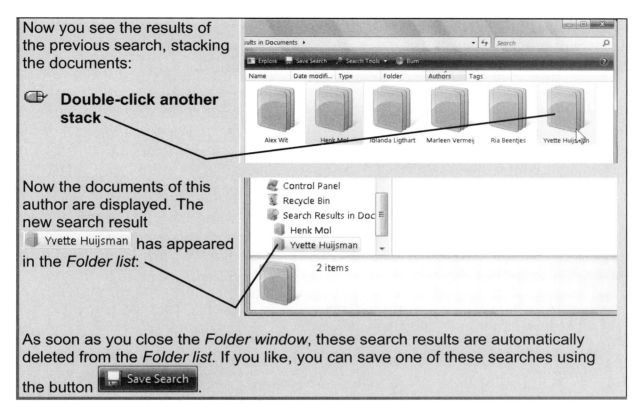

Now the documents of this author are displayed. The new search result Yvette Huijsman has appeared in the *Folder list*:

As soon as you close the *Folder window*, these search results are automatically deleted from the *Folder list*. If you like, you can save one of these searches using the button Save Search.

Tip

Group and sort
Another way to quickly create order in a large folder is to *group* the files. When you group files, the files that belong to a group are displayed in an organized list.

In this example the *File list* is grouped using the column *Authors:*

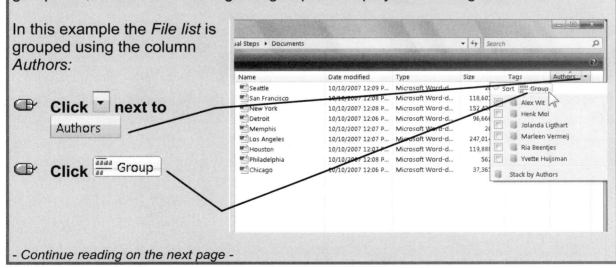

 Click ▾ next to
Authors

 Click ⊞ Group

- Continue reading on the next page -

Now you see different groups, each containing the files of a specific author:

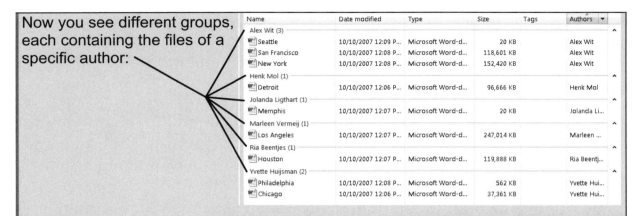

The option 'group' changes the way the files are displayed. For every folder, *Windows Vista* remembers the last view you used for this folder. When you open this folder again later, the files will be displayed as groups again.

If you want to display the files as an alphabetical list, select *sort* instead of group. This is how you sort the files by file name:

👆 **Point to** Name

👆 **Click** ▾ **next to** Name

👆 **Click** △ Sort

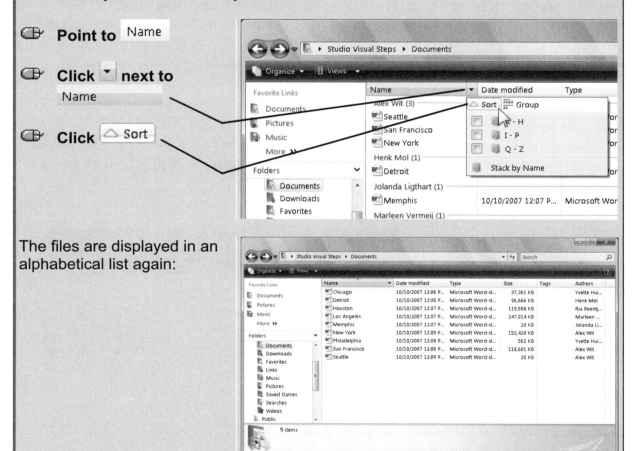

The files are displayed in an alphabetical list again:

Tip

Searching using natural language
In this chapter you have been introduced to the *Search Box* in the top right corner of the *Folder window*. This *Search Box* can be used to filter the contents of the folder currently open, for example by file name or tag.

The *Search Box* has more possibilities. When you activate the option *Use natural language search*, it becomes very easy to perform elaborate searches. From a *Folder window* you can activate this search method like this:

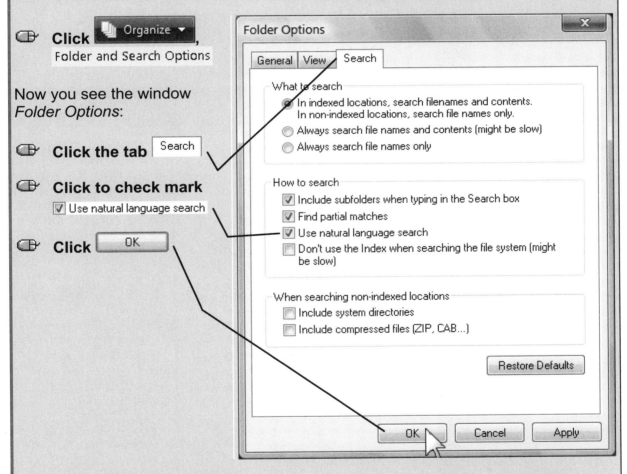

You can still use the *Search Box* like you did before. But now you can phrase the search terms in the same way you would use to describe them to another person.

- Continue reading on the next page -

For example, this allows you to search for

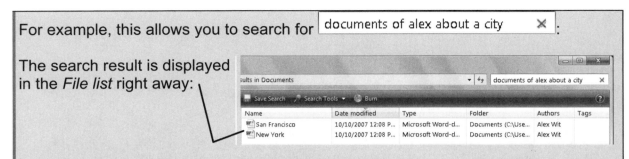

The search result is displayed in the *File list* right away:

Other examples of natural language searches:
- e-mail from Michael received yesterday
- documents that were changed last month
- classical music rated with ****

Please note: when you use the *Search Box*, the search is only performed in the folder that is currently opened in the *Folder window*. If you want to search the whole computer, select Computer in the *Folder list*.

10. Useful Vista Programs

Windows Vista includes many fun and useful programs. In this chapter you will be introduced to three of these programs.

The first program in *Windows Calendar*. This program is a worthy replacement of your hand-held appointment book or organizer. Just like you do in your regular calendar, you can use it to schedule tasks and appointments. But *Windows Calendar* goes one step further: you can also invite other persons for an appointment by e-mail. You can receive invitations for appointments yourself as well. These appointments you receive by e-mail can be imported in your calendar.

Using the *Snipping Tool* you can capture screenshots (snips) of objects on your screen quickly and easily. You can edit these *snips* or save them for use in another program.

Windows Photo Gallery is a useful program to manage, organize and view your photos and videos on your computer.

In this chapter you are introduced to:

- *Windows Calendar*;
- the *Snipping Tool*;
- *Windows Photo Gallery*.

10.1 Windows Calendar

Windows Calendar is a program you can use to replace your paper calendar. You open *Windows Calendar* like this:

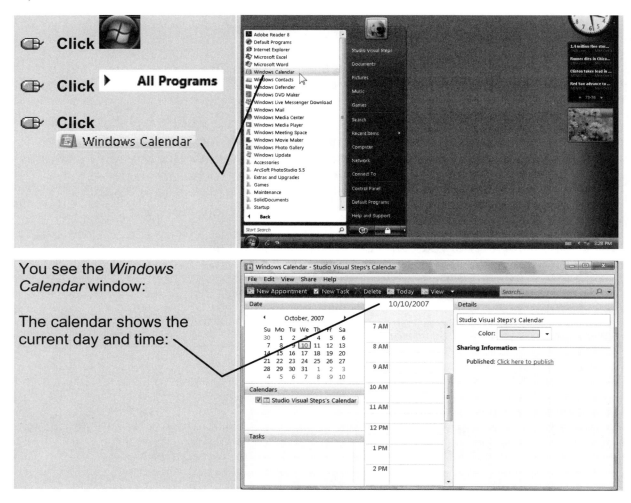

You see the *Windows Calendar* window:

The calendar shows the current day and time:

💡 **Tip**

Changing the view

You can change the view of the calendar using the button 🔲 View ▼ on the toolbar. Is that button invisible? Maximizing the window will show all available buttons on the toolbar:

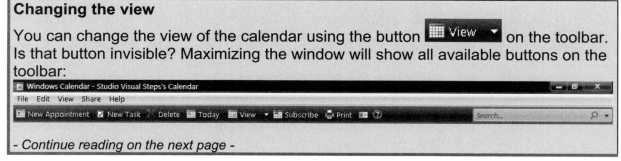

- Continue reading on the next page -

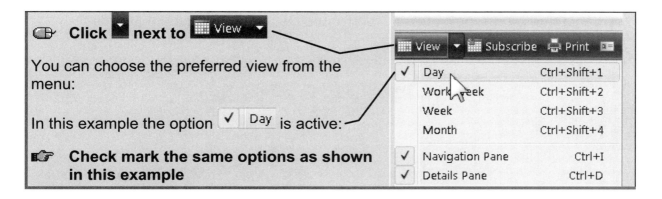

10.2 Adding a New Appointment

You can use *Windows Calendar* to keep track of your appointments. To add a meeting that will take place next Wednesday at 10:00 AM:

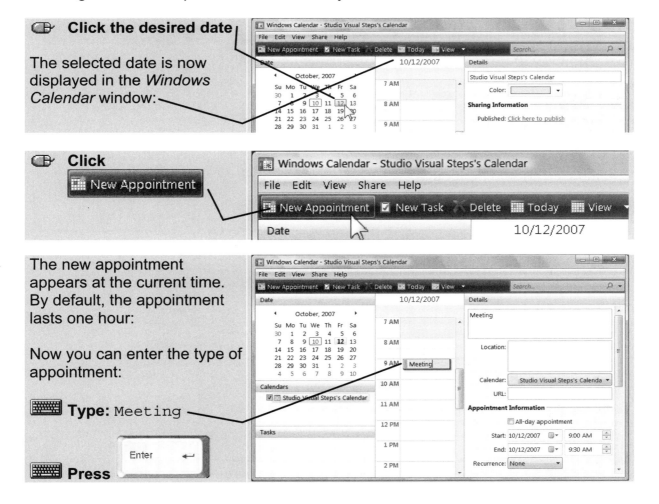

You can enter the details of this meeting in the *Details Pane* on the right side:

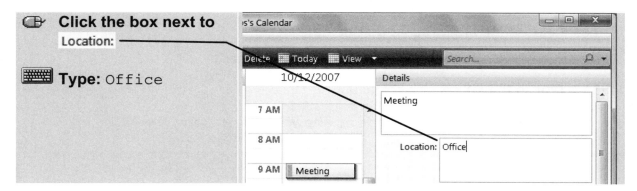

Click the box next to Location:

Type: Office

Below **Appointment Information** you can add more details for this meeting, such as the correct start and end time. You can type these times, but you can work faster by dragging the whole appointment to the correct time. Try that:

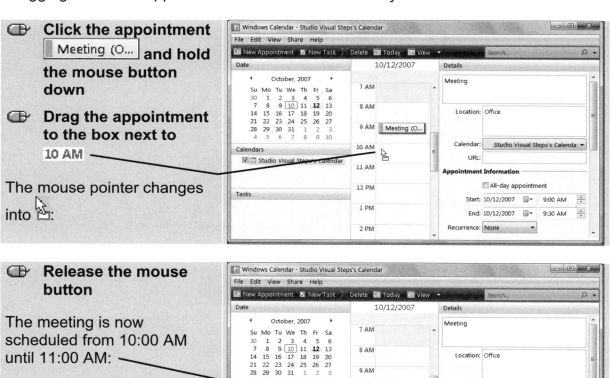

Click the appointment Meeting (O... **and hold the mouse button down**

Drag the appointment to the box next to 10 AM

The mouse pointer changes into :

Release the mouse button

The meeting is now scheduled from 10:00 AM until 11:00 AM:

For a recurring appointment you can click None next to Recurrence:. Then you choose the interval, such as weekly, monthly, etcetra.

Tip

Quickly set a date and time
In *Windows Calendar* you can quickly set a date and time for an appointment:

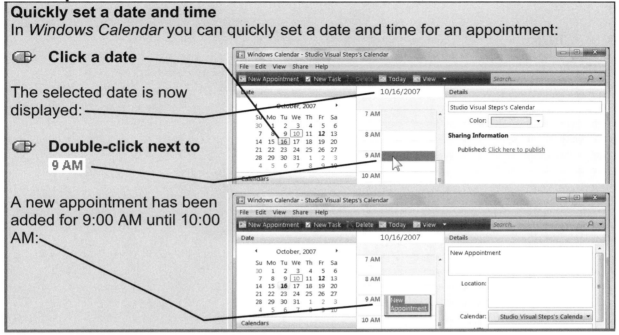

☞ **Click a date**

The selected date is now displayed:

☞ **Double-click next to** 9 AM

A new appointment has been added for 9:00 AM until 10:00 AM:

10.3 Inviting Others for an Appointment

Would you like to invite other people for an appointment? You can do that by e-mail.

➡️ **Please note:**

The people you invite for an appointment must use *Windows Calendar* or a comparable calendar feature, for example the one in *Microsoft Outlook*. Otherwise they can not read the invitation.

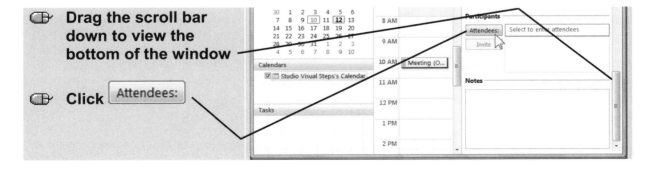

☞ **Drag the scroll bar down to view the bottom of the window**

☞ **Click** Attendees:

A new window appears where you can select a name. To be able to see what happens when you receive an invitation, you are going to add yourself as a contact:

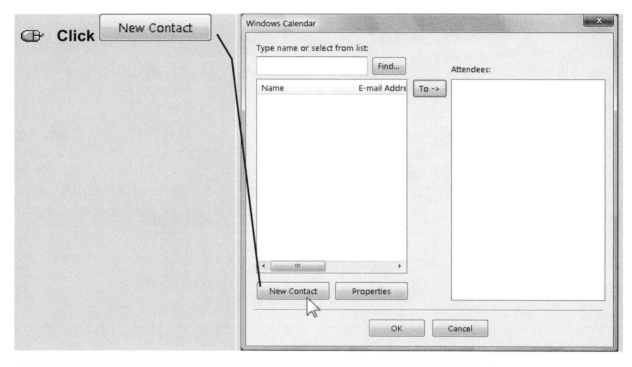

Click New Contact

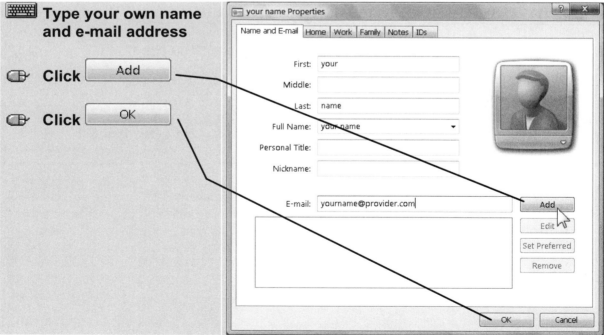

Type your own name and e-mail address

Click Add

Click OK

Your name is added to the *Contacts* folder.

Click your name

Click `To ->`

Your name is added to the list of attendees:

Click `OK`

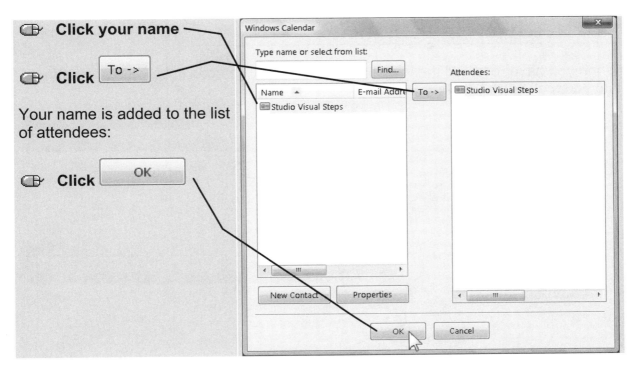

If necessary, you can add more people to the list of attendees.

You send the invitation as follows:

Click `Invite`

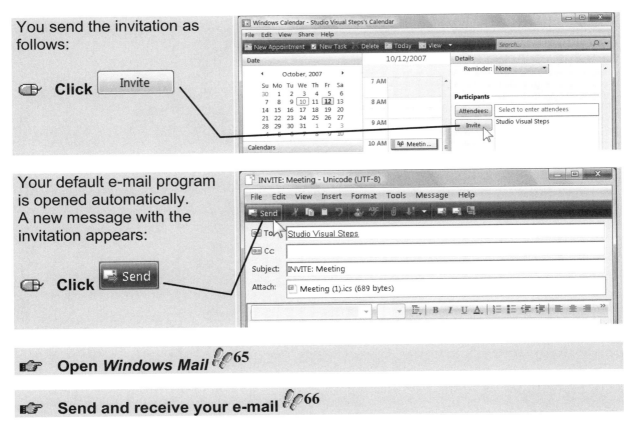

Your default e-mail program is opened automatically.
A new message with the invitation appears:

Click `Send`

☞ **Open** *Windows Mail* ⸨⸩**65**

☞ **Send and receive your e-mail** ⸨⸩**66**

10.4 Receiving an Invitation

When you have received the invitation in your *Inbox*, you can import the appointment into your calendar. Like this:

☞ **Double-click the message**
      INVITE: Meeting

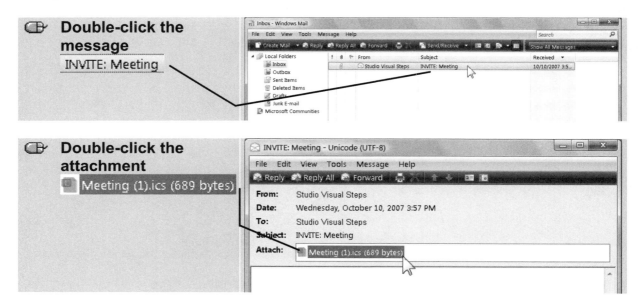

☞ **Double-click the attachment**
      Meeting (1).ics (689 bytes)

The attachment is a .ICS-file. ICS is the extension for *iCalendar*-files. *iCalendar* is the standard for exchanging calendar data. This means you can add appointments in this format to your own calendar.

☞ **Click** Open

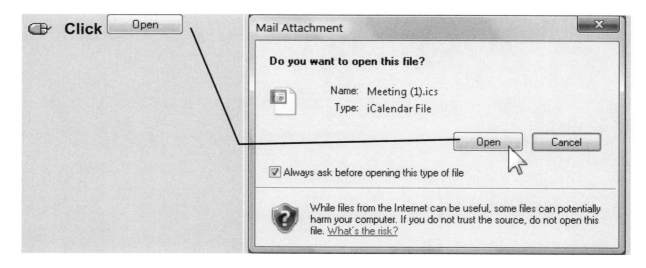

When you receive an invitation by e-mail, you can import it in *Windows Calendar.*

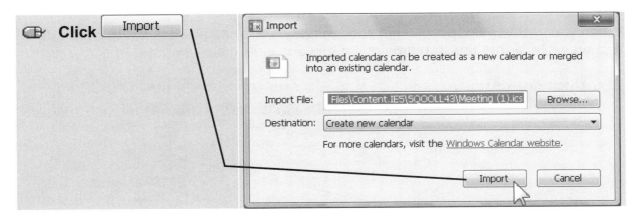

The appointment has been added to your *Windows Calendar.* A new calendar is created for imported appointments:

Here you see the names of the calendars you can view:

Here you see both appointments. The imported appointment is displayed in a different color:

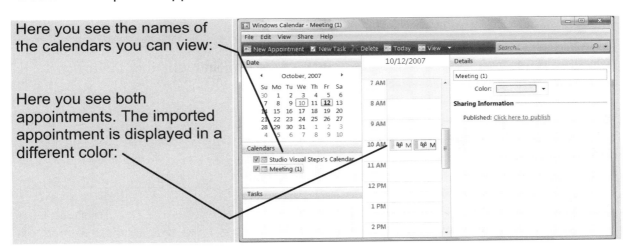

 Tip

Deleting an appointment
To delete an appointment from the calendar:
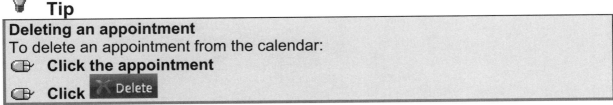

10.5 Setting and Receiving a Reminder

When you enter an appointment in your calendar, you can also set a reminder.
A short while before the start time of the meeting, you will be warned.

☞ Click one of the appointments

☞ Click None next to Reminder:

You see a list:

☞ Click 15 minutes

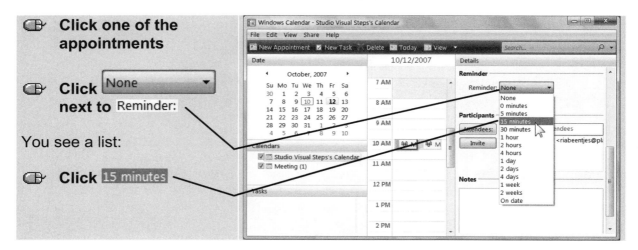

Fifteen minutes before the planned start time of the appointment, this window will appear to remind you:

☞ Click Dismiss

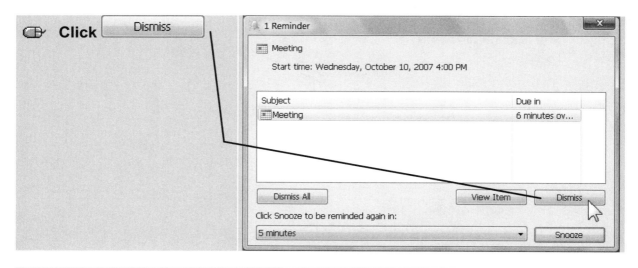

☞ Close all windows 📖1

You have learned how to work with *Windows Calendar*. In the next section you are introduced to the *Snipping Tool*.

10.6 Snipping Tool

Windows Vista contains a useful program that you can use to capture a screenshot (snip) of any object on your screen. You open the *Snipping Tool* like this:

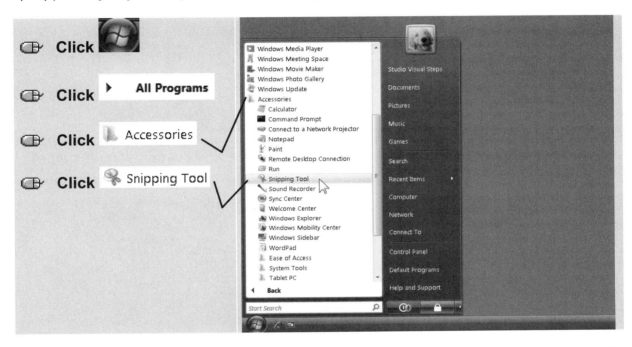

When you start the program for the first time, this window appears:

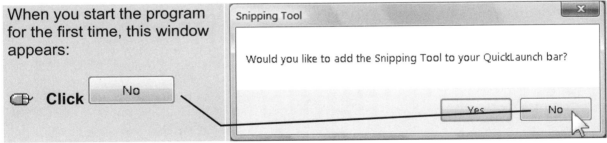

Your screen becomes foggy and you see the *Snipping Tool* window. First you choose the type of snip you want to capture.

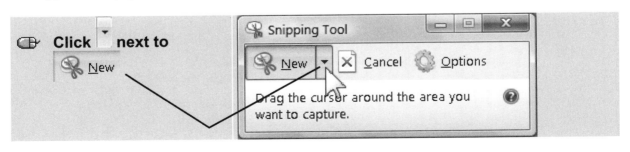

You can choose between a *Free-form snip*, a *Rectangular snip*, a *Window snip* or a *Full-screen snip*. Try the *Free-form snip*:

Now you can draw a free form around an object on your screen, for example part of *Windows Sidebar*.

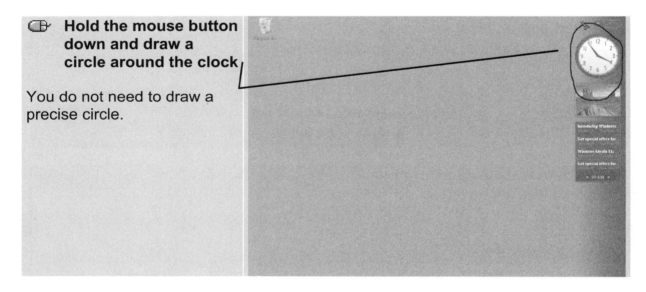

After you capture a snip, it is automatically copied to the mark-up window of the *Snipping Tool*. In this window you can edit the snip in various ways.

Use the pen or highlighter to add something (writing or drawing) to this snip. With the eraser you can erase your addition.

Use the button to save the snip.

With you copy the snip so you can paste it in another program.

Use this button to send the snip by e-mail.

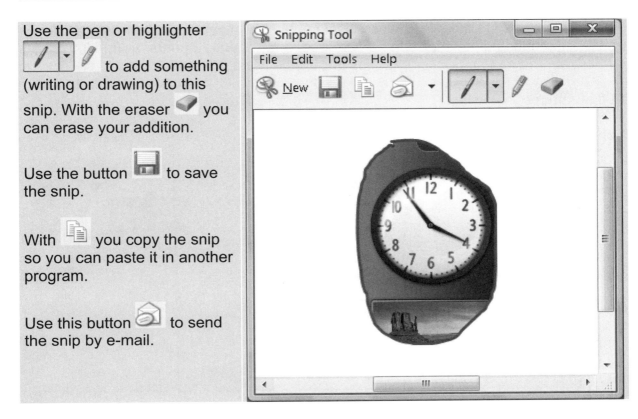

If you are not satisfied with your snip, just try again with a new one. In this window:

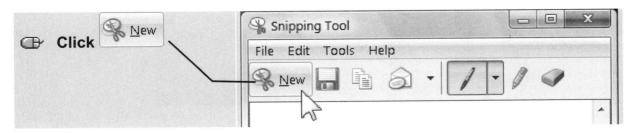

☞ **Click** New

This time select *Window snip*:

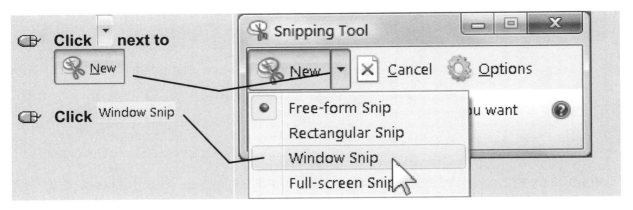

☞ **Click** ▾ **next to** New

☞ **Click** Window Snip

Now you just point to the window you want to capture. As soon as there is a window under the mouse pointer that can be captured, a red frame appears around it. At the same time, the mouse pointer changes into a little hand.

At first, the red frame surrounds the whole desktop. But you are going to 'snip' the clock window:

☞ **Point to the clock**

As soon as you see the red frame around the clock:

☞ **Click the clock**

Now you have a nice image of the clock in the mark-up window:

You can close the *Snipping Tool* window.

☞ **Click** [x]

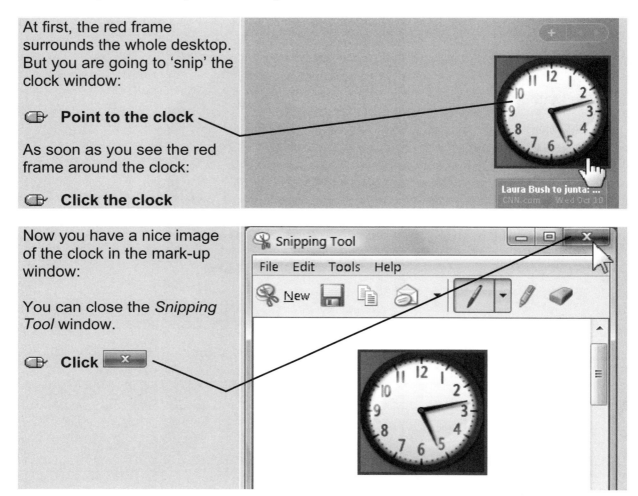

A window appears where you are asked if you want to save the changes to the snip. That is not necessary.

☞ **Click** [No]

You have seen how easy it is to create a snip of any object on your desktop.

10.7 Windows Photo Gallery

Windows Photo Gallery is a useful program to manage, organize and view the images and videos on your computer. You find the program in the list *All programs* in the *Start menu*:

Click

Click ▶ **All Programs**

Click
🖼 Windows Photo Gallery

Windows Photo Gallery is opened. The window displays all photos and videos stored in the folder *Pictures.* In the example only the *Sample Pictures* and *Sample Videos* included in *Vista* are shown. You may see different photos on your computer.

On the left side you see the *Navigation Pane* with the thumbnails of the images next to it:

In the *Information Pane* on the right side, the properties of a selected image will be shown:

If you do not see this part of the window:

Click 🏷 Info **on the toolbar**

Click all arrows ▷ **next to** ▷🖼 All Pictures and Videos , ▷🏷 Tags **and other options in the *Navigation Pane***

All options are now opened.

You can enlarge the thumbnail of an image:

☞ **Place the mouse pointer on an image**

In a few seconds, a larger version of the image and its properties are displayed:

10.8 Tags and Ratings

Finding a specific photo on your computer can be difficult when you have a large photo collection. *Windows Photo Gallery* offers useful tools to quickly find your photos:

☞ **Click** ⊞ ▾

A menu appears:

☞ **Click** Group By

In the submenu you see a list of options to group your photos by:

☞ **Click** Tag

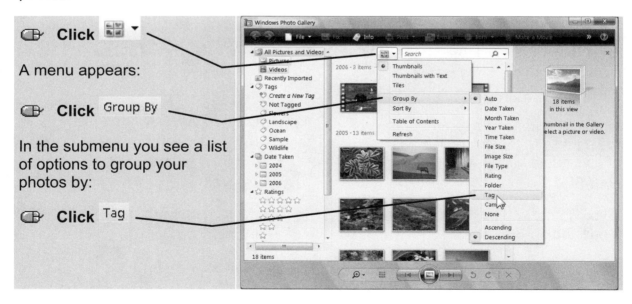

The images are now displayed grouped by their tags. Tags are small pieces of information that you can create yourself and attach to your photos and videos. These tags will make it easier to find and organize your photos and videos. If you specify a tag when you import photos and videos, it will automatically be added to each file.

In this collection five items have the tag *Flowers*
Flowers - 5 items:

Below that you see another tag Landscape - 8 items:

You can create a new tag like this:

Click 🏷 *Create a New Tag*

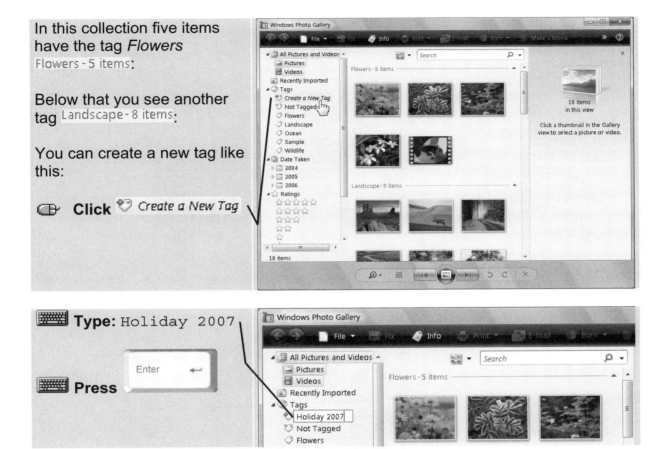

⌨ **Type:** Holiday 2007

⌨ **Press** Enter ↵

A new tag is created. Now you can add this tag to an image:

🖱 **Click an image**

🖱 **Drag the image to** 🏷 Holiday 2007

🖱 **Release the mouse button when you see**

The tag is added to the image. You can do the same thing for a group of images: select the series of images and drag them altogether to 🏷 Holiday 2007.

Tip

Nesting tags

To keep the number of tags manageable, you can 'nest' groups of related tags. This means that you add multiple lower level tags to a top level tag.

You can add a lower level tag by right-clicking an existing tag, and select `Create Tag` in the menu that appears. Here you see an example:

You can also view images grouped by the date each photo was taken, or by its rating (the number of stars). You can add stars to your images in the *Information pane* on the right side:

☞ Click an image

The properties of the image are displayed. If you want to give the image a five-star rating:

☞ Click the fifth star ☆

In the *Navigation Pane* you can choose to display all images with a five-star rating.

10.9 Adding Folders to Windows Photo Gallery

By default, *Photo Gallery* shows all photos and videos in the *Pictures* folder, but you can add other folders to *Photo Gallery* as well. You can add folders one at the time, so you need to repeat the following steps for each folder you want to add.

☞ Click `File ▼`

☞ Click `Add Folder to Gallery...`

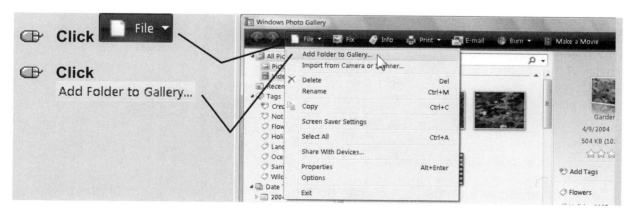

In this window you can choose which folder you want to add:

By clicking the arrows ▷ you show the subfolders:

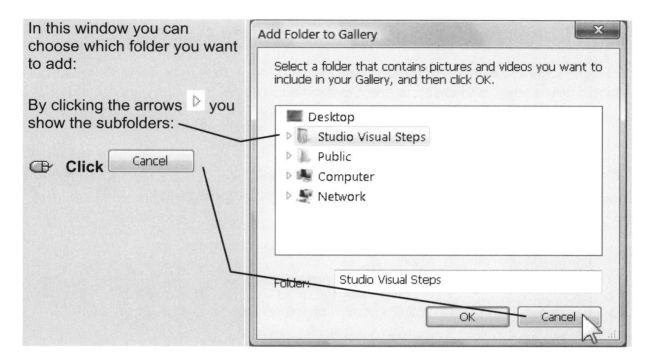

☞ **Click** [Cancel]

⇨ **Please note:**

You should avoid adding certain folders to *Photo Gallery*. The *Local Disk* folder ▷ 💾 Local Disk (C:) , for example, is called the root folder because it represents your entire hard disk. It is possible that you have a very large number of images on your hard disk. For example images from websites that were temporary stored on the hard disk while you were surfing the Internet. Adding this folder to *Photo Gallery* will make it run very slowly. You should avoid adding the *Windows* folder and other system locations to *Photo Gallery* for similar reasons.

10.10 Other Features of Windows Photo Gallery

This was a short introduction to *Windows Photo Gallery*. One of the best things about *Vista* is how easy it is to create a great looking slide show. You can play around some more with some of the other features in *Windows Photo Gallery*. In the *Windows Photo Gallery* window you see these additional buttons:

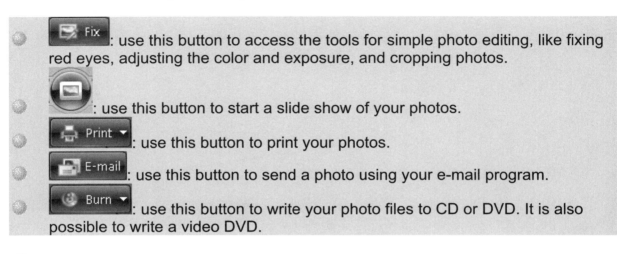

Fix: use this button to access the tools for simple photo editing, like fixing red eyes, adjusting the color and exposure, and cropping photos.

: use this button to start a slide show of your photos.

Print ▼: use this button to print your photos.

E-mail: use this button to send a photo using your e-mail program.

Burn ▼: use this button to write your photo files to CD or DVD. It is also possible to write a video DVD.

💡 Tip

Would you like to find out more about working with photos?
In the book **Photos, Videos and Music with Windows Vista for SENIORS** (ISBN 978 90 5905 065 5) you will learn a lot more about *Windows Photo Gallery*.

This book is centered around the multimedia programs included in *Windows Vista*. Subjects like photo and video editing, viewing slide shows and videos are explained in a simple, step by step manner. Other subjects include playing music, copying music from audio CDs to your hard disk and writing an audio CD with your favorite tracks. You can do all of this with *Vista*. You can turn your computer into a great source of entertainment!

For more information about this book, visit our website **www.visualsteps.com**.

☞ **Close all windows** 1

In this chapter you have been introduced to some very useful *Vista* programs. In the next section you can practice a little more with some of the things you learned.

10.11 Exercises

Have you forgotten how to do something? Use the number beside the footsteps to look it up in *Appendix B How Do I Do That Again?*

Exercise: A New Appointment

In this exercise you can practice using *Windows Calendar*.

☑ Open *Windows Calendar*. 🐾 **67**

☑ Display the day after tomorrow in the calendar. 🐾 **68**

☑ Create a new appointment and name it *lunch*. 🐾 **69**

☑ Enter *Beverly Hills Hotel* as the location for this appointment. 🐾 **70**

☑ Change the time for the appointment by dragging the appointment to 12:00 noon. 🐾 **71**

☑ Close *Windows Calendar*. 🐾 **1**

Exercise: An Invitation

Try to send, receive and import an invitation.

☑ Open *Windows Calendar*. 🐾 **67**

☑ Display the day after tomorrow in the calendar. 🐾 **68**

☑ Click the lunch appointment you created in the previous exercise.

☑ Invite yourself to this appointment. 🐾 **72**

☑ Send and receive your e-mail. 🐾 **66**

☑ Import the appointment you received by e-mail in your calendar. 🐾 **73**

☑ Close *Windows Calendar*. 🐾 **1**

Exercise: Snips

In this exercise you create a *Window snip* and a *Free-form snip*.

✔ Open *Windows Calendar.* 𝒷𝒷 67

✔ Open the *Snipping Tool.* 𝒷𝒷 74

✔ Create a *Window snip* of the *Windows Calendar* window. 𝒷𝒷 75

✔ Create a *Free-form snip* of the *Date* box. 𝒷𝒷 76

✔ Close *Windows Calendar.* 𝒷𝒷 1

✔ Close the *Snipping Tool.* 𝒷𝒷 1

✔ Do not save the changes. 𝒷𝒷 77

Exercise: Photo Gallery

In this exercise you are going to add a tag and a rating to an image.

✔ Open *Windows Photo Gallery.* 𝒷𝒷 78

✔ Display the *Information Pane* (if necessary). 𝒷𝒷 79

✔ View a random photo in the *Information Pane.* 𝒷𝒷 80

✔ Give this photo a three-star rating. 𝒷𝒷 81

✔ Add the tag *Holiday 2007* to the photo. 𝒷𝒷 82

✔ Close *Windows Photo Gallery.* 𝒷𝒷 1

10.12 Background Information

Glossary	
Contact	A collection of information about a person or organization. Contacts are stored in the *Contacts* folder in your *Personal Folder*.
Free-form snip	In *Snipping Tool*: use this type of snip to draw an irregular line, such as a circle or a triangle, around an object that you want to capture.
Full-screen snip	In *Snipping Tool*: use this type of snip to capture the entire screen. This is similar to pressing the Print Screen key.
ICS file	ICS is the extension for an *iCalendar* file. *iCalendar* is the standard for exchanging calendar data.
Importing	In *Windows Calendar*: adding an invitation you received from another person to your calendar.
Information Pane	In *Windows Photo Gallery*: part of the window where you can view the properties of a photo.
Navigation Pane	In *Windows Photo Gallery*: part of the window where you can choose from which folder you want to display the photos in the main window.
Rating	Five-star rating system that can be used to indicate which photos you like best. Up to five stars for the highest, one for the lowest. A photo may also be *not rated*. Helps to manage your photos.
Rectangular snip	In *Snipping Tool*: use this type of snip to draw a precise line, or rectangle, around an object that you want to capture.
Reminder	In *Windows Calendar* you can set a reminder for an appointment. This reminder is displayed in a window, on a time you specified before the start of the planned appointment.
Snip	Object captured using the *Snipping Tool*.

- Continue reading on the next page -

Snipping Tool	Program in *Windows Vista* you can use to create a screen capture (snip) of any object on your screen.
Tag	Word or short phrase you add to the properties of a file. For example, you can use tags to organize your photo collection and find certain photos more easily.
Window snip	In *Snipping Tool*: use this type of snip to select a window, such as a browser window or dialog box, that you want to capture.
Windows Calendar	Program in *Windows Vista* to schedule your appointments and tasks. You can also invite others by e-mail for an appointment, and receive invitations yourself.
Windows Photo Gallery	Program in *Windows Vista* to manage, organize, edit and view the images and videos on your computer.

Source: Windows Help and Support

10.13 Tips

 Tip

Pasting a snip in a *WordPad* document
You can copy and paste a snip you created in the *Snipping Tool* in a *WordPad* document:

☞ **Open the *Snipping Tool*** 👣74

☞ **Create a *Window snip* of the clock** 👣75

👆 **Click** 📄 **on the *Snipping Tool* toolbar**

☞ **Open *WordPad*** 👣2

👆 **Click** Edit

👆 **Click** Paste

Now the snip is in the document: ———

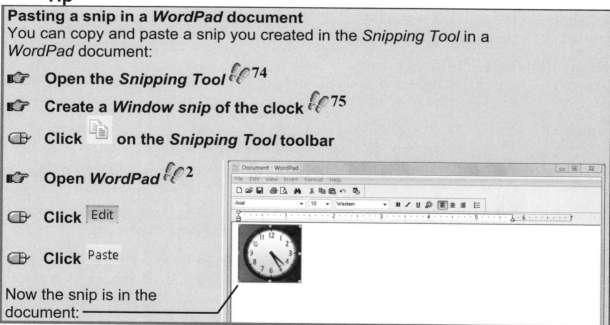

11. Word Processing with WordPad

All word processing programs work more or less the same. The word processing program *WordPad* is included in *Windows Vista* like it is in all versions of *Windows*. *WordPad* can be considered *Microsoft Word's* little sister. That is why it is an excellent program to practice with. The basic features of the two programs are the same, but *Microsoft Word* is a more extensive program.

In the book **Windows Vista for SENIORS**, basic tasks like typing and editing text were covered. Furthermore, attention was given to formatting text, showing you how to create bold, italicized or underlined text.

In this chapter you go one step further. You will read how to create bulleted lists and indentations in text. You will also see how you can make neat rows and columns for tables.

In this chapter you will learn how to:

- create a bulleted list;
- change the format of paragraphs;
- indent a paragraph;
- create a normal or hanging first line indent;
- indent a paragraph on the right side;
- create tables;
- set tab stops;
- use the portrait or landscape page orientation.

⇨ Please note:

To be able to work with this chapter, the folder ⌐ Practice files should be copied from the CD-ROM you received with this book to the folder *Documents* in your *Personal Folder*.
For step by step instructions, please refer to **Appendix A Copying the Practice Files to Your Computer** at the end of this book.

11.1 Selecting Text

The book **Windows Vista for SENIORS** provided an extensive explanation on how to select text in *WordPad*. To refresh your memory, here is a summary:

Action:	What is selected:
drag the mouse over text	one or more characters or words
click a word twice	the word
click a word three times	the paragraph
click the margin once	the line
click the margin twice	the paragraph
click the margin three times	the complete text
drag the mouse in the margin	multiple lines

11.2 Lists

WordPad includes a special format for lists like this one:
- first
- second

You are going to learn how to create these lists. First you open *WordPad*:

☞ **Click** , ▶ **All Programs**

You see the list of all programs that are installed on your computer:

☞ **Click** Accessories

The contents of the folder *Accessories* are displayed:

☞ **Click** WordPad

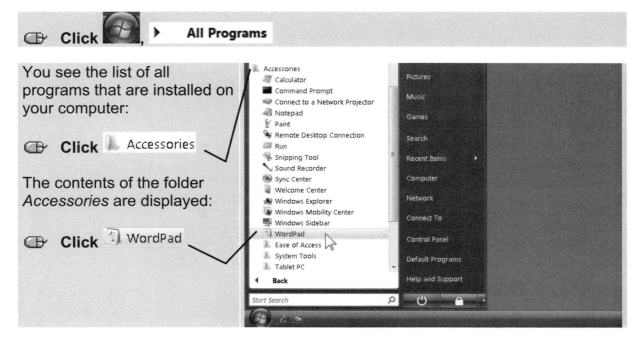

You see the *WordPad* window.

Please note:

Make sure all bars are visible in *WordPad*:

Click View

Click to check mark Toolbar, Format Bar, Ruler **en** Status Bar

First you type the text for the list. You format the text afterwards:

Type:
List
first
second
third

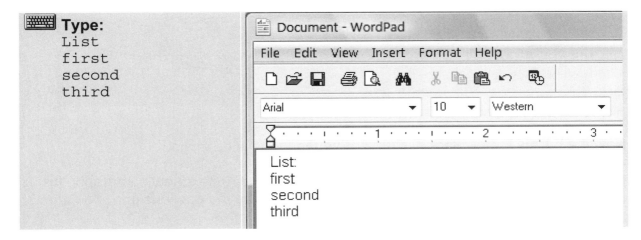

To be able to add bullets to the lines, you have to select the lines first:

Select the last three
lines 83

Click

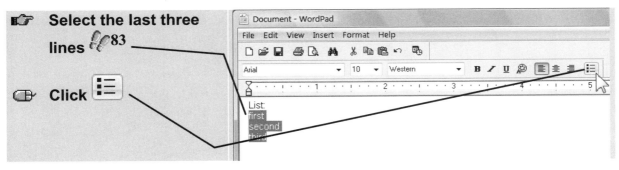

The lines are indented and a
bullet • is added.

A bullet is a small black circle.

Note that the button is
now 'pressed':

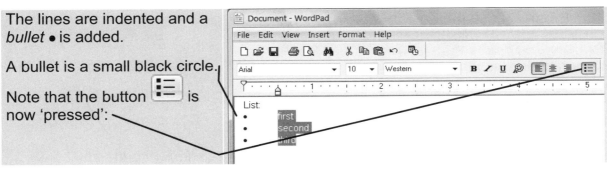

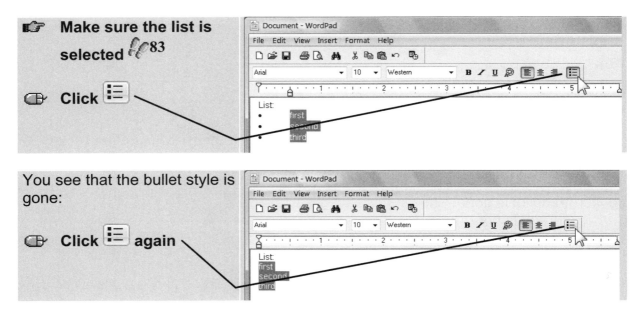

☞ **Make sure the list is selected** 𝓁𝓁83

🖰 **Click** ⊞

You see that the bullet style is gone:

🖰 **Click** ⊞ **again**

Now the bullets (small black circles) are added to the lines again.

Formatting is associated with a paragraph. When you create a new paragraph, this paragraph will automatically get the same formatting as the previous one. You create a new paragraph by pressing the │ Enter ← │ button. Take a look at this:

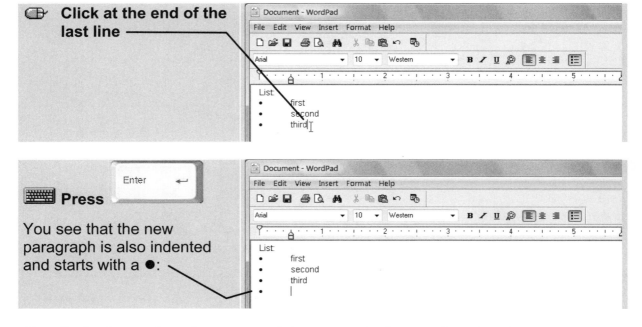

🖰 **Click at the end of the last line**

⌨ **Press** │ Enter ← │

You see that the new paragraph is also indented and starts with a ●:

Usually the formatting of a paragraph is automatically transferred to the next paragraph. But for bulleted lists a special rule applies.

11.3 Never an Empty List

A special rule applies to bulleted lists: a bullet always has to be followed by text. If you do not type anything in the new paragraph, it will get the regular formatting instead of the bullet style. It is not possible to create an empty list, take a look:

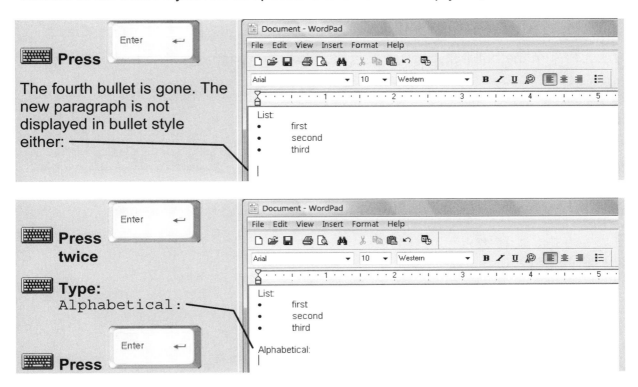

⌨ **Press** Enter ↵

The fourth bullet is gone. The new paragraph is not displayed in bullet style either: ——

⌨ **Press twice** Enter ↵

⌨ **Type:**
Alphabetical: —

⌨ **Press** Enter ↵

11.4 Applying Bullet Style in Advance

You can also turn the next paragraph into a bulleted list in advance. Give it a try:

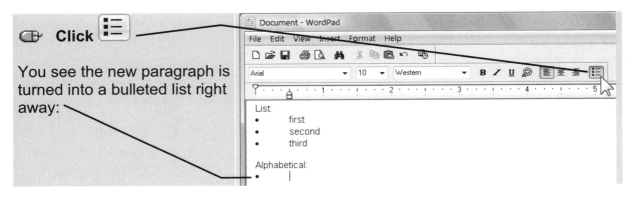

🖱 **Click** ▤ ——

You see the new paragraph is turned into a bulleted list right away: —

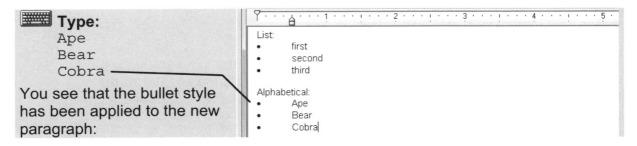

Type:
Ape
Bear
Cobra

You see that the bullet style has been applied to the new paragraph:

You can turn the bullet style off to give the next paragraph regular formatting:

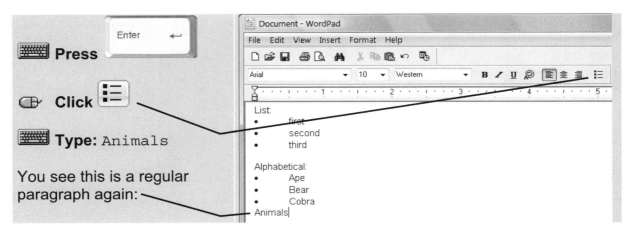

Press [Enter ←]

Click [≔]

Type: Animals

You see this is a regular paragraph again:

You have learned how to create bulleted lists. You do not need to save this document.

☞ **Start a new file, and select the document type Rich Text Document** 🐾84

In a Rich Text Document you can format the text. By default, an empty Rich Text Document is opened when you open *WordPad*. If you choose a different document type when you start a new file, for example Text Document or Unicode Text Document, you can not format the text. Then the *Format* toolbar will not be available in the *WordPad* window.

💡 **Tip**

Bulleted list with aligned text below

If you want to create a bulleted list with an explanation below each item, you can align the explanation with the list text by pressing the keys [⇧ Shift] and [Enter ←] simultaneously when you create the new paragraph for the explanation.

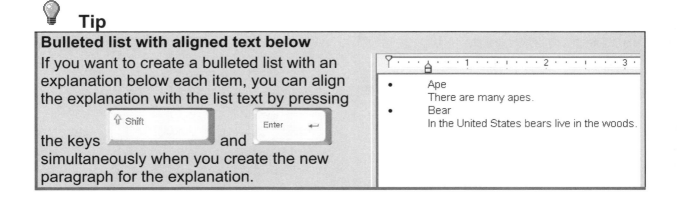

11.5 Paragraph Formatting

In *WordPad* you can *align* the paragraphs. Alignment is the way the lines of a paragraph are arranged between the margins:

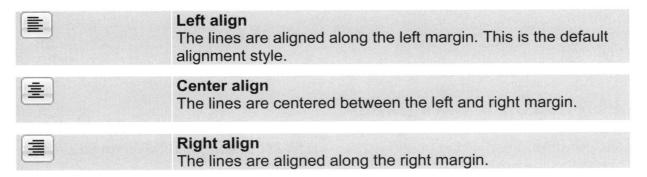

Left align
The lines are aligned along the left margin. This is the default alignment style.

Center align
The lines are centered between the left and right margin.

Right align
The lines are aligned along the right margin.

First you type a practice text:

Type: This is a short paragraph.

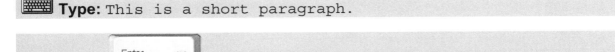

Press

Type: A long paragraph may consist of several sentences. This is the second sentence of the same paragraph. On the screen, the paragraph consists of several lines.

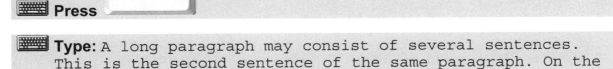

Press

You are going to right align the paragraph. Before you can align an existing paragraph, you have to select it first.

➡️ **Please note:**

Select first...then act.

☞ **Select the second paragraph** ✐85

🖱️ **Click**

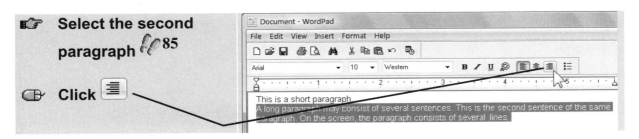

You see that both lines are aligned along the right margin:

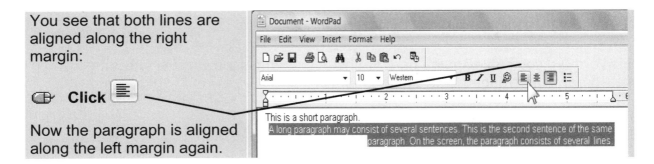

☞ **Click** ▤

Now the paragraph is aligned along the left margin again.

11.6 Indenting Paragraphs

It is possible to add an indentation to the first line of a paragraph, which means the text in the line is placed farther away from the margin.
You can adjust the indentation of paragraphs and lines using these special buttons on the ruler.

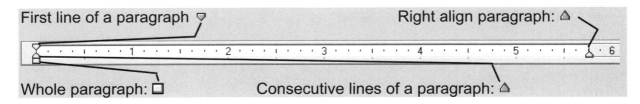

First line of a paragraph ▽

Right align paragraph: △

Whole paragraph: □   Consecutive lines of a paragraph: △

You can drag these buttons to change the indentation of the paragraph.
To be able to indent an existing paragraph, you have to select it first. The paragraph is already selected. Give it a try:

☞ **Place the mouse pointer on** □

☞ **Drag the button** □ **to the right up to the 1**

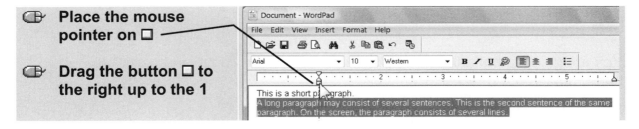

You see that both other buttons ▽ and △ move as well.

The paragraph now shows a 1 inch indent, measured from the left margin:

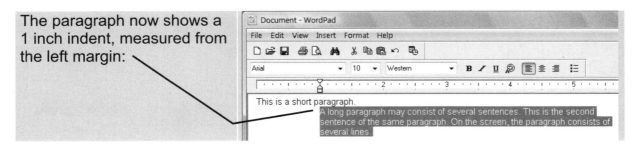

11.7 Hanging Indentation

You can also make a separate setting for the first line of a paragraph. This is how you create a 'hanging' indentation:

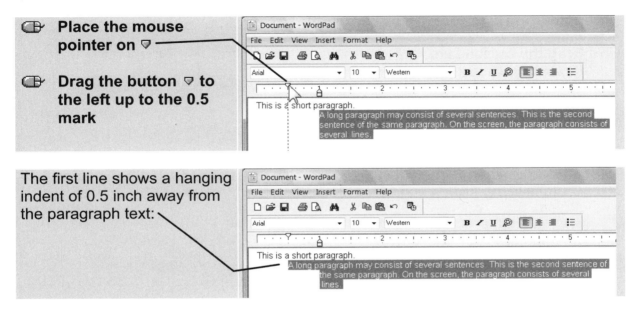

Place the mouse pointer on ▽

Drag the button ▽ **to the left up to the 0.5 mark**

The first line shows a hanging indent of 0.5 inch away from the paragraph text:

11.8 Indenting the First Line

You can also use normal indentation for the first line of a paragraph:

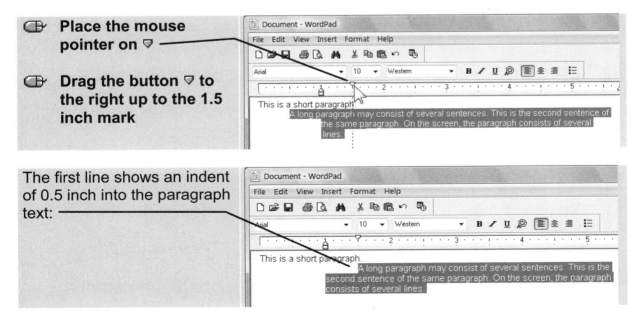

Place the mouse pointer on ▽

Drag the button ▽ **to the right up to the 1.5 inch mark**

The first line shows an indent of 0.5 inch into the paragraph text:

11.9 Undoing the Indentation

You can return the alignment of the paragraph back to the left margin like this:

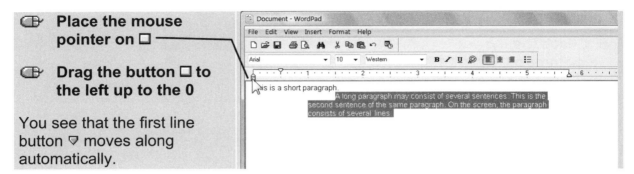

☞ **Place the mouse pointer on □**

☞ **Drag the button □ to the left up to the 0**

You see that the first line button ▽ moves along automatically.

The button □ controls the setting for the complete paragraph. Both other buttons ▽ and △ automatically slide along with it.

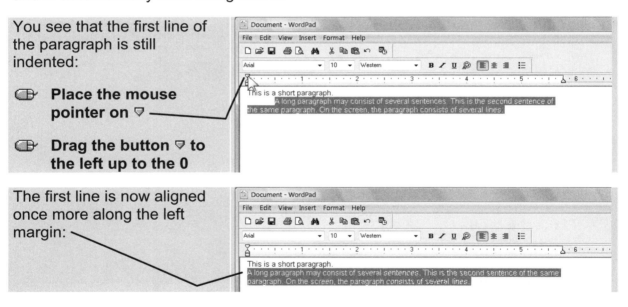

You see that the first line of the paragraph is still indented:

☞ **Place the mouse pointer on ▽**

☞ **Drag the button ▽ to the left up to the 0**

The first line is now aligned once more along the left margin:

11.10 Right Indentation

You can also add an indentation on the right side of a paragraph. Give that a try:

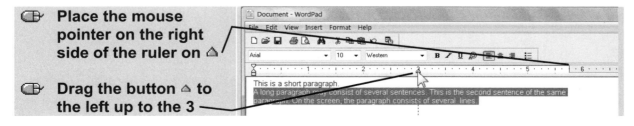

☞ **Place the mouse pointer on the right side of the ruler on △**

☞ **Drag the button △ to the left up to the 3**

You see that the paragraph
has become 3 inches
narrower:

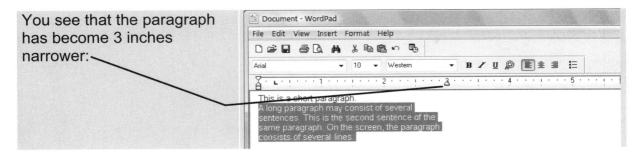

You have learned how to indent paragraphs now.

 Start a new file, do not save the changes 84

💡 **Tip**

Do you want to indent all paragraphs?
First select the whole text, then set the indentation on the ruler.

11.11 Tables

A table consists of horizontal rows and vertical columns. It is not very difficult to
create a table with the entries in the columns exactly outlined, for example to keep
the score of a game:

Scores	Bob	Sarah	Joe	Lynn	Chris
Game 1	20	10	30	20	15
Game 2	10	20	10	20	25
	---	---	---	---	---
Total	30	30	40	40	40

You create this type of tables using the Tab key [⇤ Tab].

The Tab key is to the left of
the letter Q:

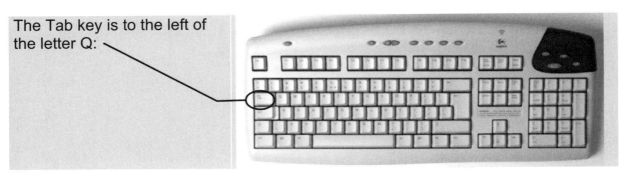

When you try to create a table using spaces, it will not be possible to precisely outline the entries in the columns. The table will then often look like this:

Scores	Bob	Sarah	Joe	Lynn	Chris
Game 1	20	10	30	20	15
Game 2	10	20	10	20	25
	---	---	---	---	---
Total	30	30	40	40	40

You are going to create a score table yourself:

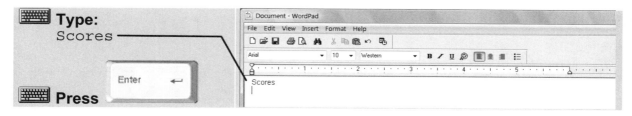

Now you can type the names. Use the ⟵Tab key after every name:

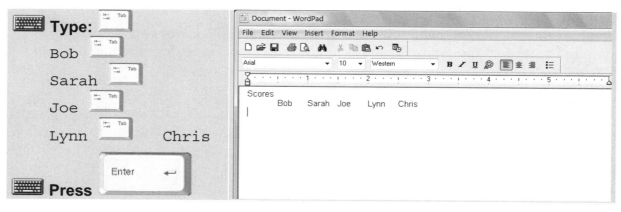

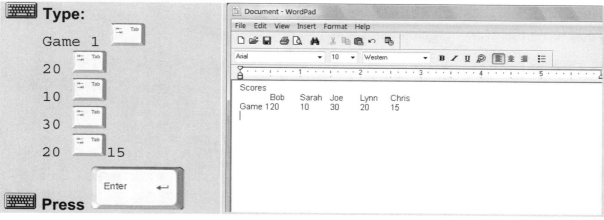

You see that the scores are positioned exactly below the names. That is because you are using the Tab key. You can create another three rows below:

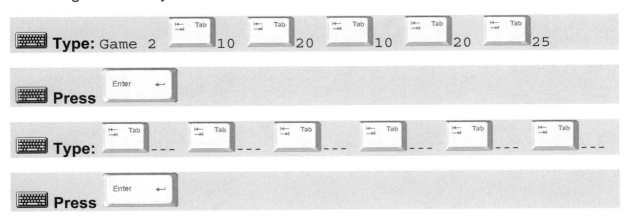

Finally you type the row with the total scores:

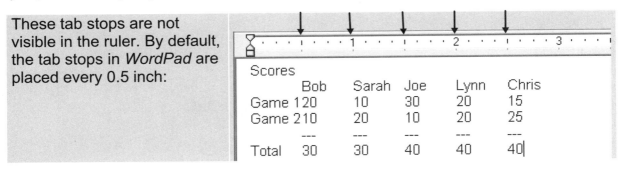

The columns are nicely aligned. Sometimes you might want to change the space between the columns.

11.12 Tab Stops

You see that the entries in the columns are placed exactly below the column titles. That is because of the tab stops in *WordPad*. A 'tab stop' is the location the cursor jumps to when you press the Tab key.

These tab stops are not visible in the ruler. By default, the tab stops in *WordPad* are placed every 0.5 inch:

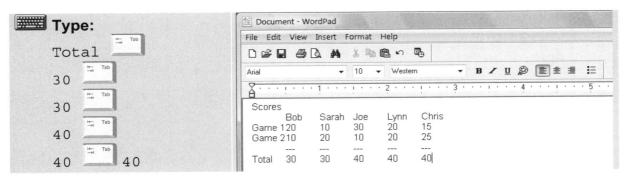

In this case, the names and scores fit in between the tab stops. See what happens if you make one of the names longer:

 Click behind Sarah

Type: Jones

You see that the alignment in the last three columns is off:

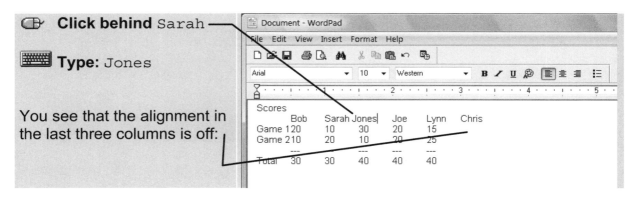

You can solve this problem by creating tab stops on the ruler yourself. You can place a new tab stop on the ruler by clicking the ruler.

➡️ **Please note:**

Select first... then act.

☞ **Select rows and columns of the table**

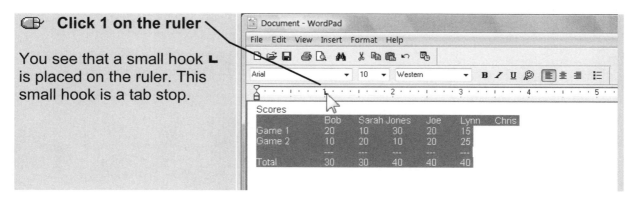

Now you can place the tab stops:

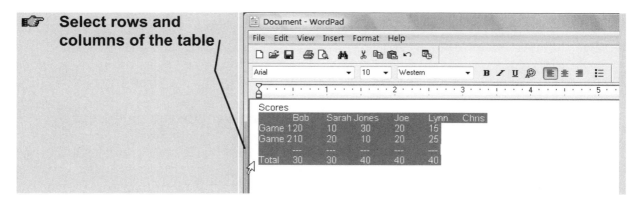 **Click 1 on the ruler**

You see that a small hook **L** is placed on the ruler. This small hook is a tab stop.

Now you can place the other tab stops, for example every inch:

 **Click 2, 3, 4 and 5**

You see that the space between the columns is enlarged and the last three columns are nicely aligned again:

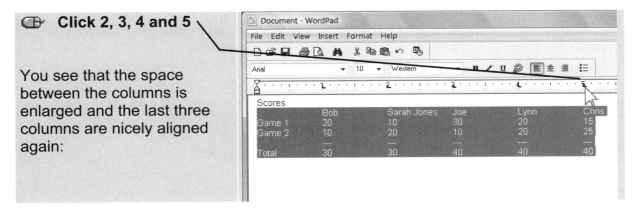

You can adjust the space between the columns by dragging the tab stops on the ruler:

➡ **Please note:**

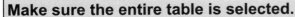
Make sure the entire table is selected.

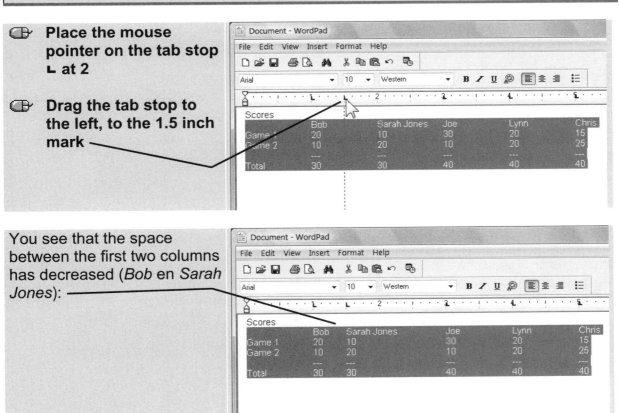

☞ **Place the mouse pointer on the tab stop L at 2**

☞ **Drag the tab stop to the left, to the 1.5 inch mark**

You see that the space between the first two columns has decreased (*Bob* en *Sarah Jones*):

11.13 Removing a Tab Stop

Tab stops can also be removed, for example when you have placed one tab stop too many. Give it a try:

 Please note:

Make sure the entire table is selected.

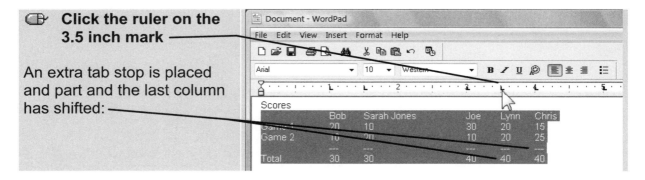

☞ **Click the ruler on the 3.5 inch mark**

An extra tab stop is placed and part and the last column has shifted:

You can remove the tab stop at 3.5 inches by dragging it out of the ruler:

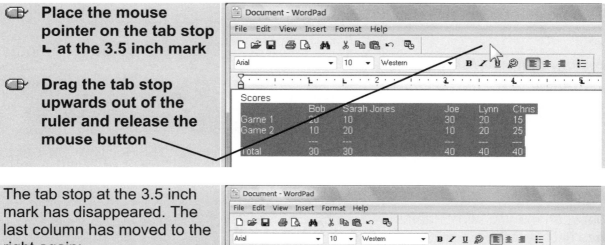

☞ **Place the mouse pointer on the tab stop ⌞ at the 3.5 inch mark**

☞ **Drag the tab stop upwards out of the ruler and release the mouse button**

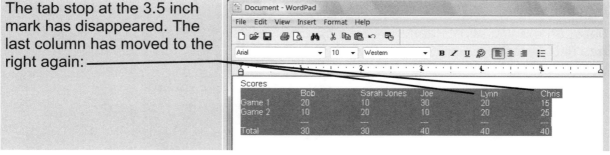

The tab stop at the 3.5 inch mark has disappeared. The last column has moved to the right again:

11.14 Selecting All

There is one important rule of thumb to avoid confusion when working with tables:

Before you change anything: **select the entire table first**.

See what will happen if you forget to do that:

☞ **Select the row *Game 1***
      7

🖰 **Place the mouse pointer on the tab stop ∟ at 3**

🖰 **Drag the tab stop to the 3.5 inch mark**

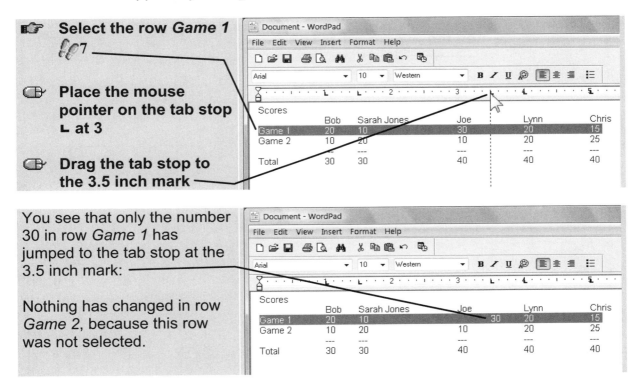

You see that only the number 30 in row *Game 1* has jumped to the tab stop at the 3.5 inch mark:

Nothing has changed in row *Game 2*, because this row was not selected.

You can undo this 'shift' by dragging the tab stop back to its previous position:

🖰 **Click the tab stop ∟ at the 3.5 inch mark and drag it to 3**

Now the columns are nicely aligned again:

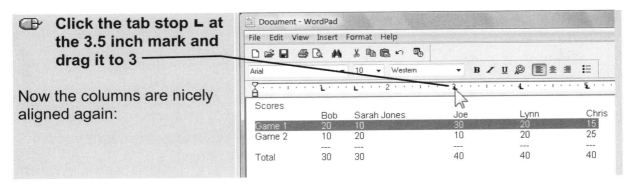

☞ **Save this table in your practice files folder and name it *Scores*** *86*

11.15 Paper Orientation

Usually you work with *Portrait* oriented pages. If you work with tables however, you might find that the page is not wide enough. In that case you can choose the *Landscape* orientation instead:

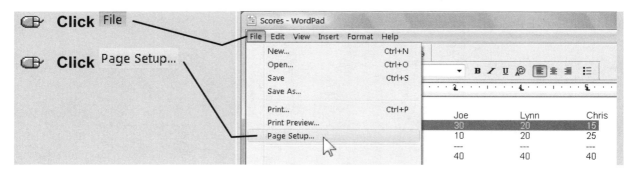

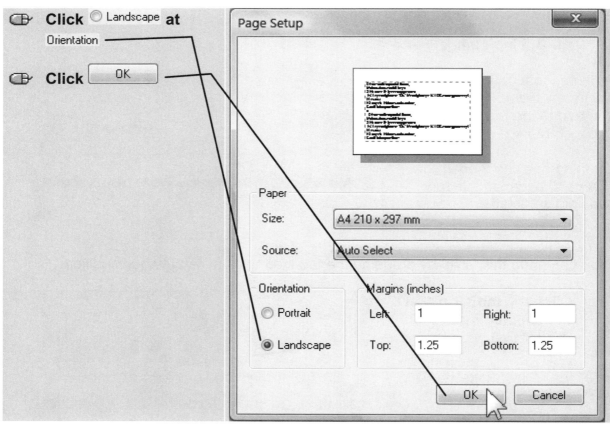

In the *Print Preview* you can see the effect of this change:

☞ **Click** 🔍

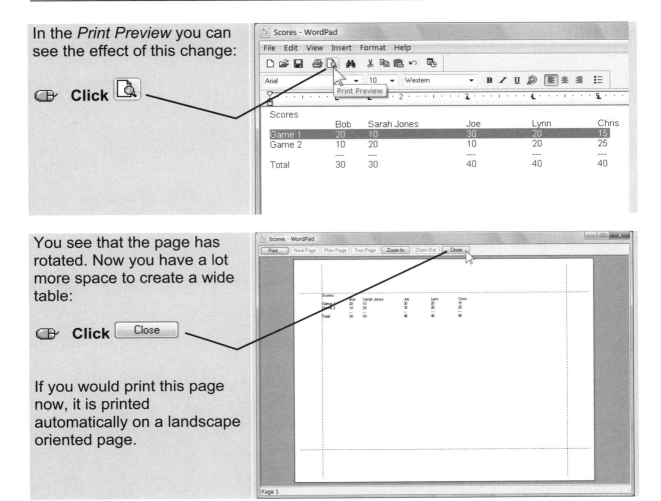

You see that the page has rotated. Now you have a lot more space to create a wide table:

☞ **Click** [Close]

If you would print this page now, it is printed automatically on a landscape oriented page.

☞ **Save the changes** 𝓁𝓁⁸⁷ **and close** *WordPad* 𝓁𝓁¹

In this chapter you have learned how to create bulleted lists and use indentations in *WordPad*. In the next exercises you can repeat what you have learned.

11.16 Exercises

Have you forgotten how to do something? Use the number beside the footsteps to look it up in *Appendix B How Do I Do That Again?*

Exercise: Bulleted List

In this exercise you add the correct layout to a list:

✔ Open *WordPad*. $\mathscr{U}^2$

✔ From the folder *Practice files, Chapter 11*, open the text titled: *Practice File Lists.* $\mathscr{U}$**88**

> **Adding new peripherals to your computer**
> You can add the following peripherals to your computer:
> printer
> double-layer dvd-writer
> webcam
> Are you interested in digital photography? Then you might consider a:
> scanner
> photo printer
> •   These peripherals are available at your local computer retailer or camera shop.

✔ Create a nice bulleted list using the buttons mentioned in the text. $\mathscr{U}$**89**

✔ Remove the bullet in the last paragraph. $\mathscr{U}$**90**

> **Adding new peripherals to your computer**
> You can add the following peripherals to your computer:
> •   printer
> •   double-layer dvd-writer
> •   webcam
> Are you interested in digital photography? Then you might consider a:
> •   scanner
> •   photo printer
> These peripherals are available at your local computer retailer or camera shop.

✔ Close the text and save the changes. $\mathscr{U}$**87**

Exercise: A Neatly Aligned Table

Use this exercise to practice working with tables.

✔ Open the text you previously saved with the name *scores*. 📖 **88**

✔ Decrease the space between the columns with tab stops placed at the: 0.75 - 1.5 - 2.5 - 3.25 - 4 inch marks: 📖 **91**

```
Scores
            Bob         Sarah Jones   Joe       Lynn        Chris
Game 1      20          10            30        20          15
Game 2      10          20            10        20          25
            ---         ---           ---       ---         ---
Total       30          30            40        40          40
```

✔ Print this text. 📖 **92**

✔ Close the text and save the changes. 📖 **87**

Exercise: Indenting Paragraphs

In this exercise you add indentations to the paragraphs.

✔ From the folder *Practice files, Chapter 11*, open the text titled: *Practice File Indentations.* 📖 **88**

✔ Create the following indentations for the paragraphs in the text: 📖 **93**

Halloween
Halloween, is a holiday celebrated on the night of October 31. Traditional activities include trick-or-treating, Halloween festivals, bonfires, costume parties, visiting "haunted houses", viewing horror films, and going on haunted hayrides.
Halloween originated from the Pagan festival Samhain, celebrated among the Celts of Ireland and Great Britain. Irish and Scottish immigrants carried versions of the tradition to North America in the nineteenth century. Other western countries embraced the holiday in the late twentieth century.
Halloween is now celebrated in several parts of the western world, most commonly in Ireland, the United States, Canada, Puerto Rico, the United Kingdom and sometimes in Australia and New Zealand. In recent years, the holiday has also been celebrated in various other parts of Western Europe.

✔ Close the text and save the changes. 📖 **87**

11.17 Background Information

Glossary	
Alignment	The way the lines of a paragraph are placed between the margins.
Bullets	A typographical symbol used to introduce items in a list.
Indenting	Setting a line or paragraph further away from the margin.
Ruler	Toolbar you can use to indent lines and paragraphs.
Tab stop	Location the cursor jumps to when you press the Tab key.

Format text
You can format text using these buttons on the right side of the format bar:

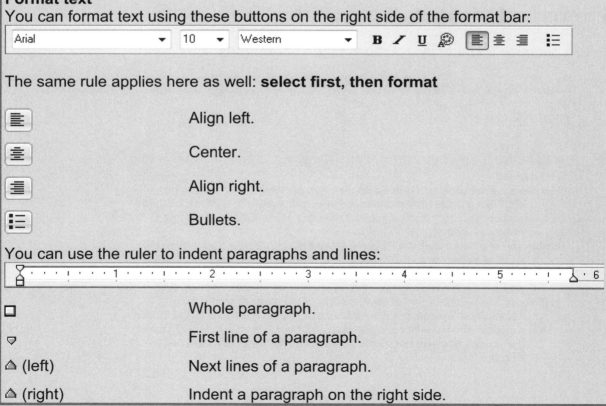

The same rule applies here as well: **select first, then format**

Align left.
Center.
Align right.
Bullets.

You can use the ruler to indent paragraphs and lines:

□	Whole paragraph.
▽	First line of a paragraph.
△ (left)	Next lines of a paragraph.
△ (right)	Indent a paragraph on the right side.

12. Managing and Maintaining Your Computer

Just like your home, your computer also needs regular maintenance. You probably want to buy and install new software, or remove unused software from your computer. In this chapter you practice removing and installing software. For this exercise we will use the program *Adobe Reader*, a program for viewing *PDF files*. You will also install a fun extra gadget for *Windows Sidebar*.

The hard disk of your computer is the central location where everything is stored. Every now and then you need to do a little spring cleaning. You can do that using the tools *Disk Cleanup* and *Disk Defragmenter*.

Disk Cleanup removes unnecessary files from your hard disk.

The *Disk Defragmenter* improves the performance of your computer. Over time, the files on the hard disk become fragmented, and your computer slows down as it has to look in many different places to find parts of a file. You can solve this problem by defragmenting your hard disk. *Disk Defragmenter* is a tool that rearranges the data on your hard disk and puts fragmented files back together so your computer can run more efficiently.

At the end of this chapter you will read about what to do when you are having problems with your computer.

In this chapter you will learn how to:

- uninstall programs;
- install programs;
- clean up your hard disk;
- defragment your hard disk;
- solve common problems.

12.1 Uninstalling Programs

Your computer probably contains programs that you no longer use. It is very easy to remove these programs from the hard disk of your computer. When you install a program, an uninstall program is usually installed at the same time. The uninstall program removes the program files and removes the program name from the *Start menu.* You are going to practice uninstalling a program by removing the program *Adobe Reader* from your computer.

 Please note:

Even if you use *Adobe Reader* frequently, you can still remove the program from your computer. In the next section you will install the latest version of *Adobe Reader* from the CD-ROM you received with this book.
If you do not have *Adobe Reader* installed on your computer, then you can just read through this section.

You can remove a program like this:

☞ Open the *Control Panel* ⫯18

You see the *Control Panel*:

Click Uninstall a program

below Programs

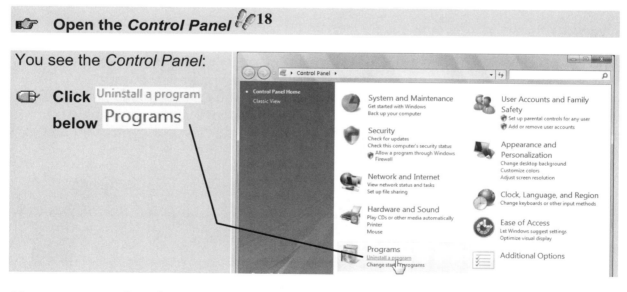

You now see a list of programs that can be uninstalled if necessary. You choose Adobe Reader, version 7 or version 8. In this example version 8 is removed.

 Please note:

If you have *Adobe Reader* version 7 installed, then you can uninstall the program the same way. If *Adobe Reader* is not installed, then you can just continue reading without performing the tasks. You can use the information in this section some other time when you want to uninstall a different program yourself.

First you select the program.

Click

Adobe Reader 8.1.0

Then you uninstall the program.

Click Uninstall

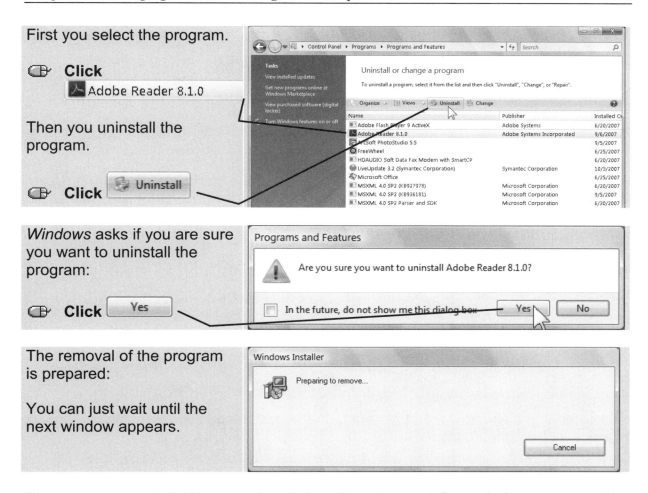

Windows asks if you are sure you want to uninstall the program:

Click Yes

The removal of the program is prepared:

You can just wait until the next window appears.

The screen goes dark. You see the window *User Account Control* where you need to give your permission to continue.

Click Allow

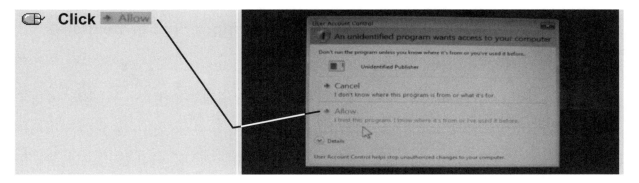

You see the progress of the program removal:

The program *Adobe Reader* requires that you restart the computer when the program is uninstalled. This will not be necessary for every program you remove, but if the instructions tell you to, you will need to do so.

You are asked if you want to restart the computer now:

 Click [Yes]

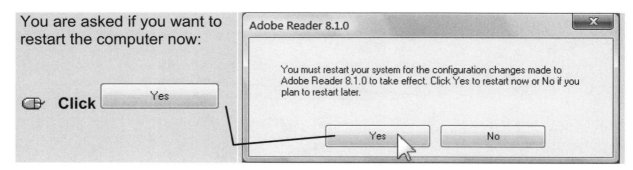

The computer is shut down and restarted. In the next section you are going to practice installing a program.

Tip

Do you want to uninstall another program?
Always do it the same way as it was described in this section. Removing an icon from your desktop or removing the program name from the *Start menu* is not enough. That way you only remove references to the program and the program files themselves stay behind.
Never try to remove a program from the program folder on the hard disk of your computer. You only remove part of the program that way, and a lot of unnecessary files remain on the hard disk. Furthermore, it is easy to make mistakes that way and you might remove the wrong files.

12.2 Installing Programs

A program must be installed on the computer before it can work. This means all of the program files are copied to the program folder, the program is included in the list of available programs and (sometimes) an icon is placed on the desktop.
All this is accomplished by an installation program, also called a *setup* program.

For many software packages, the setup program is automatically started when you insert the CD-ROM in the computer. Sometimes you may have to start the setup program yourself, for example with programs you downloaded from the Internet.

A setup program usually has one of the following names:

- **setup** (setup.exe);
- **instal** (instal.exe);
- **install** (install.exe);
- **crypticEightLetterName** (crypticEightLetterName.exe).

The full file name is shown in parentheses; the extension *.exe* indicates that the file is a program. To start a setup program, you always have to search for a program with one of the names listed above.

Some programs do not have a separate setup program. Then the complete program and the setup part are packed into one file. This is also the case with the program *Adobe Reader.*

As an exercise you are going to install version 8 of *Adobe Reader* from the CD-ROM you received with this book.

☞ **Insert the CD-ROM in the computer**

Make sure the printed side of the CD faces up.

12.3 Installing Adobe Reader 8

☞ **Open the *Computer* window** ✌**19**

You see the different drives
and devices of your
computer.

🖱️ **Double-click your**
CD/DVD drive

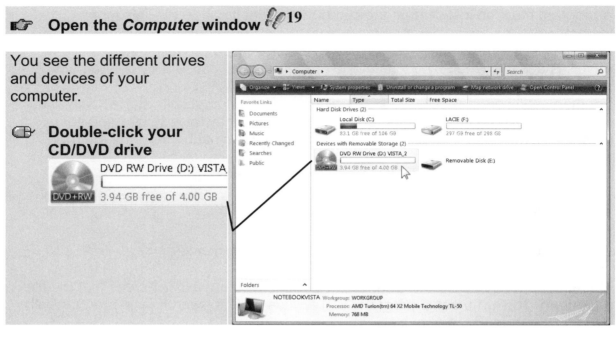

You see the folders on the
CD-ROM: ——————————

The folders may be displayed
differently on your computer.
This depends on the settings
of your computer.

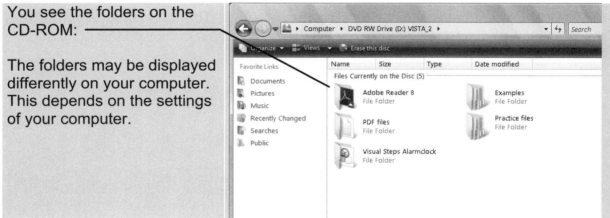

On most program CDs you will see the setup program now.
On this CD-ROM the setup program is stored in a separate folder named *Adobe*
Reader 8.

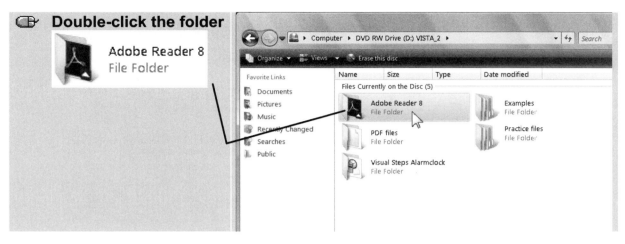

Double-click the folder

Adobe Reader 8
File Folder

Now you see the setup program named

AdbeRdr810_en_US

Some setup programs include an extra file called *readme*. This is a text file created by the manufacturer containing extra tips or a description of the changes in the software. In this example there is no such file present.
You can start the installation of the program:

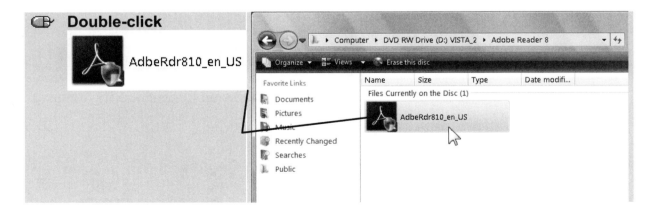

Double-click

AdbeRdr810_en_US

You see a security warning:

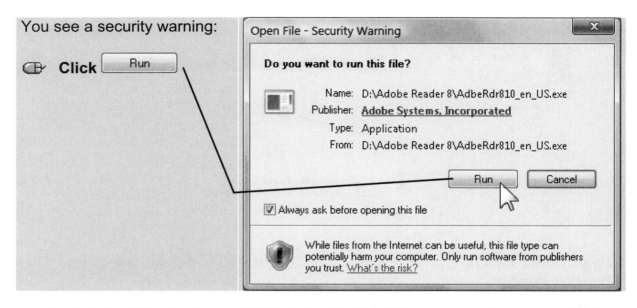

⊂⧸ **Click** [Run]

You see this window. The green bar shows the progress of unpacking the setup program:

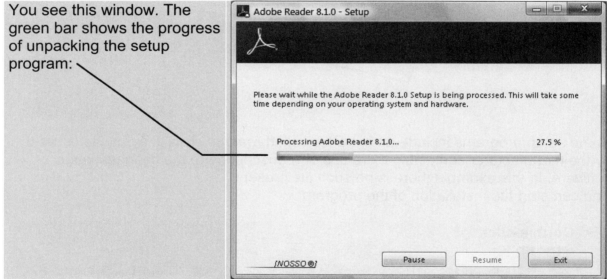

Your screen goes dark and you need to give your permission to continue by pressing the *Continue* button.

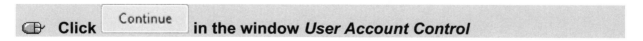

⊂⧸ **Click** [Continue] **in the window *User Account Control***

With many programs you will see a sequence of windows appearing during the installation so that you can enter your preferences. Usually you can choose the folder where you want to install the program, and you can decide whether or not you want to add a shortcut (an icon) to the desktop or the *Start menu*.

When you install *Adobe Reader* you can only choose the folder where you want to install the program.

A destination folder is suggested by the setup program:

☞ **Click** [Next >]

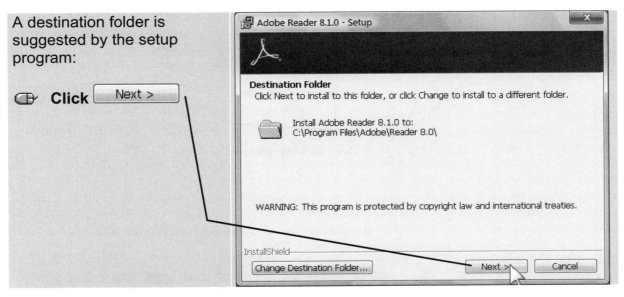

Now you can start the installation:

☞ **Click** [Install]

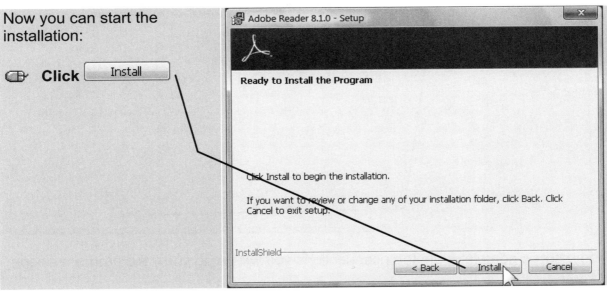

The installation is started. You see the progress and an estimation of the time remaining:

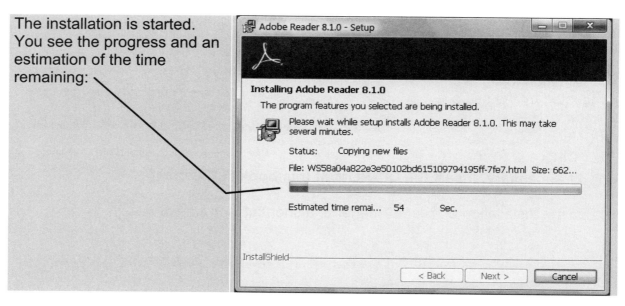

The final setup window appears.

Click [Finish]

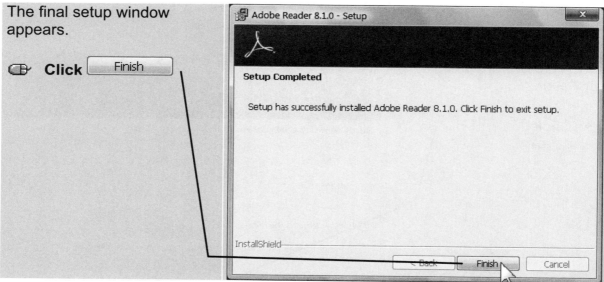

The setup is completed. In the next sections you will get to know the program *Adobe Reader* better.

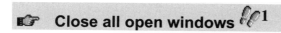 **Close all open windows**

12.4 Opening Adobe Reader

Adobe Reader is a useful free program that you can use to view PDF files. The abbreviation PDF stands for *Portable Document File*. This file format is used very often for information that you can download from the websites of businesses or institutions. The CD-ROM you received with this book contains a few PDF files as well. You are going to take a look at one of these.

☞ **If necessary, insert the CD-ROM of this book in the computer**

During the installation of *Adobe Reader 8*, a shortcut icon was placed on your desktop. You can use this shortcut to start the program:

When you start the program for the first time, you have to accept the *License Agreement*:

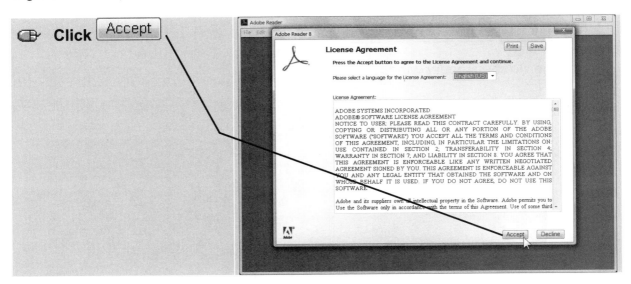

A window appears, containing information about other *Adobe* products. This information will appear every time you open *Adobe Reader 8*. You can choose to change this:

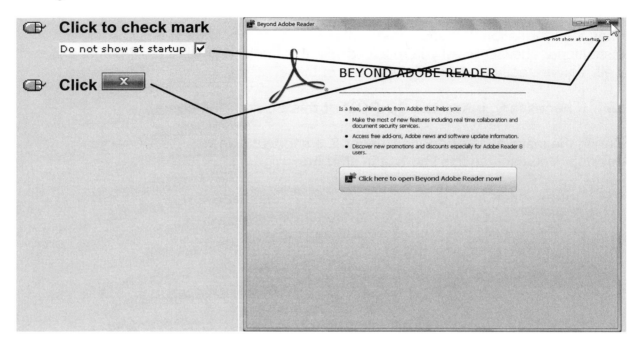

12.5 Opening a PDF File

You see the *Adobe Reader* window:

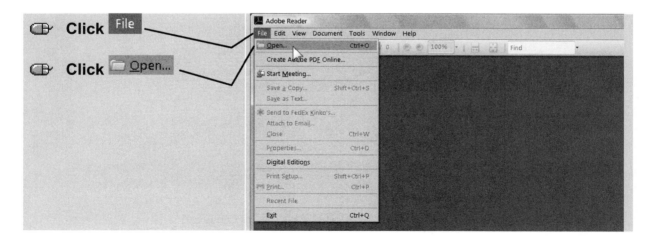

You are going to open a file from the CD-ROM you received with this book.

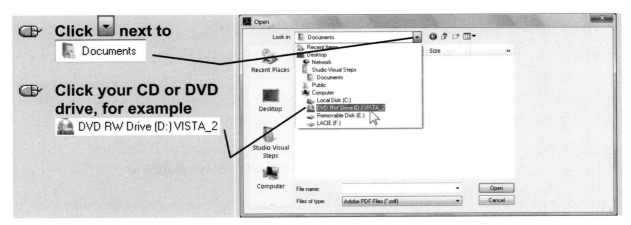

In the folder *PDF files* you find a PDF document:

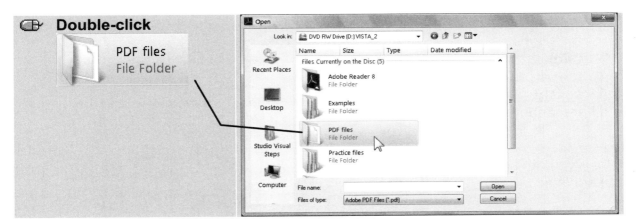

You choose the guide that teaches you how to work with *Adobe Reader 8*:

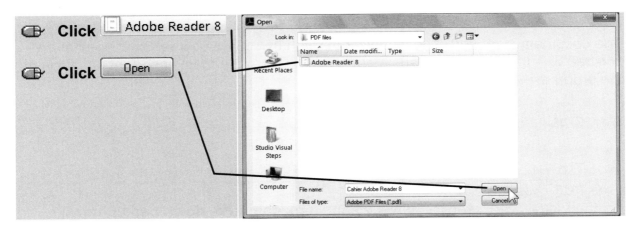

The document appears in the window:

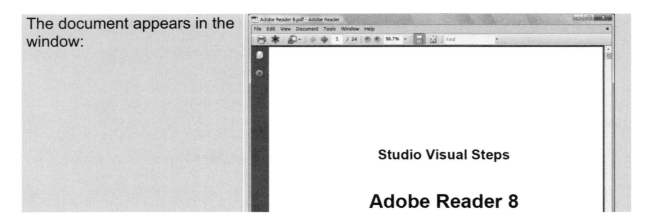

If you do not have any experience with *Adobe Reader 8,* you can work through this guide yourself. You can do that more easily when you print the guide. In *Adobe Reader 8* you can do that like this:

☞ **Check if your printer is on**

☞ **Click** 🖨

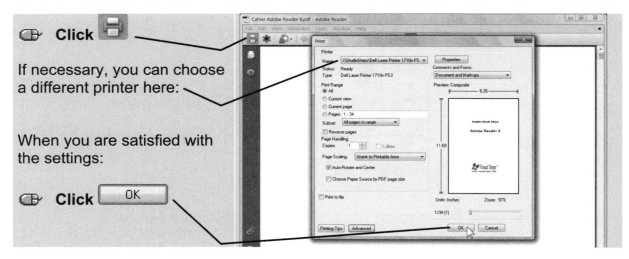

If necessary, you can choose a different printer here:

When you are satisfied with the settings:

☞ **Click** OK

The document is printed. You can work through this guide yourself after you have finished with this chapter. This is a quick way to learn the most important functions of the program.

☞ **Close all open windows** 1

💡 **Tip**

Free PDF guides
On the Visual Steps website, **www.visualsteps.com/info_downloads.php,** you find free PDF guides about various subjects available for download. You have just looked at an example of these guides on the CD-ROM you received with this book.

12.6 Installing the Gadget Visual Steps Alarm Clock

The installation of *Adobe Reader* took you through a sequence of several windows. That is not always the case when you install a program. You can see the difference when you install an extra gadget for *Windows Sidebar*. A gadget is a miniature program that is displayed in *Windows Sidebar*.

☞ **Check if *Windows Sidebar* is displayed on your desktop**

If not:

☞ **Click** , ▶ **All Programs** , Accessories , Windows Sidebar

You find the gadget *Visual Steps Alarm Clock* on the CD-ROM that came with this book:

☞ **If necessary, insert the CD-ROM in the computer**

☞ **Click** , Computer

☞ **Double-click your CD/DVD drive**

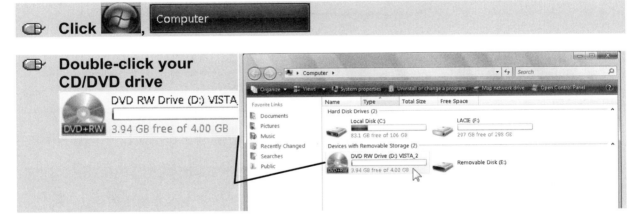

☞ **Double-click the folder**

Visual Steps Alarmclc
File Folder

You see the program named  .

Now you can start the installation of the program:

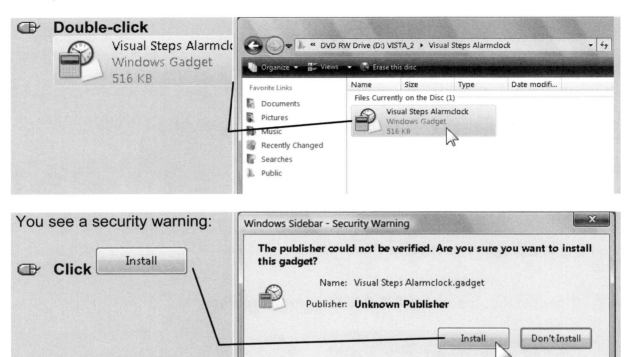

Double-click

You see a security warning:

Click `Install`

You do not need to enter any preferences when you install this gadget.

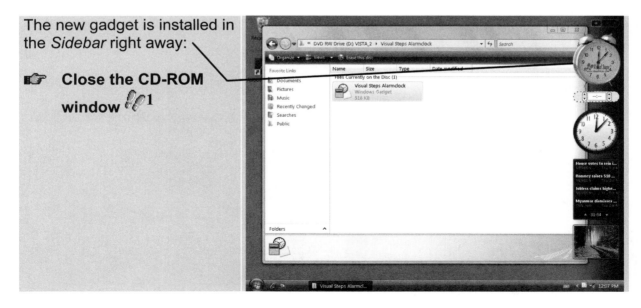

The new gadget is installed in the *Sidebar* right away:

☞ **Close the CD-ROM window** $\mathcal{U}$1

You have seen how a gadget is installed. You can use the gadget *Visual Steps Alarm Clock* right away. The *Alarm Clock* displays the correct time and you can set the time you want to be alerted.

You can set an alert time using the feature  below the *Alarm Clock*.

Using the arrows in this feature you can set the hours and minutes.
The *Alarm Clock* will make a sound. To be able to hear that:

☞ **Turn on the speakers of your computer**

To set the hour:

☞ **Click ⏷ on the left side**

To set the minutes:

☞ **Click ⏷ on the right side**

When you hold the mouse button down, the hours and minutes will change quickly.
When you keep clicking the set time will change one number at the time.
For example, set the alert time to a time a couple of minutes later than the current time displayed in the *Alarm Clock*.
At the set time the *Alarm Clock* will jump into action. You see the *Alarm Clock* move back and forth and the clock hands turn around quickly. You also hear a ringing sound.

After about ten seconds this will stop.
You can also turn the ringing *Alarm Clock* off yourself:

☞ **Click somewhere in the center of the *Alarm Clock***

Now the sound and the animation stop immediately.

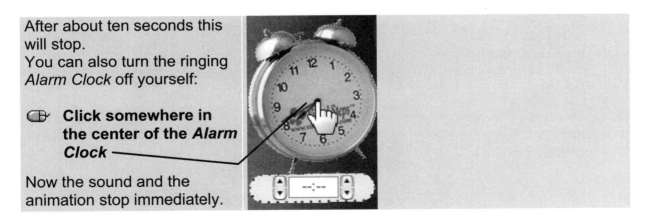

For example, you can use the *Visual Steps Alarm Clock* to protect yourself from RSI, to prevent hand and wrist complaints due to prolonged computer use. If you set the *Alarm Clock* one or two hours later every time, you are reminded to take a break.

Tip

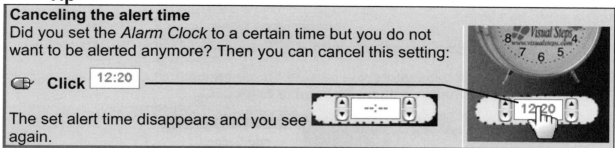

Canceling the alert time
Did you set the *Alarm Clock* to a certain time but you do not want to be alerted anymore? Then you can cancel this setting:

Click 12:20

The set alert time disappears and you see [___] again.

The *Alarm Clock* also gives - when it is not ringing - direct access to the Visual Steps website:

Click in the center of the *Alarm Clock*

Internet Explorer will be started automatically and a connection with the Internet is made.

You see the opening page of the Visual Steps website **www.visualsteps.com** :

Use the button
Free Downloads to open the webpage containing the free PDF computer guides:

Close the window 𝒪1

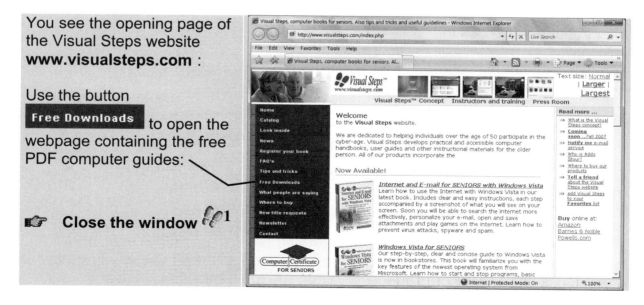

12.7 Removing a Gadget

You can also remove a gadget from *Windows Sidebar*, for example the default *Windows* clock. Like this:

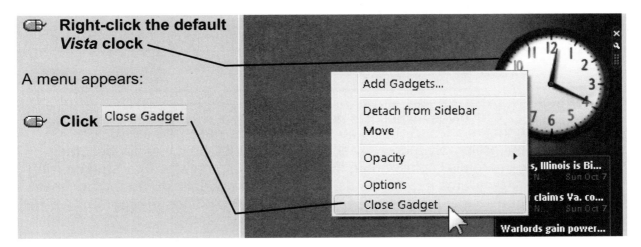

☞ **Right-click the default *Vista* clock**

A menu appears:

☞ **Click** Close Gadget

The default *Vista* clock has disappeared from the *Sidebar*.

12.8 Cleaning Your Hard Disk

When you use your computer frequently, more and more files are collected on the hard disk of your computer. For the most part this happens automatically, for example when you surf the Internet. That is why it is advisable to do some cleaning from time to time. This is especially important when your hard disk is getting full. You can check that like this:

☞ **Open the *Computer* window** 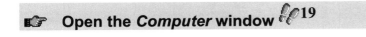 **19**

You see the window displaying the drives and devices of your computer:

In this view, a blue bar and text show how much space is still available on your hard disk (C:):

Local Disk (C:)
81.8 GB free of 106 GB

HELP! My window looks different.

When you do not see the available space on your hard disk you can change the view of the window:

☞ **Click ▼ next to** [≡▼ Views]

☞ **Click** [≡ Tiles]

 Tip

10% free
A rule of thumb that is often used, is you should keep at least 10% of the disk capacity free, but preferably more. Experience shows that the computer becomes slower when the hard disk is fuller than that. Also, some programs may start causing problems. Many programs use the hard disk for temporary data storage. When there is not enough free space, temporary data can not be stored and the programs will not function properly anymore.

You can also display the available space on your hard disk like this:

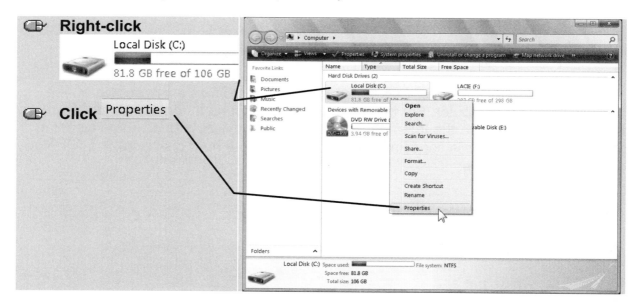

The *Local Disk (C:) Properties* window is opened.

In this pie chart you see the amount of used and available hard disk space:

There is a special program for cleaning your hard disk. You can open it like this:

☞ **Click** `Disk Cleanup`

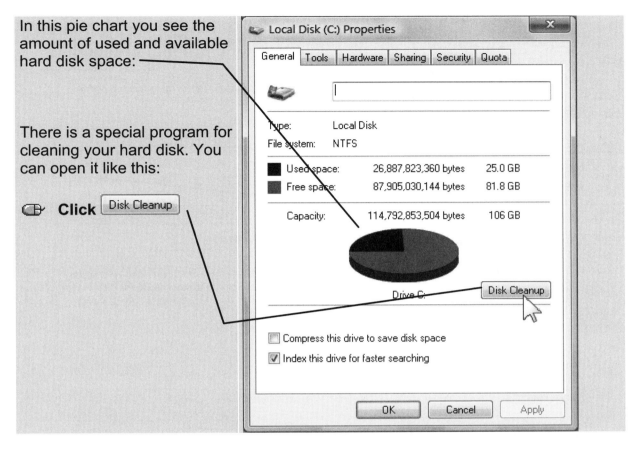

Now *Vista* asks which files you want to clean up. You choose to clean up your own files only:

☞ **Click**

➔ My files only

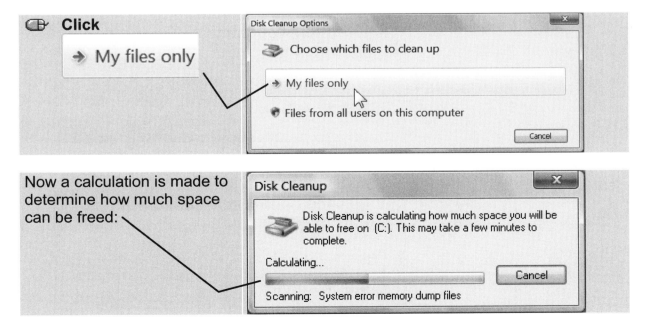

Now a calculation is made to determine how much space can be freed:

In this window you can choose which file types you want to delete:

You can empty the *Recycle Bin* for example:

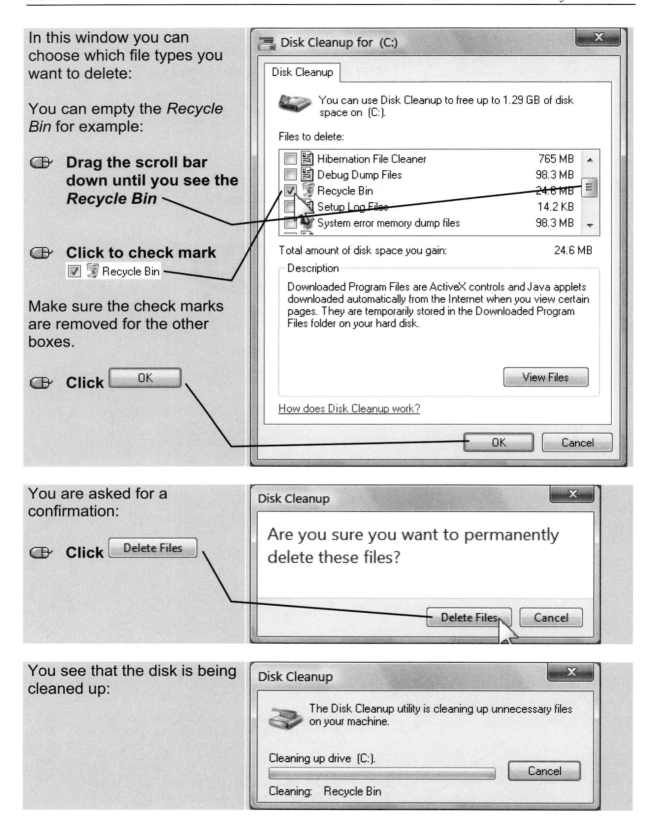

🖰 **Drag the scroll bar down until you see the *Recycle Bin***

🖰 **Click to check mark**
☑ 📁 Recycle Bin

Make sure the check marks are removed for the other boxes.

🖰 **Click** [OK]

You are asked for a confirmation:

🖰 **Click** [Delete Files]

You see that the disk is being cleaned up:

Tip

Unnecessary programs Is your hard disk becoming too full? Then you can always consider removing the programs you do not use. In this chapter you have read how to uninstall programs.

12.9 Defragmenting Your Hard Disk

Over time, the files on the hard disk become fragmented, and your computer slows down as it has to look in many different places to find parts of a file. You can solve this problem by defragmenting your hard disk. *Disk Defragmenter* is a tool that rearranges the data on your hard disk and puts fragmented files back together so your computer can run more efficiently.

You start the disk defragmentation like this:

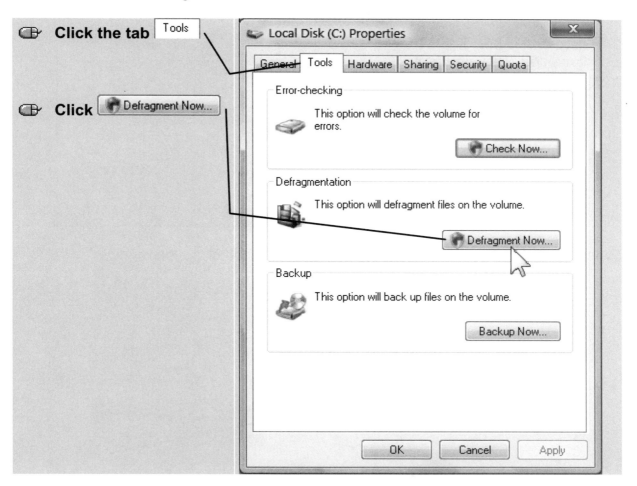

Your screen goes dark and you need to give your permission to continue by clicking the *Continue* button.

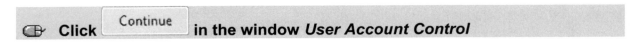

You see the window *Disk Defragmenter*.

Usually the disk defragmentation runs automatically every week:

You can also start the disk defragmentation yourself:

☞ **Click**
   Defragment now

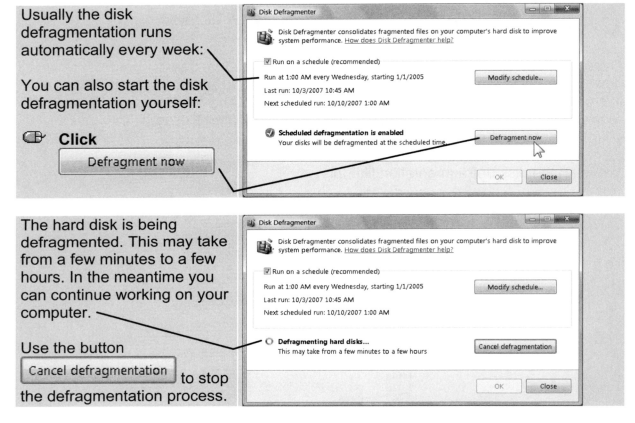

The hard disk is being defragmented. This may take from a few minutes to a few hours. In the meantime you can continue working on your computer.

Use the button
   Cancel defragmentation to stop
the defragmentation process.

When the disk defragmentation has completed, you can close the window:

☞ **Click** Close

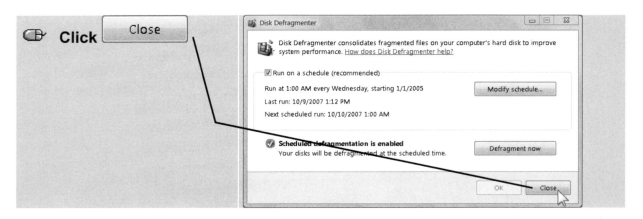

Tip

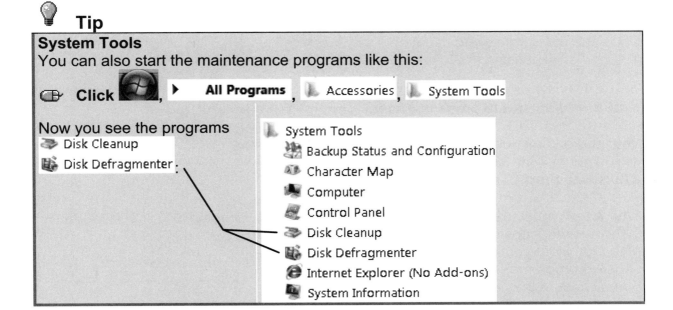

System Tools
You can also start the maintenance programs like this:

⊕ **Click** [⊞], ▶ **All Programs**, 🗒 Accessories, 🗒 System Tools

Now you see the programs

🗁 Disk Cleanup

📇 Disk Defragmenter

🗒 System Tools

 🗎 Backup Status and Configuration

 🜄 Character Map

 🖳 Computer

 🗒 Control Panel

 🗁 Disk Cleanup

 📇 Disk Defragmenter

 🅔 Internet Explorer (No Add-ons)

 🗒 System Information

12.10 Common Problems

 HELP! A program is not working properly.

Does the program inexplicably hang or crash, or will it no longer start?

A common first step you always have to try is the following:
☞ Shut down the computer, wait a few minutes, then start it up again.

That did not help?
☞ Reinstall the program. This way all the files will be 'refreshed'.

That did not help?
☞ First uninstall the program, then reinstall it.

That did not help?
☞ Check the software manufacturer's website to see if your problems are described there and if there is a solution. Sometimes you can download and install a software *update* or *patch*.

That did not help?
☞ Contact the software manufacturer's help desk (by telephone or e-mail). It is important that you can describe the problem well. If you contact them by phone, make sure you are sitting at your computer and that the computer is on. That way you can immediately try out the solution while you have them on the line.

HELP! One of my programs hangs.

Does one of your programs suddenly stop working?
You can close it using the following 'emergency' procedure:

⌨ **Simultaneously press the keys** [Ctrl] , [Alt] **and** [Delete]

Your screen goes blue and you see a couple of options.

🖰 **Click** *Start Task Manager*

After a few moments you see the window *Windows Task Manager*. Here you see a list of active programs. Somewhere in that list you find the program that is not working. Usually its status will say *Not responding*.

🖰 **Click the program**

🖰 **Click** [End Task]

You will have to wait a few moments as *Windows* tries to end the program.

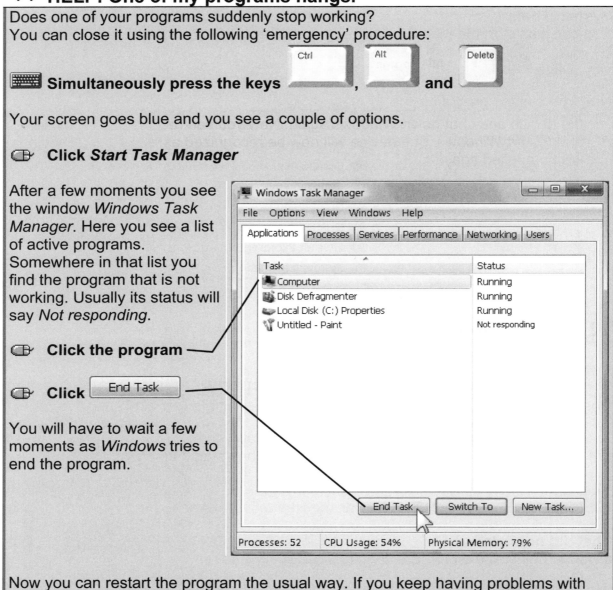

Now you can restart the program the usual way. If you keep having problems with this program, read *Help! A program is not working properly* on the previous page.

HELP! My computer is not working properly.

Is a device such as a printer or scanner not working properly?

☞ Reinstall the accompanying software. All files will be refreshed.

That did not help?
☞ Shut down *Windows* and disconnect the device. Restart your computer without the device and shut down *Windows* again. Now you can reconnect the device and restart *Windows.* The device will now be recognized as 'new' and all settings will be applied again.

That did not help?
☞ Check the device manufacturer's website to see if your problems are described there and if there is a solution. Sometimes you can download and install a device driver *update*.

That did not help?
☞ Contact the device manufacturer's help desk.

 HELP! Problems with Windows.

Are you having problems with one or more components of *Windows*?
Take a look at the *Microsoft* website: **www.microsoft.com**

This website contains an extensive **support** section:

You can search these pages in different ways to find a solution for your problems.

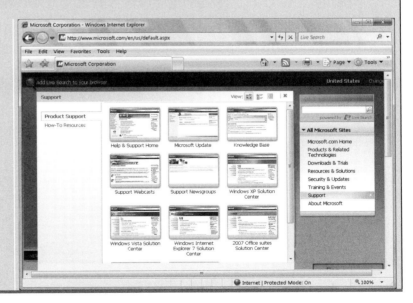

12.11 Exercises

Have you forgotten how to do something? Use the number beside the footsteps to look it up in *Appendix B How Do I Do That Again?*

Exercise: Maintenance

In this exercise you use the features *Disk Cleanup* and *Disk Defragmenter* again.

☑ Open the *Computer* window $\ell\ell$ **19**

☑ Take a look at the properties of your hard disk. $\ell\ell$ **94**

☑ Start *Disk Cleanup*, choose your own files. $\ell\ell$ **95**

☑ Delete the files in the *Recycle Bin*. $\ell\ell$ **96**

☑ Start the *Disk Defragmenter*. $\ell\ell$ **97**

☑ Cancel the *Disk Defragmenter*. $\ell\ell$ **98**

☑ Close all windows. $\ell\ell$ **1**

12.12 Background Information

Glossary

Adobe Reader	Program you can use to view PDF files.
Disk Cleanup	Tool you can use to clean up unnecessary files on the hard disk and free disk space.
Disk Defragmenter	Tool that rearranges the data on your hard disk and puts fragmented files back together so your computer can run more efficiently.
.EXE	File extension that indicates the file is a program.
Gadget	Miniature program that is displayed in the *Windows Sidebar*.
Installation program	Also called *setup program*: utility tool that installs a software program on your computer.
Installing	Placing a program on the hard disk of your computer. During this process all files are copied to the appropriate folder and the program is added to the list of available programs.
PDF file	The abbreviation PDF stands for *Portable Document File*. This file format is often used for information you can download from websites of businesses or institutions.
Readme file	This is a text file created by the software manufacturer containing extra tips and remarks or a description of the changes in the software.
Setup program	Also called *installation program*: utility tool that installs a software program on your computer.
System Tools	Collection of tools you can use to perform maintenance on your computer or to improve the performance of your computer.
Windows Sidebar	Vertical bar that is displayed on the side of the desktop. This bar contains miniature programs (gadgets).

Source: Windows Help and Support

12.13 Tips

Tip

Defragmentation and disk cleanup in Windows Live OneCare
Do you use the program *Windows Live OneCare* on your computer?
Then the program feature **Performance Plus** checks regularly if the performance
of your computer is still optimized.

If you have *Live OneCare*:

☞ **Open *Windows Live OneCare*** 102

🖰 **Click** ▸ View last tune-up report **at Performance Plus**

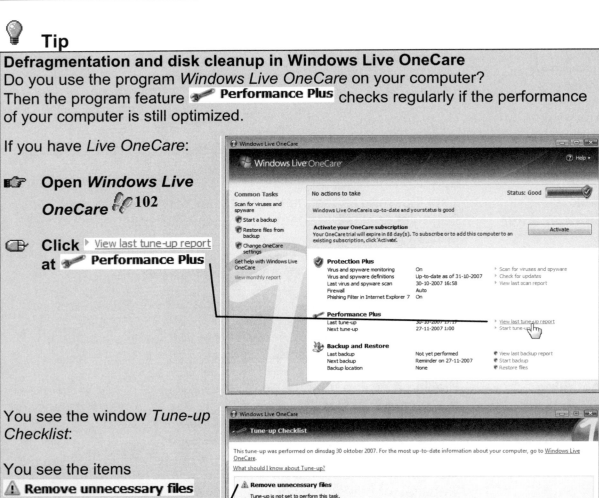

You see the window *Tune-up Checklist*:

You see the items
⚠ **Remove unnecessary files**
and
⚠ **Defragment the hard disk**:

When you have the program
Windows Live OneCare,
these tasks will be performed
automatically at set times so
you do not have to perform
these tasks manually
yourself.

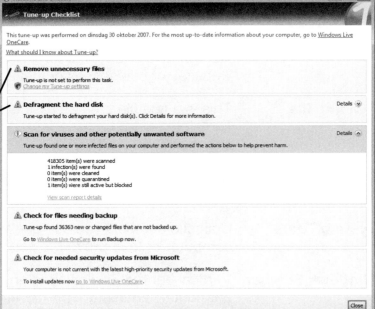

Appendices

A. Copying the Practice Files to Your Computer

To be able to work through all the chapters you need the practice files that can be found on the CD-ROM that came with this book. Copy the practice files folder from the CD-ROM to the hard disk of your computer.

The CD-ROM is stored in a sleeve that is bound between the pages of the book. Carefully open the sleeve to take out the CD. Do **not** try to rip the sleeve out of the book, as this might damage it. When you are done working, you can store the CD-ROM in the sleeve again. This way you always have the CD-ROM at hand when you work with this book.

<table>
<tr>
<td>

☞ Insert the CD-ROM that accompanies this book in the CD or DVD drive of your computer

Make sure the printed side of the CD-ROM faces up.

</td>
<td>

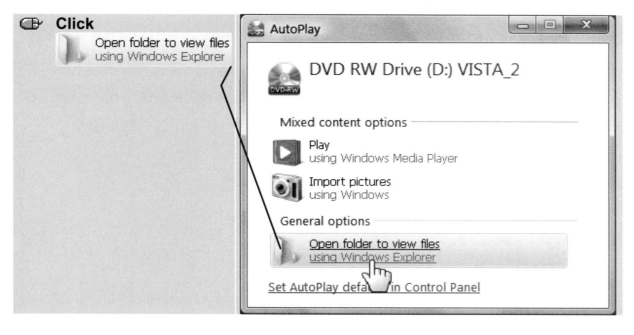

</td>
</tr>
</table>

In most cases, the following window appears automatically after a few moments:

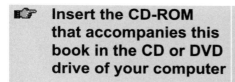

HELP! I do not see that window.

If different *AutoPlay* settings have been made for CDs on your computer, it is possible that a different window appears or a program is opened.
In that case do the following:

☞ **Close the (program) window** $\ell\!\ell$1

⏳ **Click** [⊞] , [Computer]

Now you see the *Computer* window:

You may have other drives and devices displayed on your computer than the ones shown here.

⏳ **Double-click your CD or DVD drive**

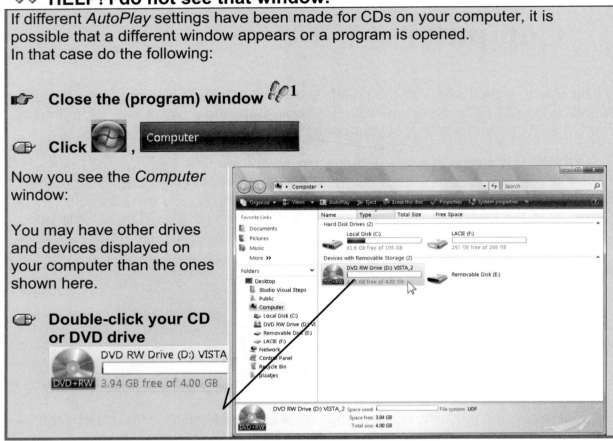

You see a *Folder window* that displays the contents of the CD-ROM on the right side:

The folders may be displayed differently on your computer. In that case you look for the folder named

Practice files
File Folder

⏳ **Right-click**

Practice files
File Folder

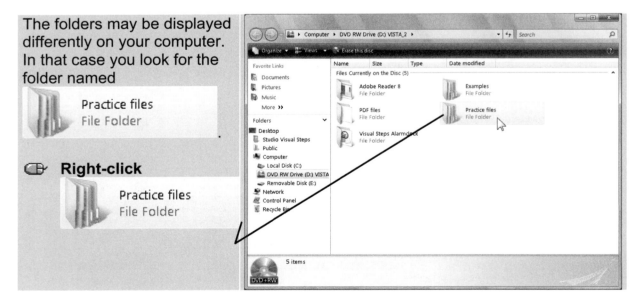

Now a menu appears:

Click Send To

Another menu appears:

Click 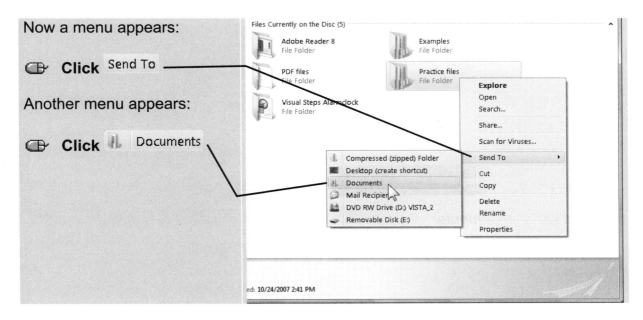 Documents

The folder *Practice files* is now copied to the hard disk of your computer:

You can follow the progress in this window:

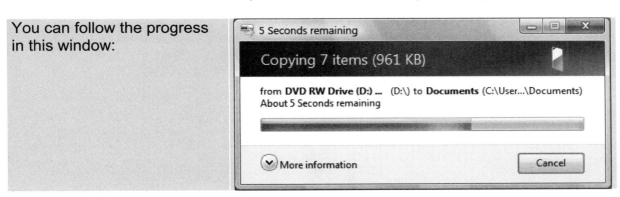

When all items have been copied:

☞ **Close the *Folder window*** [1]

When you are done working, return the CD-ROM to the sleeve in the book. This way you will always have it at hand when you work with this book.

☞ **Store the CD-ROM in the sleeve in the book**

The folder *Practice files* is now in the folder *Documents* on your computer.

B. How Do I Do That Again?

In this book some actions are marked with footsteps: 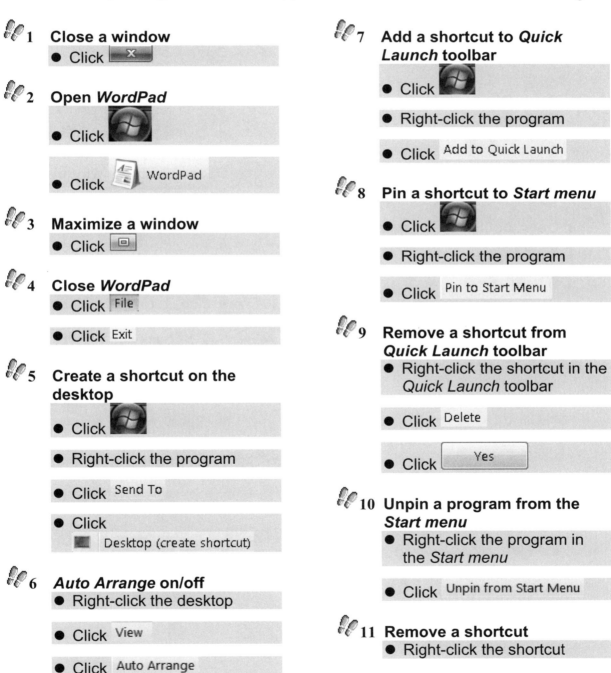1
Find the corresponding number in the appendix below to see how to do something.

1 Close a window
- Click [X]

2 Open *WordPad*
- Click [windows icon]
- Click [WordPad icon] WordPad

3 Maximize a window
- Click [□]

4 Close *WordPad*
- Click File
- Click Exit

5 Create a shortcut on the desktop
- Click [windows icon]
- Right-click the program
- Click Send To
- Click [icon] Desktop (create shortcut)

6 *Auto Arrange* on/off
- Right-click the desktop
- Click View
- Click Auto Arrange

7 Add a shortcut to *Quick Launch* toolbar
- Click [windows icon]
- Right-click the program
- Click Add to Quick Launch

8 Pin a shortcut to *Start menu*
- Click [windows icon]
- Right-click the program
- Click Pin to Start Menu

9 Remove a shortcut from *Quick Launch* toolbar
- Right-click the shortcut in the *Quick Launch* toolbar
- Click Delete
- Click [Yes]

10 Unpin a program from the *Start menu*
- Right-click the program in the *Start menu*
- Click Unpin from Start Menu

11 Remove a shortcut
- Right-click the shortcut

- Click Delete

- Click Yes

12 Display properties of the taskbar and *Start menu*
- Right-click the taskbar

- Click Properties

13 Open *Windows Help and Support*
- Click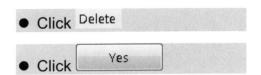

- Click Help and Support

14 Open *Default Programs* window
- Click

- Click Default Programs

15 Open *Set Associations* window
In the Default Programs window:
- Click Associate a file type or protocol with a program

16 Set program as default program
In the Default Programs window:
- Click Set your default programs

- Click the program, for example 🔵 Internet Explorer
- Click → Set this program as default

17 Check which extensions are opened
In the Default Programs window:
- Click  → Choose defaults for this program

18 Open *Control Panel*
- Click

- Click Control Panel

19 Open *Computer* window
- Click

- Click Computer

20 Open file / folder
- Double-click the file or folder

21 Remove file from desktop
- Click the file

- Press Delete

22 Open folder with practice files *Chapter 4*
- Click

- Click Documents

- Double-click  Practice files File Folder

● Double-click

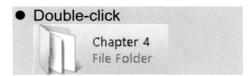

Chapter 4
File Folder

23 Copy file to a compressed folder
- ● Right-click the file
- ● Click Send To
- ● Click
  _i_ Compressed (zipped) Folder

24 Add a file to a compressed folder
- ● Point to the file
- ● Press the left mouse button and hold it down
- ● Drag the file to the compressed folder

When you see the notification
+ Copy .
- ● Release the mouse button

25 Open a compressed folder
- ● Double-click the compressed folder

26 Remove a file from a compressed folder
- ● Right-click the file
- ● Click Delete

In the Delete File window:
- ● Click Yes

27 Extract a compressed folder
- ● Double-click the compressed folder

● Click  Extract all files

● Click Extract

28 Return to the previous folder
- ● Click ⬅

29 Open *Windows Security Center*
- ● Click
- ● Click Control Panel
- ● Click
  Check this computer's security status

30 Check the detailed *Firewall* status
- ● Click Firewall

31 Open the *Windows Update* window
From the Security Center:
- ● Click Windows Update

32 Open the *Windows Update* settings
From the Windows Update window:
- ● Click Change settings

33 Open the *Windows Defender* window
From the Security Center:
- ● Click Windows Defender

34 Perform a quick scan
- ● Click ▾ next to Scan

- Click Quick Scan

35 Stop the scan
- Click Stop Scan

36 Open the *Manage Accounts* window
- Click [Windows logo]

- Click Control Panel

- Click
  Add or remove user accounts

Your screen goes dark:
- Click Continue

37 Create a new standard user account
- Click Create a new account

- Type a name for the account

- Click the option ◉ Standard user

- Click Create Account

38 Change account picture
- Click the user account you want to change

- Click Change the picture

- Click the picture you want to use

- Click Change Picture

39 Change account name
- Click Change the account name

- Type the new name

- Click Change Name

40 Remove a user account
- Click Delete the account

- Click Delete Files

- Click Delete Account

41 Open the *Backup and Restore Center*
- Click [Windows logo]

- Click Control Panel

- Click Back up your computer at
  System and Maintenance

42 Change day for automatic backup
- Click ˇ next to What day:

- Click the day you want to use

- Click
  Save settings and start backup

43 Create a system restore point
- Click
  Create a restore point or change settings
  in the *Backup and Restore Center*

- Select which disk you want to use for the system restore point

- Click Create...

- Type a name for the restore point

- Click Create

- Click OK

- Click OK

44 Format using the *Live File System*

In the window Burn a Disc:

- Click ⌄ Show formatting options

- Click ⊙ Live File System

- Click Next

45 Select multiple files

- Click the first file

- Hold Ctrl down

- Click the next files you want to select

- Release Ctrl

46 Write using the *Live File System*

- Click Burn

47 Delete files from CD/DVD-RW or from queue

- Select the file(s) you want to delete

- Press Delete

- Click Yes

48 Erase a CD/DVD-RW

- Click Erase this disc

49 Format using the *Mastered* file system

In the window Burn a Disc:

- Click ⌄ Show formatting options

- Click ○ Mastered

- Click Next

50 Add files to queue (Mastered)

- Click Burn

51 Remove file from queue

- Click the file

- Press Delete

- Click Yes

52 Write queue to data disc

- Click Burn to disc

- Click Next

- Click Next

- Click Yes

- Click Finish when the writing process has completed

⫙ 53 Display the *Preview Pane*

● Click Organize ▾

● Click ⬚ Layout

● Click ▣ Preview Pane

⫙ 54 Open *Personal Folder*

● Click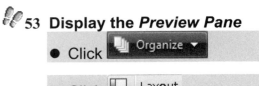

In the Start menu:
● Click your name in the top
  right corner of the *Start
  menu*, for example
  Studio Visual Steps

**⫙ 55 Open a folder using *Favorite
Links***

● Click ▧ Pictures

**⫙ 56 Open a folder using the
Folder list in the *Navigation
Pane***

● Click the name of the folder
  in the *Navigation Pane* on
  the left side

**⫙ 57 Preview a file in the *Preview
Pane***

● Click the file

⫙ 58 Change rating
In the Details Pane:
● Click the star ☆ you want to
  use

● Click Save

⫙ 59 Add a tag to a file
In the Details Pane:
● Click Sample; Wildlife; or
  Add a tag

● Type: nature

● Press [Enter ⏎]

⫙ 60 Search using the *Search Box*

● Click the *Search Box* in the
  top right corner of the *Folder
  window*

● Type: nature

⫙ 61 Save a search

● Click ▦ Save Search

● Type: nature photos

● Click Save

**⫙ 62 Open folder using the
address bar**

● Click the name of the folder
  in the address bar, for
  example Searches

⫙ 63 Run a saved search
In the folder Searches:
● Double-click the search you
  want to use

**⫙ 64 Associate file type with a
program**
In the Default Programs window:
● Click Associate a file type or
  protocol with a program

● Click a file type, for example
  BMP File

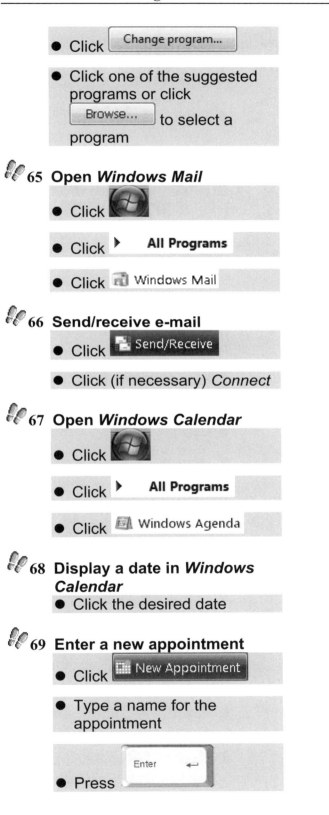

- Click Change program...

- Click one of the suggested programs or click
  Browse... to select a program

65 Open *Windows Mail*

- Click 🪟

- Click ▶ **All Programs**

- Click 📩 Windows Mail

66 Send/receive e-mail

- Click 📧 Send/Receive

- Click (if necessary) *Connect*

67 Open *Windows Calendar*

- Click 🪟

- Click ▶ **All Programs**

- Click 📅 Windows Agenda

68 Display a date in *Windows Calendar*
- Click the desired date

69 Enter a new appointment

- Click 📅 New Appointment

- Type a name for the appointment

- Press Enter ⏎

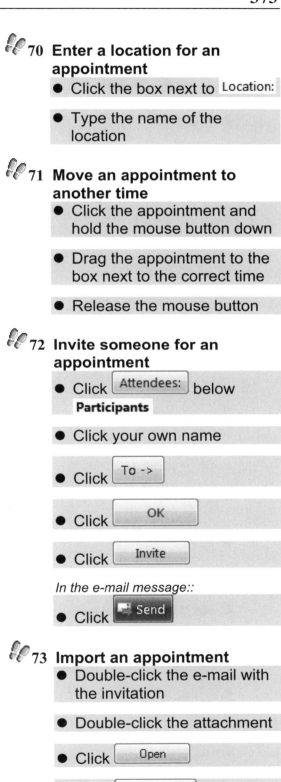

70 Enter a location for an appointment
- Click the box next to Location:

- Type the name of the location

71 Move an appointment to another time
- Click the appointment and hold the mouse button down

- Drag the appointment to the box next to the correct time

- Release the mouse button

72 Invite someone for an appointment
- Click Attendees: below **Participants**

- Click your own name

- Click To ->

- Click OK

- Click Invite

In the e-mail message::
- Click 📧 Send

73 Import an appointment
- Double-click the e-mail with the invitation

- Double-click the attachment

- Click Open

- Click Import

74 Open *Snipping Tool*

- Click

- Click ▶ **All Programs**

- Click 📁 Accessories

- Click ✂ Snipping Tool

75 Create a *Window snip*

- Click ▼ next to ✂ New

- Click Window Snip

- Point to the window you want to capture

When you see the red frame around the window:
- Click the window

76 Create a *Free-form snip*
In the Snipping Tool window:

- Click ✂ New

- Click ▼ next to ✂ New

- Click Free-form Snip

- Hold the mouse button down and draw a shape around the object you want to capture

- Release the mouse button

77 Do not save changes to the snip
When the Snipping Tool is closed:
- Click No

78 Open *Windows Photo Gallery*

- Click

- Click ▶ **All Programs**

- Click 🖼 Windows Photo Gallery

79 Display the *Information Pane*
- Click 🏷 Info

80 View a photo in the *Information Pane*
- Click the photo

81 Rate a photo
For three stars:
- Click the third star ☆

82 Add a tag to a photo
- Click the photo

- Drag the photo to the correct tag in the *Navigation Pane*

- Release the mouse button when you see

83 Select lines
- Click the margin next to the first line

- Hold the left mouse button down

- Move the mouse pointer in the margin to the last line

- Release the mouse button

84 Start a new file - do not save the changes
- Click `File`

- Click `New...`

In the window New:
- Click `OK`

Question: Save changes?
- Click `Don't Save`

85 Select a paragraph
- Click a word in the paragraph three times

86 Save a new document to the folder with practice files
- Click `File`

- Click `Save As...`

- Type at `File name:` the name of your document

- Check the address bar to see if the folder `Chapter 11` is opened

- Click `Save`

87 Save an exist document
- Click `File`

- Click `Save`

88 Open a document
- Click `File`

- Click `Open...`

- Click the name of the document

- Click `Openen`

89 Create a bulleted list
- Select the paragraphs

- Click

90 Remove a bullet style
- Select the paragraphs

- Click

91 Adjust tab stops
- Select the lines

- Drag the tab stops ∟ to the right place on the ruler:

92 Print a document
- Click `File`

- Click `Print...`

- Click `Print`

93 Indent paragraphs
- Select the paragraphs

- On the ruler, drag △ or ☐ to the right:

94 Display the properties of the C:-disk
- Right-click

  Local Disk (C:)

  85.2 GB free of 106 GB

- Click `Properties`

95 Start *Disk Cleanup* for your own files
In the Properties window:
- Click `Disk Cleanup`
- Click `→ My files only`

96 Remove files from the *Recycle Bin* using *Disk Cleanup*
- Drag the scroll bar down until you see the *Recycle Bin*
- Click to check mark ☑ Recycle Bin
- Click `OK`
- Click `Delete Files`

97 Start the *Disk Defragmenter*
- Click the tab `Tools`
- Click `Defragment Now...`
- Click `Continue`
- Click `Defragment now`

98 Cancel the disk defragmentation
- Click `Cancel defragmentation`

99 Open *Adobe Reader*
- Double-click `Adobe Reader 8`

100 Open a file
- Click `File`
- Click `Open...`
- Select the file
- Click `Open`

101 Print a file
- Click 🖶
- Click `OK`

102 Open *Windows Live OneCare*
- Click
- Click ▶ **All Programs**
- Click Windows Live OneCare

103 Open *Internet Explorer*
- Click
- Click Internet Explorer

104 Connect using the *Dial-up Connection* window
- Type your user name and password if necessary
- Click `Connect`

105 Go to a website in *Internet Explorer*
- Click in the address bar and type the web address
- Press `Enter`

C. Index